THE
FEINER
POINTS
OF
LEADERSHIP

THE
FEINER
POINTS
OF
LEADERSHIP

THE FIFTY BASIC LAWS THAT WILL MAKE
PEOPLE WANT TO PERFORM BETTER FOR YOU

MICHAEL
FEINER

WARNER
BUSINESS
BOOKS™

NEW YORK   BOSTON

Warner Business Books

Time Warner Book Group
1271 Avenue of the Americas, New York, NY 10020
Visit our Web site at www.twbookmark.com.

The Warner Business Books logo is a trademark of Warner Books, Inc.

Printed in the United States of America

First Printing: June 2004
10   9   8   7   6   5   4   3   2   1

Library of Congress Cataloging-in-Publication Data
Feiner, Michael.
    The Feiner points of leadership : fifty basic laws that will make people want to perform
better for you / Michael Feiner. — First Warner Books printing
    p. cm.
    ISBN 0-446-53276-2
    1. Leadership. 2. Management. I. Title.

HD57.7.F45 2004
658.4'09—dc22   2003015646

For
Lisa
Matthew, Allison, Meredith, and Kate

Contents

PART III
Situation-Specific Leadership

PART IV
Values-Based Leadership

Introduction

Most organizations don't work. With alarming frequency, companies under-perform, organizations fail, and leaders underachieve, derail, or lead people astray. The now familiar litany of infamous organizational failure—Enron and Andersen, WorldCom, the FBI and 9/11—reflects only the most visible flameouts. In many, many organizations, results don't reflect the collective effort, and work is more misery than pleasure. Too often the best people don't get hired, and existing employees don't get assessed fairly. The right people don't get promoted. Communication within and between organizational units doesn't always take place. The best decisions don't get made. And conflict, when it occurs, isn't addressed effectively, if at all.

It isn't for lack of trying. An entire literature of business books, squadrons of management consultants, countless magazines, case studies, conferences, and celebrity speakers—all are dedicated to improving businesses for their owners, employees, and customers. And yet the struggle continues. Why is it so damn hard to run a business well?

Throughout my career, first as an aspiring executive, then as a senior corporate leader, and more recently as a management consultant, I've wrestled with this question.

For twenty years at PepsiCo, ten as Chief People Officer for Pepsi-Cola worldwide, one of my primary responsibilities was to coach and counsel executives on what they might do more of or less of in order to become more effective leaders. You might say that one of my key roles was as a kind of corporate consigliere. Watching leaders at all levels of an organization in a variety of countries allowed me to see what worked, as well as what didn't work, and to learn close up what it takes to lead.

Beyond the responsibility to help leaders grow and develop, I led my own organization, which at one point numbered some four hundred people in over sixty locations worldwide. I had my own successes and failures in trying to motivate people, hold them accountable, and achieve great results. I saw how challenging it was to lead people, to keep people focused on the key priorities, to keep high-potentials from quitting because of their desire to get promoted quickly, to handle tough bosses, to get the cooperation of peers. By the time I retired, my organization was recognized as one of the most distinctive, innovative, and prestigious Human Resources organizations in the world—but I made my share of mistakes along the way.

Since 1995, I've been providing management consulting support to a wide variety of companies. I'm retained by CEOs or COOs to assess their executive teams and to help them lead their teams more effectively. As part of this process I often interview their subordinates to learn what they see as their boss's strengths and weaknesses. Not surprisingly, I hear the same complaints, the same frustrations, the same disappointments I heard as an executive at Pepsi. My clients fall into the same traps that I tried—and continue to try—to help leaders avoid.

For the past five years I've also taught MBA students at Columbia University Graduate School of Business. What's striking is that, while nearly all are pursuing their MBA as a way of fast-tracking the achievement of fame and fortune, many if not most of my students were prompted to return to school because of bad bosses or bureaucratic organizations that didn't allow them to feel appreciated or valued. The course I teach, High-Performance Leadership, has become extremely popular among second-year students, partly because they want to avoid making the mistakes they saw their bosses making.

These three different experiences—as a corporate executive, a management consultant, and a business school professor—have taught me just how difficult it is to engage people, motivate people, and lead people to achieve great results. But they've also taught me that effective leadership can be learned. There *are* some hard-won insights that *can* be conveyed, and that stand the test of time. This book, then, is my attempt to gather and distill the leadership lessons of a career.

The book is in four parts. Part I looks at what we mean by leadership, and makes the case that a focus on managing relationships is what distinguishes successful leaders. It further argues that knowing *what* leaders do isn't nearly as important (or helpful) as understanding *how* they do it. Part II moves on to discuss *relational* leadership, and presents the hows of managing relationships—with subordinates, bosses, teams, and peers—in the form of leadership laws. Part III then gives laws for *situation-specific* leadership, that is, laws for situations where conflict, change, or difference of ethnicity or gender are significant factors. Finally, Part IV unites the various laws with an overarching thesis of *values-based* leadership, a single predicate for the laws of motivating, galvanizing, and energizing people. Whatever your technical skills and mastery of the tactics of leadership, the lesson I've learned time and time again is that your values make a difference—in the final analysis, *it's your values that build followership*. After Parts II and III have presented the hows of leadership, then, Part IV examines the role of values in leadership in more detail (and since I started work on this book, the shortcomings of our corporate leadership in this area have been starkly exposed).

To help you remember the laws, they are illustrated with stories from my corporate, consulting, and teaching careers. These

stories are all true, and they're told as faithfully as possible—the
ending isn't always happy, I don't always do the right thing, and the
characters don't always express themselves politely. Together, they
point out the thousands of mistakes I made before I came to understand the laws of leading bosses, peers, and subordinates, and
they attempt to dramatize the leadership equation.

But what's the purpose of this effort? Why does the world need
yet another book on leadership? The reasons are twofold. First, I've
been immersed in organizational life for my entire career. What
I've seen and continue to see is alarming—and sad. Far too many
people find working in organizations to be under-nourishing and
unsatisfying. It's not just people in factories or call centers who feel
unappreciated. It's not just first-line supervisors who feel taken for
granted. I find that people at all levels, including senior management, feel undervalued—that they don't count and don't matter.
With this book, then, and its focus on the hows of effective leadership, I want to help aspiring leaders and seasoned managers alike,
regardless of where they reside in the organizational hierarchy,
make organizations more fulfilling and more fun—yes, even fun—
for their subordinates, their bosses, and their colleagues. And for
themselves.

The second reason has to do with the institution of business itself. There is enormous pressure on organizations, and the leaders
who run them, to achieve great results. This isn't new. Yet this pressure to outperform the competition continues to increase, at an increasing rate! And this pressure has created the conditions for the
kinds of scandals and shenanigans we've been reading about in the
past few years. That these sordid deviations from ethical conduct
were perpetrated not by corporations but by individuals sometimes
gets forgotten. We read about Enron or Andersen or Tyco or the
rest so frequently that we forget that it's people, not inanimate corporate entities, that go astray. So my second reason for writing this
book is that I want to provide leaders with a visceral understand-

ing of how crucial their value system is in motivating, galvanizing, and energizing people to achieve the great results they're under such tremendous pressure to produce, and to show them how to achieve these results without breaking the law, without cooking the books, and without violating people's need for dignity and respect.

PART I

What Exactly Is Leadership?

The concept of leadership is often misunderstood. Part I examines what leadership is (and is not), what leaders do, and the critical difference between leadership and management.

1	*Beneath the Tip of the Iceberg*

In the early stages of my career as an executive, I felt I needed to direct people to do certain things. I knew I was supposed to be sensitive and allow my people to have a sense of involvement, but all the same I believed that they expected me, as their leader, to tell them or show them what to do—to prescribe a course of action. I was attempting, without fully realizing it, to conform to the "heroic individual" concept of leadership.

So when I took my senior team to Hurricane Island, off the coast of Maine, on a six-day Outward Bound team-building exercise, I carried this concept of leadership with me. I had been successful leading this way and there was no need to fix something that wasn't broken.

The Hurricane Island experience began with a day of land-based exercises. My eight-person team was pumped and ready to go. After a few hours of orientation, we were asked to confront our first challenge: to get the entire team over a fifteen-foot-high wooden wall. We contemplated the wall, each of us thinking about a solution to this puzzle. After a few seconds, people began to volunteer their ideas, each realizing the flaw in the suggested solution the longer he or she explained it. I waited, infinitely patient and super-sensitive leader that I was. After about five minutes, people became quieter, and my moment to lead had arrived.

I presented my analysis of the problem, and laid out the solution I had in mind. The team listened to my instructions carefully. On the first attempt, six of us were able to scale the wall in no time, but we weren't able to get the two remaining members of the team over. I outlined another approach, which again stranded two team members. After a little more deliberation, and then more pushing and shoving, the third plan I suggested ended in pretty much the same way. Fast-forward two hours: We were at Plan N, and it was becoming clear to me that I wasn't moving any closer to getting all of us over the wall. I began to feel desperate—here I was, the captain of the ship, with a crew that expected me to save the day, to solve this problem, and to lead them to success, and we were getting precisely nowhere. It was at this moment that Anita, one of my most trusted subordinates, moved to my side, carefully positioning herself so that the rest of the team couldn't hear what she was saying.

"Mike, try backing off a bit and ask us to think as a team about how to get over this friggin' wall."

I heard this whispered comment, but at first I couldn't process the suggestion. What was she talking about? How could I let my team know I didn't have the answers? How could I turn to the team for advice at this point without their losing respect for my leadership authority? Wasn't I expected to know more? Hell, that's how I'd gotten to be the leader. I looked again at Anita, my desperation mounting. She shot me a reassuring glance. I called a time-out.

"Folks, I'm obviously better at going through walls than over them." The team laughed politely, though tempers at this point were a little frayed. "How about we step back and talk about this for a bit? This is trickier than we thought."

The change was dramatic—and instantaneous. People began to brainstorm, asking rather than telling. "What do you think of this approach . . . ?" became a common starting point. In a matter of about thirty-five minutes, we—the team—had sorted out the most plausible options and twenty minutes later the entire group was over the wall, the preceding two hours of futility behind us.

But what surprised me most was that, after this episode, people acted no differently toward me even though I had been the living embodiment of the leader who had the answer to every problem (at least, that's how I had seen it). What worked in this situation was not strategy, was not oratory, was not a sense of mission. It was not my following a "heroic individual" approach. Rather, what worked was stepping back, asking a question, and understanding that I didn't need to single-handedly lead the team out of the wilderness. Most importantly, though, this didn't detract from my leadership. Quite the opposite. In this instance, giving the team a say in the decision enhanced my leadership, and enabled us to succeed.

When it comes to common perceptions of leadership, however, the heroic individual model—what has been called the Myth of the Great Man—has proven remarkably resilient. It holds that a leader is a larger-than-life, heroic individual; a leader is valiant, courageous, and stands alone at the summit of an organization; a leader devises strategy, delivers moving oratory, defines a grand vision. This is the concept of the leader that many of us carry around in our heads, and we continue to do so despite a number of recent attempts by some of the best thinkers in the field to redefine leadership in less swashbuckling terms.

Perhaps the most prominent voice in this movement is that of

Warren Bennis. In his groundbreaking book *Organizing Genius*, Bennis provides six case studies that show leaders achieving success not as individuals, but through their skill at working with their teams. Bennis points out that Steve Jobs, generally assumed to be the lone genius behind the creation of the Apple Macintosh, was not a technical expert (that was his best friend, Steve Wozniak), but was supported by a large team of developers who put in the hundred-hour weeks necessary to the success of the project. Bennis shows us that Walt Disney, hailed as the father of animation, brought a vision of a transformed entertainment industry, but relied on a team of skilled animators to see that vision to fruition (Disney himself, we learn, didn't draw a single frame of his first full-length feature film). And Bennis and Howard Gardner, another assailant of the Great Man Myth, both point to J. Robert Oppenheimer and the Manhattan Project as the classic example of harnessing the talents of others: Oppenheimer led the project to a successful conclusion, despite his reserved demeanor, despite his inexperience leading large groups (twenty-five hundred scientists were recruited to work at Los Alamos), and despite the fact that he was not the most technically able scientist on the team (seven Nobel Prizes were awarded to Manhattan Project physicists later in their careers; Oppenheimer was not among them).

What Bennis and Gardner challenge, in these various examples, is our tendency to attribute successes of human endeavor to a single individual. We often think of Jobs as the father of the Mac, Disney as the father of animation, and Oppenheimer as the father of the atomic age. Did Jobs, Disney, and Oppenheimer possess incredible talents? Of course they did, perhaps even genius. Yet each only achieved what he did through others. And arguably each would have achieved much less were it not for skills at energizing, motivating, and inspiring people that are greatly removed from the vision-strategy-oratory skills that most of us associate with leadership. The revised thinking encourages us to view leadership not as "an inherently individual phenomenon,"[1] where we intertwine leadership with solitary heroics, but rather as a process of harnessing and directing the talents of others. Bennis, in place of the theory of the Great Man, offers us the model of the Great Group.

There is another reason that the Great Man model is nearer myth than reality: If we examine the enormity of the challenge facing the modern leader, it becomes clear that individual leadership is simply not feasible. The world is far too complex for a man or woman to be able to single-handedly resolve the problems of the day. As the march of globalization continues, and as technology places ever more information ever more quickly at our fingertips, it's virtually impossible for a leader to be smart enough or to be able to understand enough of the overall picture to *unilaterally* resolve every question an organization, large or small, faces every day. Further, organizations and the problems they face are themselves too complex for a person to lead by himself or herself. The human dimension complicates exponentially the rational and logical model of the way these organizations are supposed to work. So complexity—of the world, and of the organizations in it—means that leadership can *never* be something practiced by an individual in isolation.

But despite these assaults, and despite the impossibilities of individual leadership in the modern world, the Great Man Myth is still alive and kicking. When I ask audiences, whether composed of MBA candidates, experienced managers, or people at any level in between, to name figures, living or dead, who embody great leadership, the lists are always remarkably similar. Winston Churchill, Napoleon Bonaparte, George S. Patton, Martin Luther King, Jr., Mahatma Gandhi, John F. Kennedy, and Abraham Lincoln—with an occasional Margaret Thatcher or Michael Jordan or Jack Welch thrown in. When I ask these audiences what the great leaders on their list have in common, their responses usually reflect the concept of leadership as an individual, heroic phenomenon (and, judging by the lists my audiences generate, an almost exclusively male phenomenon at that). Leaders are great speakers, they have a clear vision, they've overcome adversity, they make difficult decisions single-handedly, and so on.

These audiences are generally composed of intelligent people with not insignificant experience in the professional world. Yet this tendency to deify leaders, and to ascribe to them superhuman powers, persists. Why?

Leaders do a huge number of different things each day. Some are visible to us; most are not. When we think of great leaders, we (not surprisingly) think of *visible* leaders, and of what those leaders do that we see. We then (again, not surprisingly) equate those things that we see these leaders doing with what great leaders do—and what we see, primarily, are speeches and articles and interviews about vision and strategy, hence our view of the leader as the orator who single-handedly shapes the future path. *But leadership is like an iceberg: Ninety percent of it is hidden below the surface.* To form our impressions of leaders based on only their public activities relies on a dangerously biased sampling of what really goes on. Yet this is precisely what most of us do.

This book attempts to set the record straight, by revealing the ninety percent of leadership beneath the tip of the iceberg. We'll see that this ninety percent has comparatively little to do with strategy, oratory, or technical skills, and everything to do with *managing relationships* up, down, and across an organization. Leadership is the aggregation of hundreds upon hundreds of small interactions—most of which take place out of our sight—projected across layer upon layer of relationships, day in and day out. It is these relationships that form the substance of organizational life—a fact that the Great Man Myth, centered as it is on the power of the *individual*, largely fails to take into account. Anything that an organization achieves is achieved by a group of people working together: At the simplest level, the leader is a leader because he or she can enable that group to deliver—*and the only way to do this is through the relationships that define the group.*

Saying that leadership is about managing relationships, however, isn't nearly enough. To see leadership as the ability to achieve great success through others is a critical advance—in that it moves beyond the mythology of individual genius—but this approach still has a key shortcoming. It stops short of offering a visceral understanding of *how* leaders do what they actually do. We are told that leaders build Great Groups or Hot Teams; we are told that leaders Establish Direction, Align People, and Motivate and Inspire;[2] we are told that leaders have employees who feel empowered. But these are *whats*, not *hows:* Understanding them doesn't enable you to go to the office tomorrow and behave differently. This isn't news you can use.

The people I once coached at Pepsi, my current clients, and my MBA students all want to know *how* they go about dealing with the endless array of leadership challenges. They want the tactical details of how to handle a difficult subordinate or an unreasonable boss, how to manage conflict, or how to lead a change process. What distinguishes truly great leaders—and what is required of any discussion of leadership if it is to be helpful to current or aspiring leaders—is an understanding of these *hows*. *How* do you build a great team? *How* do you motivate and inspire your people? *How* do you take people with you?

A detailed understanding of the hows of leadership marks what we'll call a *High-Performance Leader*. It's what enables a leader to tap into something greater than himself or herself. It's what leads to energized employees, effective teams, and enhanced business results. It's also the only way I know of to teach people to become better leaders.

The remainder of this book, then, goes beneath the tip of the iceberg to reveal the invisible ninety percent of leadership, and presents this ninety percent as a series of hows. It provides a basic framework of laws for the High-Performance Leader, which encompass the hows of leading subordinates, bosses, and peers. Because my ego still hasn't quite recovered from the battering it took on Hurricane Island and needs all the help it can get, I call them Feiner's Laws. There aren't seven laws or ten commandments: Leadership isn't that simple. In fact, there are fifty laws in this book, provided to tackle the endless array of challenges we face in organizational life.

We should address two characteristics of the hows of leadership in advance. First, you'll see that High-Performance Leaders achieve much of their success in managing relationships not through distant communications (by memos or speeches or video broadcasts), but through direct, up-close, personal interaction. They challenge, argue with, and persuade people up and down the organization regarding their ideas. They give and solicit feedback. They get to know their people and what makes them tick. They coach and mentor. They encourage debate, and the conflict of ideas. They hold people accountable. They tell uncomfortable truths. They dive deep into the details. They build coalitions and alliances. In order to ensure that people in the organization are pulling on the oars in unison, High-Performance Leaders engage in what I call HTHC—*Hand-to-Hand Combat*. They do this every day, sometimes in formal, scheduled interactions (staff meetings or one-on-ones), but also in informal, unscheduled, and frequent transactions with members of their team. They recognize that leaders can't overcommunicate, and they understand that, in fact, the opposite applies: It's through what feels like overcommunication that people come to embrace the vision or internalize the priorities, and that relationships are fostered and maintained. You'll see these HTHC activities in many of the laws we'll discuss throughout the book.

The second characteristic of the hows of leadership is this: To excel in all of them is far from easy. The laws are surprisingly difficult to implement with any level of consistency. They call for courage, yet it's unbelievably difficult to summon the courage to tell your boss that he or she is making a huge mistake, or to give a peer candid performance feedback. They call for a leader to provide purpose and meaning, yet it's unbelievably difficult to infuse an overriding purpose into every aspect of your team's work. They call for unwavering commitment, yet it's unbelievably difficult to display the sort of commitment to a subordinate that places their own interests ahead of yours when the chips are down. They call for leaders to own outcomes, yet it's unbelievably difficult to do this to such an extent that you never reflexively blame others for problems, but only address what you can do to resolve them. And they call for leaders to uphold values, yet it's unbelievably difficult to stand up for decency, dignity, and honesty when competitors both inside and outside the firm seem to be willing to break all the rules to get ahead. If there's anything heroic about leadership, then, it's this: *The ninety percent of it that we don't see demands incredible application, stamina, and dedication.* Any effective leader must sustain a huge number of relationships, and this requires heroic (and largely unseen) effort.

Although processes and systems are important tools for leaders, we'll devote very little time to them here. This is not an oversight on my part. While it's true that leaders must leverage all kinds of processes—for decision making, resource allocation, strategy formulation, change, and learning, to name only a few—in order to achieve great results, process skills alone don't make a leader. No matter how well-conceived and well-designed processes are, they're used and implemented by people, not by automatons. If a leader can't manage relationships with his or her people, then, process design talent won't help.

And, lest my argument here seem too simplistic, I'm not suggesting that strategy or technical skills are unimportant. Technical skills are often the price of admission to the leadership game, and there are certainly times when strategy must be front and center of a leader's thinking. But these occasions are much rarer than most people assume, and a new strategy is generally developed by a *team* of people, not by an all-seeing, all-knowing individual leader. A good example of this is the recent meltdown at AOL Time Warner. When the business model upon which Steve Case and Gerald Levin (both of whom have now left the company) had constructed their merger became invalid, Dick Parsons, the new CEO, needed to build a new strategy—with the help and involvement of his entire team. "I see my job as to make sure that we have the best team on the field," Parsons commented.[3] He could well have added that it's his job to manage the relationships within that team so that they deliver the best result possible.

When you read the laws, you may feel that they're common sense. *But if they are common sense, there's very little evidence they're in common use.* If they were, organizational life would be much more rewarding than it is for many of us—and we wouldn't be reading in the papers every day about corrupt executives and accounting scandals, which are clearly failures of leadership at a variety of levels.

If the laws are applied, however, magic happens. When a leader summons the commitment to lead as the laws suggest, bosses, peers, and subordinates respond. The laws, because they address the hows of leadership, operate at the immediate, practical level, and the results are likewise immediate and palpable. The laws have been pressure-tested through thirty-five years of corporate and consulting experience. They are built on the conviction that the genius of leadership is a mastery of the details, and that a leadership book, to be truly helpful, must speak to these underlying fundamentals of human relationships. And collectively, they take us beneath the tip of the leadership iceberg.

2	*The Difference Between Leadership and Management*

One of the things that makes leadership such a daunting proposition for most of us is the range of skills required. On the one hand, leaders need to convincingly communicate the urgency and importance of an organization's journey through the corporate cosmos. The people around them need to feel that they are engaged in a mission that matters, and they need to see a leader who exemplifies courage, commitment, and values in pursuing this mission. On the other hand, leaders must astutely navigate the internal landscape of a firm, composed as it is of meetings, requests for information, resource allocation and budgeting decisions, and the like. They must take responsibility for predicting and controlling the conditions under which their people are asked to perform. *To be successful, then, leaders must engage in two very different sets of activities.* In the discussion that follows, we'll begin to distinguish between those activities that could be called leadership and those that could be called management. Because these terms are often used interchangeably, it's difficult to help leaders understand which set of skills is needed in a certain situation. Or whether it was their leadership or management skills that accounted for their success. Or, for that matter, what the difference between leading and managing really is.

One of my most memorable career experiences was working for Pete, a division head. Pete was a really nice guy. He was very smart and well organized, and treated everyone with respect. His workdays, which started at 7:00 A.M., were as well planned and tightly scheduled as those of a U.S. President. Because he wanted to stay in touch with what was happening in the organization, he would schedule lunches two weeks in advance with key managers throughout headquarters. His follow-up system was flawless, his calendar management was exemplary. He was a talented navigator through the corporate bureaucracy, and a strong problem solver. And his integrity was unimpeachable.

Pete was one of the great managers of all time. If we analyze his strengths, we find he excelled at three key sets of activities, most of which we've seen in basic management texts for many years.[1]

First, Pete was a master of *Planning and Budgeting*—actions that occur at almost every level of an organization. Managers are expected to establish a plan for accomplishing their key goals for the coming month, quarter, or year and then to estimate the budget and resources necessary to meet these goals. Depending on the size of the organization, many months can be devoted to developing annual operating plans in great detail. While planning and budgeting are often viewed as tedious and draining, without skill in these areas no manager would ever ship—that is, deliver the goods—on time and on budget.

Second, Pete had a black belt in *Organizing and Staffing*—the activities that translate goals and targets into an organizational structure. This activity typically begins with a detailed analysis of the skills and competencies needed at the various levels of an organization in order to meet the goal. The requirements generated in this analysis are carefully mapped against the talents and work capacities of available employees. Staff are then confirmed, reassigned, or hired as needed, so that the right people are in the right jobs. At the same time, the overall plan must be integrated with the revised organization so that each of the tasks that lead toward the overall goal is properly sequenced and assigned to the right group of people. Skillful organizing and staffing ensures that the firm's resources are optimally deployed against its goals.

Finally, Pete had few equals when it came to *Controlling and Problem Solving*—the activities where executives spend the majority of their time. Monitoring and control systems are essential to make sure people are doing what they're supposed to, the way they're supposed to. At the same time, these systems—such as a store sales report, or a customer retention analysis—help the organization know how it's doing against its goals and targets. Wal-Mart's control system permits it to measure results against plan, by store, by department, by day, and by individual salesperson. Retail banks closely monitor how many of their new customers leave during the first months after opening an account, and thereby obtain critical information about the quality of their service to these customers—and again, this can be tracked down to an individual bank clerk. All this monitoring helps confirm that things are going according to plan.

It also sounds the alarm when things are not. Executives at all levels of a firm are frequently, if not continuously, engaged in problem solving—that classic firefighting activity necessary because the unforeseen inevitably happens, and the unexpected invariably develops. Problem solving requires astute analytical skills (in order to identify the root causes of problems) and a talent for risk assessment ("what's the downside of this solution?"), together with the ability to make trade-offs (identifying and taking responsibility for the "as good as we can get it" solution).

Pete excelled at these activities, and organizations are filled with people like Pete. Talented, and hardworking, they dive deep into the details of their executive roles and are on top of what's going on in their departments. They know their numbers, have their people on a short leash, and are hands-on in making sure projects and programs are implemented, on time and on budget. The skills that they possess—*management skills*—are crucial in organizations. Taken together, planning and budgeting, organizing and staffing, and controlling and problem solving create *order* in an organization, necessary regardless of a company's size. *Management activity produces predictability, consistency, and control, things that every organization requires to perform well.* Pete was an outstanding manager.

But working for him was not a lot of fun.

On one occasion, for example, I had been trying to arrange a meeting between Pete and Max, the head of one of our largest unions—a union that had been militant and adversarial for years. Max, then in his late seventies, viewed everyone at headquarters as "pencil pushers," his pejorative term for stuffed suits who cared nothing about the human side of the business. To Max, executives worshipped at the altar of profits—a false deity as far as he was concerned.

Still, I had met with Max often in my first year in the job and we talked by phone every week or so. After twelve months of repeated prodding, Max finally relented and agreed to meet with Pete—then my boss—and me for lunch. Though Pete was willing to do the lunch, he wasn't confident it would help to resolve the deep-seated mutual mistrust that had existed between Pepsi and the union. But I felt it was worth a shot.

So the day before the lunch, I made sure I spent some time with Pete, prepping him. As I recall, I told Pete something like this:

"Max was hauling cases as a salesman in the thirties. He'll want to recount the glory days of the Cola Wars, when real men lugged cases up six flights of stairs in walk-up buildings. He sees himself as the John L. Lewis of the soft drink industry. He's a bit of a dinosaur, and he can be crusty and crotchety, but he's a softie in many ways. And make no mistake—he does care about the workers."

Pete wanted to focus on the details. "Mike, is there something specific we should seek to get from this lunch?"

"I really don't think so," I said. "I just want you to break the ice. Let him see you as a person, not as a faceless executive. Take an interest in some of the stories he'll tell from days gone by. And tell him some war stories of your own."

"You're sure we shouldn't use this as an opportunity to discuss the work rule problems we need to address in the next contract negotiations?" Here was Pete being fact- and issue- and data-oriented.

"I really don't think we should go there. If this lunch goes okay, there will be plenty of occasions to discuss the operational stuff. Just make him feel important. Let him see that you care about our people just like he does. Tell him our plans for upgrading the facilities. Give him a sense of our long-term vision for the division. And don't be surprised if he's a little standoffish at first."

"Okay, I'll give it a go."

The next day Max arrived right on time. We shook hands and walked to the executive dining room, where, according to plan, Pete was waiting for us at the best table. I made the introductions, we sat down, and, to get the ball rolling, I asked Max if he had ever visited our headquarters before.

"Nope," he responded curtly.

"Well, maybe we can walk around the grounds after lunch. The sculpture collection is world-renowned."

"I'm not much into sculpture." Okay, I thought, that's 0 for 1 for Mike.

Pete tried to help us recover from the chilly start. "Mike tells me you're a soft drink veteran who's seen it all, Max."

"Well, I've seen a lot. I remember dealing with Pepsi Presidents in the thirties." And Max began to tell a long story about how in the good old days the company really cared about workers as human beings.

I began to scrunch my toes in my shoes. This wasn't the start I'd hoped for. "Why don't we order?" I said, hoping the break in conversation would allow us to restart the meter.

The food arrived, but Pete was still a little stiff and uptight—probably the way Max expected a pencil pusher to be. I redoubled my efforts to get the conversation going, giving Max some easy prompts ("I bet the competitive posture with Coke has changed over the years!") and throwing Pete a softball or two ("Maybe Max would be interested in hearing about some of the new product stuff we're testing in the lab!"). But I wasn't getting anywhere—any real three-way conversation was scarce, forced, and punctuated by stretches of uncomfortable silence.

I was getting desperate. I asked Max about his wife, to whom he was totally devoted, and who was unwell at the time. I was hoping that opening a line of personal conversation would nudge Pete to let his guard down and talk about his own family. Max reported with obvious concern about his wife's need for a hip replacement.

"That's too bad," Pete responded, cryptically.

I figured we were now 0 for 2. I wasn't sure what else I should do.

Then Pete, still very serious and businesslike, began to speak. "Max, maybe I can take a minute and talk a little about the business and how the year is shaping up." My toe scrunching intensified.

And Pete began to talk about the kinds of things he was most comfortable talking about: sales volume, rates of return, market share, pricing, and the like.

Max seemed to stare at his coffee cup during Pete's monologue. I began to wonder whether I could access some magical power that might transport me to another cosmos.

Pete finished his business review and Max looked up and began to reply. "Pete, I wish you people were as interested in *my* [*sic*] workers as you are in the money you make off their backs."

The room began to swim around my head.

I heard Pete reply, "We are interested in *our* [*sic*] workers. We're interested, for instance, in why so many of them are absent every day that we can't staff our manufacturing lines to run at full speed." And we were 0 for 3. No personal connection, no understanding of where the other was coming from, no progress in breaking down the pencil pusher/union stooge stereotypes. An unmitigated disaster—and the first meeting between Pete and Max was also the last.

Pete was in many ways a fine guy to work for, but even in situations like this, when the woods were burning all around him, he couldn't deviate from his facts-and-figures, data-and-charts approach—he couldn't get past the management details. While he possessed some leadership ability, management skills dominated his repertoire. When that's the case with too many senior executives, there's a significant risk that an organization will run into trouble.

Another boss of mine, Jim, was the complete opposite of Pete. Jim, the head of a large division, had leadership talent flowing abundantly through his veins. In particular, he excelled in five areas.

First, Jim demonstrated courage. Not courage to take enormous risks, or to bet the firm on the pursuit of a radical strategy— that's recklessness. I'm talking about the courage to confront the obvious. If it was obvious that an employee wasn't living up to expectations, Jim had the courage to speak to him about it. If it was obvious that his team was headed in the wrong direction, Jim had the courage to (diplomatically) guide us back to the right path. On many occasions, he had the courage to say what everyone was thinking, but would not dare to say aloud. And he was willing to take on corporate higher-ups, who were often pushing us to increase our profit plan or shift our marketing strategy.

Second, Jim understood it was up to him to provide purpose and meaning. Those of us who worked for him knew the mission we were on, and we knew who the enemy was. But Jim did more than simply inform us of the goal. Rather, it was infused into everything he said and did, and was transformed from the end point of our journey into the very purpose of our existence.

Third, Jim was committed to his people, and showed it. If one of his people needed his advice, his door was always open. When a major decision was called for, seniority in the firm did not equate with exclusive entitlement to participate in the debate: The entire team was called on for their thoughts, and the opinions of both senior and junior staff were treated on their merits alone. While somewhat shy and reserved in style, Jim always had time to offer career advice, and was always willing to sponsor his high performers for promotion.

Fourth, Jim believed our ultimate success was in our own hands. When the corporate office threw roadblocks in our way, Jim felt it was within our capacity to push back and change what we needed to change in order to deliver the goods. I never heard him blame anyone or anything for our results—our performance was something for which *we* were totally accountable.

Finally, Jim led by upholding values. He treated everyone with dignity and decency. He was comfortable in his own skin and with his own laconic manner, and this authenticity served to better connect him to his people. He never hid the truth about how we were doing against our profit plan. While there was lots of pressure from Corporate to gild the lily, he always told it straight about how we were doing in the marketplace against our competitors. And Jim consistently and publicly chose the right course of action over the most profitable one, when those two were in conflict.

But working for Jim was, in many ways, a living nightmare.

One saga that I remember began when Yolanda, the VP-Marketing, dropped by my office for a chat. During our conversation she mentioned how under-the-gun she felt to complete an analysis Jim had asked her to undertake a few days earlier.

"What's the analysis on?" I asked.

"Jim wants us to do a crash-and-burn on the risks and opportunities of launching the Pepsi Challenge nationally."

"Wow, that's a switch—weren't we talking at last week's meeting about piloting the Challenge in Texas for a few more months before deciding on a national rollout?"

"We were. But you know Jim. Sometimes he changes his mind. I've got almost my entire group doing the analysis and running the numbers. He wants to see the data in a week, at the outside. I had to pull the agency off the ad campaign we had them working on so I could show Jim what some national Challenge spots might look like."

"Boy, you've got a full plate," I said. "Good luck." I knew from past experience that these kinds of starts and stops could drive people nuts.

A few days later I ran into our VP-Sales in the fitness center.

"Hey, Gordon, I haven't seen you down here in the past few days. How come you're slacking off?" I teased.

"Slacking off nothing. I have my whole team doing some heavy lifting for Jim."

"What's going on—what's Jim got you doing?"

"He's rethinking our Challenge strategy. He thinks we should revisit the decision to pilot it in Texas for two more months. So he wants us to look at whether we could get the bottlers to sign on if we went national right away. I've told my folks to put everything on the back burner so we can get the analysis to Jim ASAP."

As soon as Gordon started telling me his tale of woe I knew another headquarters fire drill was in motion. I didn't say anything to Gordon beyond wishing him luck, and instead headed straight for the shower.

The minute I got upstairs, I knocked on Jim's door, stuck my head in, and asked if he had a few minutes.

"Sure, come on in."

"Jim, I heard you're rethinking the game plan for the Challenge." I didn't even bother with any small talk.

"Right. I spoke to Rick [PepsiCo's COO, and Jim's boss] and we both think it's worth at least considering going national sooner. Why do you mention it?"

Here I needed to be respectful but let Jim know what was happening. I had seen this movie before. "Well, I spoke to Yolanda and she tells me she's got most of her people going flat out to get you the analysis you wanted."

"I know—I asked for a quick turnaround on this because I promised I'd give Rick our recommendations right away."

"Then what part of the plan is Gordon working on? I just saw him and he told me his folks are also pulling out all the stops on this."

A puzzled look came over Jim's face. "I only asked Gordon to look at the bottler implications. I just mentioned it when I saw him a couple of days ago."

"Jim, the thing is that Gordon and Yolanda don't know they're both working on this."

Jim was obviously embarrassed. "I didn't mean to have them both do an in-depth analysis. I just wanted the salespeople to know about this and give me their thoughts on the bottlers' reaction. It's not simply a marketing issue."

"Jim, these two are both scrambling big-time on this. Their teams have dropped practically everything else they're working on."

"That's not even close to what I wanted." Jim had a pained expression.

I was heading into sensitive territory. "I know that. But this kind of thing has happened before. You're going one hundred miles an hour thinking about an issue. So you may not realize how the team tries to respond to what they think you're asking for." Jim didn't respond so I kept going. "It would really help going forward if you could get the team together and figure out an action plan for handling this type of thing."

"You're absolutely right," Jim said, with lots of conviction.

"Right now, I think it would make sense for you to call Yolanda and Gordon, tell them you've realized there's probably some overlap on the projects they're working on, and ask them to pool their resources and work on this jointly."

And Jim did just that. After three or four days of working independently, Gordon and Yolanda figured out how to integrate their teams and efficiently complete the project. They each shook their heads and mumbled to themselves for a week afterward, realizing how foolish all the chaos looked to their people.

You won't be surprised to hear that a few months later Jim unintentionally launched another fire drill, with the organization's right hand not knowing that the left was fighting the same blaze.

This was something that happened chronically under Jim's leadership. Because Jim, just like Pete, was for the most part a one-trick pony. While he exemplified many of the *leadership* skills we'll be discussing in this book, his *management* skills were missing in action. Details, action plans, due dates, follow-up, performance measurement, and the like—these were not part of Jim's vocabulary. The result—ever changing priorities, ready-fire-aim decision making, and vague short-term objectives—created a kind of loosey-goosey, hands-off climate, which was exhausting, confusing, and frustrating.

A leader must not only give followers structure, organization, and control, but also show courage, purpose, commitment, accountability and a sense of values. It follows, then, that *both* management *and* leadership skills are indispensable. That doesn't mean that you have to be an Olympian as both manager and leader—rarely is anyone a ten in both areas. However, every High-Performance Leader I ever coached, consulted with, or observed had *both* strong management *and* strong leadership skills. So while this is a book about the hows of leading people to deliver great results, both managing and leading are absolutely essential skills to have in one's repertoire. For if a management focus produces essential *order, consistency, and predictability*, then leadership produces *change and adaptability*—to new competitors, new products, new markets, new regulations, and new customers. Both sets of skills are necessary, and both must be in balance.

And an imbalance between leadership and management can lead to problems not just for individuals, but also for entire organizations. Consider an organization with a strong focus on tightly managing its business. There are lots of systems and processes in this organization, including strategic planning systems, annual operating planning systems, reward systems, and communication systems. This is an organization like the Xerox of the seventies, eighties, and nineties—a company unaffectionately referred to by its employees as Burox. In this kind of bureaucracy, with an intense focus on management activities, the culture becomes one where red tape and command-and-control prevail. The old AT&T and General Motors (which resembled a Department of Motor Vehicles) both suffered from this type of paralyzing control obsession. Management without leadership leads to organizations that are insular and bureaucratic and myopic and slow-moving. These kinds of organizations are so internally focused that they spend little or no time looking out, either at the market or at their competitors. They're often veterans of their industries, and often dominate those industries with mature product lines and reliable revenue streams. They often think that they're safe from competition. That, essentially, is why there is no longer an American electronics industry. It's why the American steel industry is a ghost of what it once was. It's why General Motors's share of the American automobile market had shrunk from fifty percent in 1955 to twenty-eight percent in 2002. Sadly this focus on command-and-control, without an offsetting leadership focus, characterizes far too many organizations today.

Contrast this orientation with a primarily leadership focus, where management process and systems are viewed as unimportant—where the vision and mission is thought to be all the juice an organization needs to be successful. This kind of organization, where there's lots of *leadership but little management* focus, is equally dangerous, producing the cultlike, chaotic environment of the classic dot.com start-up.

There's no secret formula for determining when to lead and when to manage—High-Performance Leaders engage in both activities during any given day. When problems arise, even the most senior leaders don their management hats and dive deep into the organization to find out what's going on and to engage in fixing it.

How can you tell if you have leadership and management in the right equilibrium? The best way is to look over your daily work calendar for the past ninety days. People are always amazed at how much time they've devoted to managing, and how little they've devoted to the coaching, feedback, communication, and other relationship-building activities that characterize leadership. It's so easy to let planning, budgeting, staffing, resource allocation, and problem solving take charge of our days. It's what I call the activity trap: the mistaken idea that your volume of activity correlates with the value you create. Multiply this phenomenon across an organization where nearly everyone is nearly always managing—driven largely by the need for control and order and consistency (and short-term results)—and you have an organization that's stultified and atrophied. Or soon will be.

One interesting note here. It's much easier to think of examples of firms or individuals suffering from too much management and not enough leadership than it is to think of examples of the opposite problem. There are two reasons for this. First, business schools and universities have done a very thorough job of teaching management skills. They're easily identifiable, easily quantifiable, and easily communicated. Granted, it takes real application and discipline to become a superlative manager, but the skill set involved seems much more readily accessible to most of us. Leadership, on the other hand, is fantastically difficult to get right. Whereas most experts would agree on the essential elements of good management, a much smaller number agree on the tenets of great leadership. And if the skill set isn't even clearly agreed upon, it's not surprising that leadership skills are more often found to be lacking. The standard qualification for an executive career is a Master's of Business Administration degree. Yet few business schools, even today, have figured out how to teach not just business administration, but business leadership.

The second reason for this imbalance has to do with the nature of leadership itself. Leadership seeks to create change—and most of us are afraid of change. Indeed, our response to the threat of change, the looming possibility of the unknown, is to seek refuge in order, consistency, and predictability—to seek refuge, that is, in management. Management activities exert a gravitational pull over us that leadership activities don't. So for an organization facing a significant challenge, very often the instinct is to try to survive through management alone. Clayton Christensen has given us a fascinating chronicle of how the smaller, innovative firms in an industry can rise up to overtake and swallow the larger incumbents.[2] None of these larger incumbents—think of Digital Equipment Corporation, which, after failing to react to the new market of Unix servers, was acquired by Compaq in 1998—lacked management talent. They wouldn't have survived as large, complex firms without it. What they lacked was the ability to change, and that is the classic signal of a paucity of leadership.

Neither Pete nor Jim, by the way, rose further in the executive ranks. Although Pete was no lightweight, and although he did a creditable job of running the business at a time when the enterprise needed operational and executional discipline, in the end the imbalance between his management and leadership skills let him down. His need for so much structure in the way he ran his division meant the organization was more tightly and rigidly controlled than it needed to be. We underachieved in relation to our potential, and we didn't have much fun along the way. Pete ultimately moved to a senior administrative officer position where his analytical and planning skills were more effectively deployed.

Jim saw the writing on the wall—he wasn't going to get a more senior corporate job. Jim's persona was that of a visionary, an idea guy who didn't have the hands-on, management focus to run operationally intensive businesses. And without management discipline, his divisional results were inconsistent. He left the organization and, after a few other corporate roles, ultimately started his own business.

This discussion of the difference between leadership and management is intended to dramatize the importance of both. The character sketches of Pete and Jim should enable you to recognize a leadership/management imbalance in your bosses, your colleagues, and most importantly, in yourself. For the remainder of this book, though, we'll concentrate on the leadership side of the equation, and specifically on the hows of motivating, energizing, and galvanizing people to achieve great results.

PART II

Relational Leadership

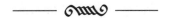

The first group of hows are organized by key relationships—with subordinates, bosses, teams, and peers. Leading subordinates is what comes most readily to mind when we consider leadership, but the other relationships are just as important. Taken together, these chapters present a 360-degree set of leadership tactics. Because relational leadership skills apply to everyone in every social system, regardless of age, gender, race, or seniority, the laws in Part II are the foundation of effective leadership—and by effective, I mean leadership that achieves business results the right way: without demeaning, demoralizing, or destroying people.

3	*Leading Subordinates*
	OF EXPECTATIONS, FEEDBACK, AND RIDING A BIKE

As a young guy about to start my business career, I used to fantasize about making it to the big time and becoming a huge success. As part of my dream I'd think about how great it would be to have lots of people working under my command, and to be able to tell them—sensitively, of course—what I wanted them to do. This is a naively simplistic view, but lots of young managers today hold these same notions of leadership that I had one hundred years ago. Frighteningly, many senior executives do as well.

The mind-set is one of power and authority: The more senior an executive, the more power and authority he or she has to command and control people. There is some truth in this notion—a leader is supposed to set direction and chart a course for his or her organization. People want to know where they're headed and what they're supposed to achieve. They need to know this.

But in a deeper sense, day-to-day leadership is much less about the use of power and much more about the empowerment of others. It's about pulling people rather than pushing people, about *taking people with you.* You don't do this primarily with speeches, strategic vision, or, for that matter, efficient management. You do it by enabling, by teaching, by coaching, and by helping your people to excel.

I discovered this about leadership after trying to live out my fantasy of leading by telling people what to do. I discovered after several years of pushing people (not always gently!) that people would comply with my direction but weren't very committed to me or my organization. I also learned that, at the opposite extreme, providing no direction can be just as deadly to a leader's success. The boss who has no interest in a particular subordinate's work is a character we all recognize, and has prompted endless war stories in class from my MBA students.

My own false steps early in my career gave me some real insights into what can happen through an overreliance on power and authority (the incident on Hurricane Island, with which we began this book, is a good case in point). After leading in this way for a number of years, I realized that my subordinates were afraid of me and my use of power: that they withheld their true opinions, that they weren't able to give me honest feedback, and that they felt intimidated. At the same time I'd watch executives whose teams were more motivated and more energized—and more productive. And I'd listen to high-potential managers, many of whom I had hired, come to me to complain—about bosses who didn't seem to have blood in their veins, bosses who didn't demonstrate any interest in the work of these managers, and bosses who rarely, if ever, gave their managers a sense of how they were doing.

From these experiences I distilled Feiner's Laws of Leading Subordinates—laws that show leaders how to enable, how to teach, how to coach, and how to help their people excel.

1. THE LAW OF EXPECTATIONS

In 1968, teachers in a California school district were told that certain third-grade students had scored well on a "late bloomer" test. The test measured the innate ability of these students: Those who scored well had considerable potential, and would likely have a learning spurt in the near future, irrespective of their classroom performance to date. At the end of the school year, the school district found that nearly all of these late bloomers had significantly better classroom achievement. IQ scores of many of these students went up as well.[1]

This really doesn't seem so surprising. The kids who had been identified as late bloomers did, indeed, bloom, so the test must have been accurate. But there was no test! The entire exercise was an experiment conducted by the school district in collaboration with Robert Rosenthal, a well-known psychologist. The students identified as late bloomers were simply selected at random. Yet their performance improved. How can this improvement be explained? The designers of the experiment suggest that, first, teachers' expectations were raised when told to expect a learning spurt. With their raised expectations, teachers gave these students more time and more attention. With the increased attention and focus they received, the students began to sense the enhanced confidence in them from their teachers, and the higher expectations of success. And this enabled them to improve their performance. (And it goes further than this. A later experiment by the same psychologist using rats suggests that these expectations are communicated wordlessly.)

The Pygmalion experiment, as this study came to be called, has some monumentally important lessons for parents and teachers— and leaders. It suggests that *people live up to their perception of our expectations of their performance.* More simply, *people respond to the level of confidence you show in them.* Many of us have had an important experience in our lives where someone has believed in us. The linkage is quite simple: My parents believe in me, or my coach believes in me, or my teacher believes in me, or my boss believes in me, so—*I believe in me.* It follows that you can have high expectations for performance if you believe—and convey the belief through your involvement and the quality of your interactions—that your subordinates will meet or exceed these expectations.

A wonderful story that illustrates this Law perfectly involves the late Billy Martin, five-time manager (and five-time fired manager) of the New York Yankees. I happened to catch an interview with him on a talk show many years ago. Cantankerous, insubordinate, and argumentative, Billy had trouble holding down a job, especially with the Yankees. Nevertheless, he managed them to a pennant in 1977 and a world championship in 1978 and also enjoyed considerable success with other clubs, young teams with low payrolls and few marquee players that were not expected to perform as well.* When asked the reason for his success, Billy responded almost immediately.

"That's very simple," he said. "At the end of spring training, as we break camp and head out to start the regular season, every one of my ballplayers believes that he's starting the season batting one thousand, not zero." Think of the genius of this perspective. Billy might have been a difficult guy to manage but he certainly knew about the Law of Expectations and its link to leading people to excel.

In sum, expectations are a ceiling on performance, not a floor under it. To raise performance, a leader must raise the ceiling.

The irony here is that we're taught and accept the dictum that leaders should not assess subordinates at the beginning of a per-

---

*Martin's career record with non-Yankees teams is as follows: In 1969 he took the Minnesota Twins from seventh to first; in 1971, he took the Detroit Tigers from fourth place to second, and to first the following year; in 1974 he took the Texas Rangers from sixth to second; and in 1980 he took the Oakland Athletics from seventh to second.

formance cycle, but should withhold evaluation until a formal performance review. Of course, these reviews are important in assessing the performance of your people. But that should not stop you
from showing your confidence from the get-go in a subordinate's
ability to meet his or her year-end targets. Given the results of the
Pygmalion experiment, it makes no sense not to show your confidence. If people respond to the level of confidence leaders show
them, it behooves a leader to be absolutely certain that the subordinate is aware of this confidence. The leader's belief must be explicit and palpable: Conveying that *you* believe your people can
and will exceed expectations gets *them* to believe it. And, finally,
convincing your people of your high expectations of their performance is an important way to show your commitment to their
success.

2. THE LAW OF INTIMACY

For ten years I had it all wrong. Being a good leader, I thought, required that I treat everyone the same. It seemed a logical and sensible approach in order to avoid playing favorites, and to create a
level playing field. But treating people the same confuses *equitable*
treatment and *similar* treatment—treating people *equitably* does
not mean treating everyone the same. Some of your subordinates
need a short leash, some a long leash. Some need lots of freedom
to perform best, some prefer structure. Equity comes from giving
each subordinate what he or she needs to perform, even though
these needs may be different.

Which means that a High-Performance Leader must really
know his or her people, and what makes them tick. What are their
hopes, dreams, and ambitions? What are their fears? Under what
conditions and type of supervision do they perform best? To answer these questions, a High-Performance Leader must practice
the Law of Intimacy. The law states that *to lead your people, you*

must know your people. And although this might seem obvious, it's incredible how infrequently it happens.

For twenty years at Pepsi I quarterbacked succession planning reviews for the entire management cadre. At these sessions, called Human Resource Planning sessions, or HRPs, managers would review their people's strengths and weaknesses, their suitability for promotion, and their long-term potential. The reviews, conducted over a three-month period, would be cascaded up the organization so that by the time the senior executive level was reached, my boss and I would be listening to senior executives reporting on the top three hundred people in the corporation.

These HRP sessions were vital to our ability to build a world-class management cadre by identifying top-flight talent early. For me, they served another different but equally important role. As executives reviewed the strengths of their people and their readiness for promotion, the HRP process allowed me to assess the executives in terms of how well they knew their people—of how familiar they were with what made their subordinates tick.

The Chairman devoted a month of his time to these sessions, and they were pretty rigorous. I essentially ran the reviews, and this was where I'd ship—that is, deliver the results expected of me.

A senior executive—we'll call him Ian—would get up and talk about his people, what they did, what they'd achieved, key questions about them, and I'd say, "Ian, what's the key question on Barbara?"

And he'd say, "The key question is, 'How high is up?' Barbara is a very high-potential member of the team, very good executive, very buttoned-up, results are great. She's ready. The question is, how high can she go? At this point, I'm not sure."

I'd say, "You know, we have an opening in California for a senior operations executive. Is Barbara ready for that job?"

"Absolutely. I mean, she's got a thirty-thousand-mile guarantee from me. There's no doubt she could do it, she's going to be stretched, but she's ready."

I'd say, "We have this opening in L.A. Would she move?"

Ian would say, "Hell yes—she's ambitious and wants to get ahead."

I'd say, "Well, we'll probably move her around November 15, after the school year is started. Is she married?"

"Yes."

"Any children?"

"Yes, she's got a couple of . . . I think two, maybe three kids."

"Know their ages?"

"Ah, I'm not sure, I believe twelve, eight, and six...or fifteen, twelve, and . . ."

"Well, high school's a tough time to move kids. Barbara's husband, does he work?"

"Yes, I think he's in advertising, or an attorney, or something like that."

And I'd say, "Well, Ian, let me ask you a question"—because Ian just shot himself in the foot—"How long have you managed Barbara?"

"About three and a half years."

I had this kind of conversation over and over again for twenty years. This is sad. This is a poignant story. Far too often your senior constituents don't know you, don't know what you're all about. And that's just the biographical stuff. So if they don't know the biographical detail, you can pretty much bet that they don't know what style of management you operate best under, what your hopes and dreams are, and so forth. But if leaders don't know their people, they can't effectively lead them.

Now, the best way—indeed, the only way—to get to know your people is to watch them, to listen to them, and, most importantly, to experiment with different approaches to leading them. It's not your job to be their shrink, but it is your job to learn as much as you can so you can bring out the best in people, so that they excel. Over time you'll find out a lot, *especially if people believe you have a genuine interest in learning who they are!* Your intentions as a leader will determine their response. If you want to know—if you display commitment to them by trying to understand them better—they'll let you know. But if you're only asking because you think you should—if you display commitment only to yourself and your career—don't expect to find out much, and don't expect people to be fooled.

A caveat here. The Law of Intimacy does not mean you need to become friends with your subordinates, or that you need to socialize with them outside of work. You do not and you should not. Even if you think you can have a personal relationship with a subordinate outside of work, and maintain an objective relationship in the workplace—which is highly unlikely—the rest of your subordinates will not believe it. One of my larger mistakes was playing racquetball several times a week with Carlos, who worked for one of my direct reports. While we didn't socialize outside of work and confined our nonprofessional activity to racquetball during lunch hours, I learned that my staff was threatened by this and felt the playing field was uneven for others at Carlos's level who didn't have such direct access to the boss. Be careful, then, that knowing your people stops short of befriending them.

Before leaving the Law of Intimacy, I want to reiterate that treating people differently makes sense because people *are* different. While your performance standards should be the same for all your people, you must determine the best way to enable a subordinate to meet and exceed these standards. Just as every person is different, so every person's way of delivering great performance is different. It's your job to know what it takes for your people to ship.

A story about my dog, Piccadilly, is worth telling, not just because it's a cute story, but because Piccadilly reminds me every day that the Law of Intimacy applies even to pets. When our family got Piccadilly about five years ago, we were new to dog ownership. So we were confused after a year or so when we noticed that some evenings she would mope while other nights she would be frisky and playful. Then we figured it out. Unless my wife or I greeted Piccadilly *first* after being away for the day—and took fifteen seconds to scratch behind her ears before acknowledging the rest of the family—she would mope. Properly tended to, Piccadilly is cheerful and contented. I'm not suggesting that subordinates are like pets. But I am suggesting that, among other things, it's important for leaders to learn which of their subordinates need more scratching behind the ear, figuratively speaking, to be fully productive.

3. THE LAW OF BUILDING A CATHEDRAL

High-Performance Leaders believe they will change the world, and they infuse their subordinates with this belief. When a leader provides meaning and purpose with this degree of fervor, with this sense of passion and significance to the future of the human race, he or she convinces people that *they're building a cathedral, not cutting stone.*

The mission—Warren Bennis calls it a "Mission from God," which captures the sense here exactly—is not make-believe. It's not invented. Rather, it's discovered within the organization, or handed down from some higher force outside the organization. It's not a Big Hairy Audacious Goal (BHAG),[2] which seeks to motivate by the *size* of the goal; rather, the Mission from God motivates by connecting the work that fills our days with a *purpose* bigger than all of us.

After I joined Pepsi, it was only a matter of months before I began to feel that beating Coke was our manifest destiny. We were engaged in the mission of taking on and defeating the world's most powerful trademark—we were the underdog, the David taking on Goliath.

I recall visiting a restaurant with my young children. As soon as we sat down, a waitress approached our table, welcomed us, and asked for our beverage orders. My kids looked at me warily—milk was the standard beverage of choice in our home—and my son ordered a Coke. My daughter quickly followed with the same request. I was flabbergasted. I quickly told the waitress "they mean Pepsi." Smiling, she replied, "Sorry, we only have Coke."

We left the restaurant. Not serving Pepsi was sacrilegious.

I hired a consultant who was helping me do some strategic work for the Chairman. He had a New Year's party. We arrived at the party, and headed to the bar to get a shooter. He only had Coke mixers. We left the party!

The Law of Building a Cathedral is not about shareholder value or return on invested capital. In a sense, these are trivial in terms of what your organization is about—and trivial not because I assert that, but because only a tiny proportion of your people will ever truly be fired up by the desire to increase operating profits. This is about believing so deeply in the mission, in the vision, in the organization, that it's a part of you. It's taken over, in a sense, who you are and what you want to be. And your subordinates and peers understand, as they spend more time working with you, that what they do is vital to the mission. They feel important to its success, and that feeling of importance engenders their motivation, responsibility, and trust.

Now, as I look back on these two instances from early in my Pepsi career, I ask myself what the hell I was thinking (and my wife still can't believe that we left the party). At the time, however, my actions felt not only reasonable but unavoidable. Pepsi's leaders had identified our mission, and had presented it not as a memo outlining the strategic vision, not as an anemic mission statement, laminated, pinned to the wall, and universally ignored, but rather as our very own cathedral construction project. Beyond presenting it, they lived and breathed it, and we lived and breathed it along with them.

4. THE LAW OF PERSONAL COMMITMENT

Every successful executive I ever worked with or consulted for became successful because of commitment. Commitment to his or her own success, that is. Corporate life is a demanding institution and it takes an intense achievement orientation to make it. It's stating the obvious to say that, to be successful, executives must be passionate about being outstanding performers, meeting or beating their targets, and driving their organization's total performance. Perhaps commitment to one's success is just another way to describe ambition.

But I use the word commitment for a reason other than trying to be linguistically elegant. And the story that follows will explain why.

I had been Vice President and Chief People Officer for Pepsi's $3 billion U.S. business for less than a year. At age thirty-nine, I was a very young guy in a very big job. And the following day I needed to brief PepsiCo's Chief Operating Officer that there was a real possibility of a work stoppage in Chicago,* our most profitable market. The issue was our desire to convert our employees from a Teamster pension plan to a company plan. A company plan would be much less expensive to Pepsi to fund, but more importantly we believed our employees were getting a raw deal—too much of Pepsi's monthly contribution to the Teamster plan was covering administrative costs (which we felt to be excessive), rather than going to actual employee benefits. The challenge was to convince our employees that our company plan would be better for them than the Teamster plan.

*The name of the city has been changed.

But I'm getting ahead of myself. My boss and I first had to convince Rick, PepsiCo's COO, that our intentions were worth the risk of a long strike in Chicago, long a bastion of Teamster support.

Because I was no expert on the technicalities of pension plan funding, I was bringing Dan, my benefits guru, to the meeting to join me and my boss in our presentation.

When Dan poked his head in my office the day before our meeting, I waved him in and asked if he was all set for the next day's presentation.

"Well, that's what I wanted to talk to you about," he said.

"I'm glad you came by," I continued, "we need to have our act together since I'm sure Andy will ask some tough questions tomorrow."

There was a long pause—Dan was obviously uneasy.

"What's the matter?" I asked. "We've been discussing Chicago for months."

More pause and then Dan, with a look of embarrassment, replied, "I can't make the meeting tomorrow."

"That's a joke, right?" I said, laughing nervously. "I don't know diddly about pensions. I know a little more about pensions than I do about turbine engines, which is nothing. So you have to help me—I'm going to introduce you, it's a multimillion-dollar issue, we could take a twelve- to sixteen-week strike over this issue in Chicago, so you're going to make the presentation."

"I'm not kidding," he offered meekly. "I won't be able to go to the meeting."

Now I was starting to get ticked off. "Look, Dan—I'm not sure what the problem is. We've had this meeting scheduled—"

"I know, but I didn't know how to tell you. I can't make it."

"Can I know why?"

"I just can't make it."

I was dumbfounded at this. The clash with the Teamsters was the first really major issue I had faced since getting this job. The possibility of a strike—a long one—in a major market such as Chicago could end up costing Pepsi a million dollars a week in operating profit. A bad presentation on my part would hardly demonstrate that the new guy understood what was at stake.

"Is there something going on I don't know about?" I asked.

He hesitated before responding. "Yes," he said finally. "I have a family commitment."

"What commitment?"

"I'd really rather not say," he replied. "It's just important and that's all I can say."

At this point I was incredulous. "You owe me a fuller explanation. What's the commitment?"

"Tomorrow's Halloween," Dan offered, blushing.

"That's great," I said. "And the sky is blue. What does that have to do with—"

"It's Halloween," he said, "and I have to take my kids trick-or-treating."

I shot back, "Dan, stop screwing around. This meeting tomorrow is a big deal. Seriously, what is the family commitment you don't want to tell me about?"

"Look," he replied, "it's a commitment I made to myself and my kids—that I'd take them trick-or-treating every Halloween."

"Okay," I replied, "I understand what you're saying and I respect how devoted you are to your kids. That's wonderful. But this is ridiculous. I mean, I'm naked here . . . I'm exposed. Halloween trick-or-treating? Maybe your wife's birthday, or your anniversary, but Halloween trick-or-treating? You'll miss it once."

"Mike, I know it may seem silly or trivial but it's something I feel I need to do. Please don't ask me to attend the meeting tomorrow. It will really disappoint my kids."

"Why didn't you mention this two weeks ago when we put this on our calendars? Why am I finding out the day before the meeting?"

"Because I thought for sure that Corporate would change the meeting date. You know how often calendars change around here, especially when Corporate is involved. And then as the meeting date got closer I was simply embarrassed to tell you—I knew what your reaction would be."

"Look," I said, still thinking I had a way to work this out. "The meeting is at five-thirty. It probably won't take more than an hour, you'll be out of here by six-thirty and home by seven."

"Mike," he said, "you know I have young kids. They'll be asleep. I'm sorry, but I need to skip tomorrow's meeting."

I tell this story because it represents what happens hundreds or thousands of times every day in all kinds of organizations, of all types and sizes. Leaders have to decide when to cut employees slack and when the organization must come first. They are faced every day with special requests from employees involving sick children or spouses or parents. Or school recitals or doctor's appointments or college visits or Little League games or varsity athletic events. Or requests for extra vacation time or long weekends. Some of these seem weighty and important; others can seem trivial.

I was angry at Dan for not telling me sooner. But my immediate concern was figuring out what to do. The most obvious solution here would have been to tell Dan that trick-or-treating, while important to him, was insignificant given the importance this meeting represented to the business—and to my own career. "Sorry, Dan, you'll have to suck it up and make other plans—I need you at tomorrow's meeting," would seem like the response any ambitious, achievement-oriented executive like myself would have given. Besides which, I didn't know what I would tell my boss, who knew I was no pension whiz, if I decided to grant Dan's request. I wasn't afraid to tell Dan that he had to attend—believe me, at Pepsi I was considered a demanding boss with relentlessly high performance standards (others may have had more colorful descriptions). On the other hand, however, Dan was a very talented manager and I wanted to give him all the consideration I could. And I didn't want to risk alienating him—and his family!

Ultimately I decided to give Dan a pass, and I did so because at that point in my career, after years of getting these situations wrong, I had come to understand the Law of Personal Commitment. It states that *if a leader wants a subordinate to be committed to the success of the leader and the leader's organization, then the leader must be committed to the subordinate*—to his or her growth and development, and to what's important to him or her both inside and outside the office.

I told Dan, "I think you're carrying this trick-or-treat thing to extremes. You've got a big job with a premier company, this meeting is a big deal, and asking for time off is something I have trouble with. But it's obviously important, very important to you. So bring me up to speed as best you can—teach me everything you can about this pension stuff. I'll have to tell the boss tomorrow that when we go see the chairman, it's going to be me. And pray, for my sake as well as yours, that I don't come off looking like a moron tomorrow afternoon."

So we spent some time cramming together, and I went to see my boss the next morning, and he said, "Are you all set for the meeting?"

And I said, "Yup."

And he said, "Dan's all set?"

And I said, "No, Dan's not all set. Actually Dan can't make it."

And he said, "Well, who's going to make the presentation?"

And I said, "I am."

"You don't know zilch about pensions. You know zippo about this stuff. I mean, I know nothing, but you know almost nothing."

I said, "No, I'm up to speed, I know it."

He said, "Mike, this is your ass on the line here, 'cause this is the big dude we're seeing, and I don't want to be embarrassed . . ."

I said, "I've got it covered. It's a lock."

So we went to the meeting, made the presentation, the COO asked three questions that I knew the answers to, we were done in fifteen minutes, and he gave us approval to take the strike.

Dan, meanwhile, was relieved and at the same time a little shocked at my decision. But the real point is that, because I put my butt on the griddle for him, Dan saw firsthand that I cared about him and about what was important to him. Of course, he knew how ambitious I was and how concerned I was about my performance and the performance of my department. But that afternoon he saw that he wasn't just another factor of production in my career dreams. He realized I was prepared to make a sacrifice for him. Dan worked in my organization for another eleven years, and was incredibly loyal and committed to me, to my success, and to our organization's performance.

The Law of Personal Commitment means that you must be committed to your subordinates' careers as well as to your own. Believe me, people understand that their bosses are committed to their own success, to their own fame and fortune. Subordinates recognize that they will succeed if they help make the boss and the boss's organization look good. People are savvy in this way about the rituals of organizational life. But they will never fully commit to a boss unless the boss demonstrates commitment to them. The Law of Personal Commitment means that *to get loyalty, you must give loyalty*. This personal commitment occurs in small ways—like getting back to a subordinate when you promised, like making sure performance appraisals are done on time, like processing the salary increase when it's due, like making yourself available when a subordinate needs to see you—and in big ways, like being actively involved in teaching and coaching, on an ongoing basis.

High-Performance Leaders, then, are committed to a subordinate's growth, development, and success as much as they are committed to their own fame and fortune. I once had a boss who would go through his mail during our meetings. I've heard all about multi-tasking, but think about the signal this sent to me. I'm discussing a tricky people issue with a boss who's processing his mail and listening to me at the same time. It made me feel like an ashtray—or something about that important. He had no interest in me as a person. He had interest in my productivity, and he had interest in whether or not I was meeting his objectives, but he had no time for me—he wasn't willing to be in my space.

If a leader cares about his or her people, if a leader commits, day in and day out, to their growth and development, and if a leader manages to convey that sense of commitment, subordinates will go to the wire, will give one hundred percent—will contribute, directly, to improved business results. That's what Dan did for me, *after* I took a risk for him.

But you can't fake it. Subordinates know when a leader is genuinely committed and when he or she is not. No matter what a leader says to his or her people, if that leader spends most of the time each day looking up the organization at his or her superiors, the words mean nothing. Your people are more concerned with your feet than with your mouth.

Younger, up-and-coming leaders have a hard time following this law. They are so obsessed with their own ambition and success that there is no room left in their solar systems for anybody but themselves. As a former MBA student of mine succinctly (and distressingly) put it, "The only thing I give a damn about in my career right now is me!" But although leaders who achieve great success do so because they're fanatical about being successful, this commitment is not only to their own success but to the success of their people.

5. THE LAW OF FEEDBACK

When former students contact me, it's often to ask for advice on how to handle the problem of the uncommunicative boss. People want feedback. They *need* feedback. One of the reasons sports are so important to people all over the world is that they allow participants and spectators alike to keep score—at any moment we know if our team is ahead or behind. And with careers, people need to know the score, need to know how they're doing.

When leaders don't give much, if any, feedback, people often assume the worst. "I must be failing." "I'm not meeting her expectations." "There's a problem here." Or, they assume something even more corrosive. "I don't really matter around here." "I'm not important enough to warrant feedback." "My boss doesn't care enough about me to give me feedback."

Unfortunately, there are leaders who feel they're too busy to give feedback, who are uncomfortable giving even positive feedback, or, more often, who lack the courage to tell a subordinate that he or she is not cutting it. What's inescapable, however, is that *if a leader withholds feedback out of a desire not to de-motivate, that leader actually retards improvement in a subordinate's performance.*

Feedback is a gift, in two ways. It's a gift to the recipient, because it provides data that can allow him or her to improve performance. But it's also a gift for the feedback giver himself or herself. By giving feedback that helps enhance the performance of the subordinate, the leader helps ensure that the unit's overall performance will improve.

Implicit here is that feedback is more than an "attaboy" or "attagirl." There's nothing wrong with telling someone "nice job," when it's warranted—people love these kudos; some need them continually. But feedback is more than this. It means telling a subordinate what he or she needs to do more of, needs to do less of, or needs to do differently to improve performance.

Leaders should offer this kind of feedback throughout the year. Too often feedback is held back, and then sprung on an employee during the annual performance review, in the form of a list of things the employee must initiate or change in order to improve. Needless to say, the list of to-dos generally comes as a shock, as it's the first time the employee has heard negative feedback. The employee is confronted with the realization that his or her performance has been thought badly of for a long time, but that he or she hasn't had an opportunity to respond to any concerns. This happens far too frequently in organizational life. It's called the Ambush.

Annual performance reviews should be a summary of the performance feedback conversations a leader has held with a subordinate throughout the year. The only key task in an annual performance review should be for the leader and subordinate to develop, together, a performance improvement plan for the coming year. Such a plan might include a special project, in-depth mentoring, a presentation skills program (like the one I needed when I started at Pepsi, as we'll see in a moment), or all of these. It's the investment of time in the feedback and performance improvement process that brings to life the teaching, coaching, and enabling role of a leader.

(We should also note, by the way, that feedback needs to go both ways. Bosses should encourage feedback from their subordinates, who will often have a much better idea of their boss's effectiveness than the boss will. It's a sad truth, however, that very few bosses have the DNA to receive feedback from subordinates when that feedback is negative or critical, and that the subordinate who will give this feedback without being asked for it is rare. We'll talk more about how to give unsolicited upward feedback in the next chapter.)

The Law of Feedback doesn't stop with the *need* for feedback: It goes beyond the requirement to tell subordinates how they're doing and what they need to do to improve their performance to specify the *type* of feedback required. It states that, to be effective, feedback must be *camera-lens:* The leader should indicate the *specifics of what he or she observed* that led to his or her judgment of the subordinate's performance.

I recall my maiden voyage presentation, as part of Pepsi's Strategic Plan Review. It was a high-powered cast of characters: PepsiCo's Chairman, President, and CFO, my boss (the Chairman of Beverages), and our CFO. I was one of the presenters, and I really prepped for it.

At the end of the twenty-five-minute session, we were walking out, and my boss said, "I need to see you in my office."

"Sure."

He closed the door, and said, "I have to tell you, that was a pretty poor presentation."

I was taken aback. "Really? I'm normally pretty good on my feet, I've given presentations, I mean . . ."

"Mike, watch my lips. That was a crappy presentation. And I've got to tell you, this is a transactional environment. We don't write lots of memos around here. How well you do on your feet has got a lot to do with how you do career-wise, and you blew it. Okay?"

"Can you give me a . . ."

"I don't want to . . . what more do you need? Let's not beat this into the ground. Mike, it sucked."

This was not helpful. A leader's telling a subordinate that he or she is unhappy with a subordinate's performance is just the start. The leader must continue by giving the camera-lens feedback that led to the assessment. In my case, I went back to my boss several days later, when he had gotten over being embarrassed by his new subordinate, and asked for the specifics.

He told me, "You seemed very nervous and that doesn't inspire confidence. Beyond that, I thought your slides were too busy, one of the numbers didn't foot, I think you could have used some humor at the end, and your summary was poor—it wasn't clear what your action plan was."

Now that's camera-lens feedback. It told me what he and others observed. It gave me a kind of videotape of my own performance. It gave me action items that I could use to nail my next presentation. And it clearly demonstrated why *feedback is a gift.*

Nevertheless, there are times, as you might expect, when people don't like the feedback a leader gives. I used to see this at Pepsi when people received 360-degree feedback from peers and subordinates as well as from their boss. I see it now when I'm passing on feedback to a COO or CEO that I've gained from interviewing their executive team. So I offer here a simple model that I learned years ago that may prove helpful. It's called the SARAH model, and each letter represents a phase people tend to go through when receiving negative feedback.

S stands for SHOCK. In this first phase, the recipient is almost paralyzed by the data. It's here that the recipient often feels—and may even suggest—that this feedback must have been miscoded, or that this is someone else's feedback.

A stands for ANGER. Symptoms of this phase can take seconds—or days—to appear. The recipient feels betrayed and unappreciated. Often they will be thinking, "After all the work I did on this project, this is the thanks I get."

R stands for REJECTION. Here the recipient simply rejects the feedback: "It isn't true. This isn't valid feedback. I absolutely do make time for my people. They're flat wrong." Symptoms include criticism of the company's feedback system, criticism of feedback systems in general, and unsolicited statements of what a waste of time it is to ask for feedback from people that stupid.

Here's the rub. Some people never get beyond the R stage. They are unable to accept the feedback. Hopefully, with a leader who knows the SARAH model, a recipient can be encouraged to think about the data and ponder why people may feel the way they do. The recipient then moves to the final two stages.

> **A stands for ACCEPTANCE.** At this point the recipient begins to recognize that others' perception of their behavior is a reality. The recipient acknowledges that the feedback is probably valid, painful as some of it may be to accept. Symptoms include a marked decrease in any discussion of feedback. Thus, the final phase arrives:

> **H stands for HELP!** Having accepted that there's some bad news in the feedback as well as good news, the recipient realizes that, in order to grow and develop, it's necessary to deal with the negative elements. With the leader's help, he or she develops a plan to respond to this negative data, and moves to implement that plan.

There is another important part to the Law of Feedback. It is essential, when giving feedback to subordinates, to explain the consequences of the feedback. In other words, a leader must connect the dots between the feedback and its impact on the subordinate's performance, the team's performance, and the subordinate's career.

When my boss told me my maiden voyage presentation was horrible, he didn't give me camera-lens feedback, but he certainly connected the dots for me. He let me know why my poor presentation was such a big deal. He explained that Pepsi was a highly interactive environment where people influenced others and impacted decisions by dint of their transactional skills. He communicated to me quite directly the implications of not being good on my feet—my career would be negatively impacted, as the eu-phemism goes.

I recall when a young manager—we'll call him Scott—joined my organization. His first week with Pepsi was, coincidentally, the week we held our annual off-site conference to review our goals for the coming year. These conferences were carefully planned, and people looked forward to them. It was a time for socializing with colleagues from all over the world while learning about key initia-tives. There were even well-known outside speakers to stimulate our thinking. After dinner on the second day of the conference, we had a fifties party, with a DJ. Toward the end of the evening, as a very well-known record (by the Platters, I recall) was playing, Scott, all of two days with Pepsi, jumped up on the stage, took the microphone, and proceeded to sing along—and badly at that. Most of the hundreds of people stopped dancing and began asking who this guy was. To make matters worse, some people began to shout out song requests, encouraging him to continue singing to the next record the DJ played.

I couldn't believe it. I wondered how the guy had the nerve to do this after two days in a culture he was in the early stages of learning about. Although I could have ignored his behavior—it wasn't that big a deal—or simply told him to knock it off, I thought something more was needed. I sought out the member of my team who was in charge of the division that Scott had just joined. We quickly connected. It was clear after a brief exchange that he felt the same way I did. He signaled the DJ that it was time for a break, and Scott's singing debut ended abruptly. A few min-utes later I saw my division head talking to him quietly in a corner of the room.

About a half hour after that, after the DJ resumed the party, Scott came over to my table and asked if I had a moment. I said I did, and we walked out of the room to a small foyer. Scott said he wanted to apologize. I asked if he knew what he was apologizing for.

"Well, I guess it was kind of rude to just take the DJ's mike. I didn't mean to embarrass him."

"Scott," I said, "you didn't embarrass him. You embarrassed yourself. To succeed here you need good situational judgment. In your job you'll be interacting with lots of people, some much more senior than you. What I'm concerned about is that, with practically no knowledge of the culture and what's appropriate behavior at these conferences, you decided to do something rash and imprudent. Most of the people here haven't yet met you. What kind of impression will they form of you now?"

"I never thought of it that way. I'm really sorry."

"Look, you didn't commit a felony. What you did was a corporate misdemeanor. And had you been here for a while and established your professional reputation on the basis of performance and results, jumping on stage and singing would be fine. It's just that your situational judgment here was flawed. And situational judgment will be critical to the relationships you form with colleagues and everyone at Pepsi you work with. These relationships will have a direct impact on how far you go here."

Scott understood—he got it. My practicing the Law of Feedback helped him see the implications of his behavior on his reputation, and therefore on his career. Scott acted more thoughtfully during the rest of the conference. He was not simply more low-key, but he tried to observe more carefully the people around him and learn as much as possible about the acceptable and unacceptable rituals of this new culture.

The Law of Feedback is not easy to practice. It takes time—a commodity that, for leaders in particular, is in very short supply—to give camera-lens feedback on an ongoing basis. It takes guts for a leader to give negative feedback to a thin-skinned subordinate, whose response is likely to follow the SARAH model. Yet when leaders summon the commitment and the courage required, subordinates respond. Not simply because they know the leader cares about their performance, but because they have a clear picture of what they can do to improve it.

6. THE LAW OF TOUGH LOVE

The Laws of Expectations, Intimacy, Building a Cathedral, Personal Commitment, and Feedback will have a crucial impact in unleashing a subordinate's potential, and practicing these laws requires discipline and resolve. But the Law of Tough Love takes real guts. You won't have to apply it often, but from time to time it will lead you to take on really difficult issues that it would be easier to duck. It addresses those situations where the leader needs to deliver a difficult message or make a tough decision about a subordinate— those situations where *it is as difficult for the leader to speak out as it is for the subordinate to hear.*

High-Performance Leaders have the courage to take on these uncomfortable issues. Issues, on a small scale, such as telling a subordinate that their style of dress is inconsistent with the corporate culture, or that their personal hygiene is a problem. Or issues on a much larger scale, such as when I noticed that a subordinate—and one of my best performers—seemed to get a bit sloppy after a few drinks at corporate dinners.

Fred wasn't anywhere near the point of being drunk at these events, but I noticed changes when he drank that made me feel that he was beyond being simply more relaxed and mellow. I wasn't sure what to do, so I let it go. After all, his performance was excellent. As the months passed, I continued to observe the same behavior becoming increasingly accentuated, albeit subtly. My instincts told me Fred had a drinking problem, but his behavior was definitely within reasonable bounds, and I remained unsure of what to do. I had a great relationship with him, which I didn't want to jeopardize.

After too many sleepless nights, however, I decided that no matter how difficult it was going to be, I had to talk with him. So at the end of a weekly one-on-one meeting with him, I said, with a large amount of anxiety, "I need to talk to you about something, and I'm not even sure how to do it. So rather than beat around the bush—are you all right?" I asked this knowing that the only response it would elicit would be, "What are you talking about?"

He said, "What are you talking about?"

I said, "I don't know—I just notice with you that . . . I can't put my finger on it, but something doesn't seem right with you at a lot of these off-sites."

He said, "What are you talking about?"

I said, "What I'm talking about is—it seems to me that after . . . after one drink you seem a little out of sorts, not yourself."

I was very nervous. I didn't want to de-motivate him, I didn't want to humiliate him, I didn't want to embarrass him: He was a key member of my team.

He said, "What do you mean?"

I took a deep breath. "Fred, it just seems to me that after a drink—not after three or four—you're in the bag. If it was just a few pops at one meeting, and you're a little bit over the edge, we wouldn't be having this conversation. But it seems to me that there's a consistent pattern of behavior where after a drink you're noticeably high, and it gets more noticeable to me after that. Is this the first time you've heard this?"

He said, "Yeah, this is the first time I've heard this: I don't know what you're talking about."

I said, "Well, I'm worried about you, I'm worried about your stepping over the line. Is this a problem?"

He paused. And then he paused again. "Mike," he said, finally,

"I've always struggled with this. I know that after a drink—it doesn't take much and I'm sort of in another place."

I said, "How long have you noticed this?"

He said, "I've noticed this for a long time. And I try to manage it, I try to control it."

I said, "You're thirty-nine years of age. If you're trying to control it, you're going to lose. Given what I know about it—which is not a lot—this is going to be a problem for you. You've got to come to terms with this."

He said, "Mike, like I said, it's never been a problem. Has anybody else said anything to you about it, in the group? Any of my people?"

"No. But I'm just concerned about what I see, and I'd like you to try to do something about it."

"I've been doing something about it for fifteen years. I try to control it, to handle it . . ."

I said, "If you've got a problem, trying to control it is just dealing with the symptoms. You need to get to the bottom of the problem. Because at some point this is an accident waiting to happen. You're going to either mess up your career, or you're going to embarrass me, or you're going to embarrass the company, and none of those are good things. You need to deal with this. You need to get into a program."

He said, "Mike, you're overreacting. I'm not an alcoholic."

I said, "I don't know what you are. But what I see makes me very uncomfortable, and I want you to get into a program. I want you to go to a doctor and get a physical—if you don't want to go to the PepsiCo doctor that's your business, you can go to your own doctor—and I want you to get into one of those programs."

"We're going from your thinking I'm a little relaxed or chatty at meetings over the past few months, to all of a sudden I'm going to a resident treatment program?"

"It's that plus what you just told me. You've been trying to handle this for fifteen years? I've seen the end of this movie. You're just masking the symptoms, hiding the issue. You're just pretending. You've got a problem."

"What about my family? You're going to tell them?"

"My sense is that they know already. Fred, if I didn't know you, didn't care about you and your career, I could duck this. I'm going to be leaving this position soon. This isn't going to be my problem, in one sense. But I can't recommend you to replace me, knowing that you've got an issue with alcohol."

"Don't do this."

"Fred, I have to."

"What will I tell my people?"

"We'll tell people you're attending an executive education program. You know how prestigious that is. They'll never know—I won't leave tracks. But you've got to go to a treatment program. Your job depends on it. This is nondiscretionary: I'm not asking you, I'm telling you."

He was emotional. "You can't do this to me. My performance . . . my family . . . my people will find out . . ."

"They won't find out from me. Listen, if I have to pay ten thousand dollars out of my budget for an executive program just so the receipt's on the record, I'll do it—I don't give a damn. That's how committed I am. But you're going to this program."

With great reservations, Fred agreed, and subsequently enrolled in the program. The good news was that he learned from his treatment program how dangerous and deep-seated his drinking problem was. He was able to get control of it, and went on to become a highly successful senior executive in the company. But this was one of the most difficult conversations I ever had to have with a subordinate. A week of root canal surgery would have been preferable. Worse, Fred was not happy about my ultimatum, and it definitely affected our professional relationship for almost two years. That was a great loss for me, because I really trusted him and valued his comradeship. In the end he realized that what I did was the right thing—for him, for me, and for Pepsi—but it took a long time.

A leader who has so much concern that he or she is willing to experience embarrassment and pain, and to cause embarrassment and pain, knowing that this will ultimately have a positive payoff for a subordinate, is following the Law of Tough Love. Tough love is hard to give, and hard to receive. But love is the operative word here. *It's the sign of the ultimate respect that a leader can show a subordinate.*

7. THE LAW OF COMPETENCY-BASED COACHING

This law sounds like a mouthful, but it is really pretty simple. *The lower a subordinate's skill and experience level, the more coaching and teaching a leader must provide.* This doesn't appear to be very complicated. Yet many leaders I worked with at Pepsi, and many of the senior executives I consult with today, sing the same refrain: "I don't have the time to coach my people."

Of course, a leader's job is very demanding. The array of to-dos is virtually endless—keeping bosses informed, customers happy, suppliers involved, and investors advised, not to mention the strategic reviews, operating plans, sales reports, budget analyses, and other requirements organizations place on leaders. For many leaders, coaching subordinates is a nice to-do, but definitely not a top-of-the-food-chain priority. When I hear this—and I hear it a lot—I'm reminded of how you learn to ride a bike.

Regardless of what culture we're from or what country we're from, it really is extraordinary that we all learned to ride a bike the same way. One day, either you decide, or your mother/father/sister/brother decides it's time for you to learn how to ride a bicycle. So, usually on a Saturday morning, you go out to your bike, mother/father/sister/brother tells you to get on the bike, asks if you're on, puts one hand on the back of seat, one hand on the handlebar, and yells, in whatever language:

"Pedal. *Pedal!* PEDAL!"

And, risking a coronary, they run alongside the bike, so that after about four or five minutes, perspiration is absolutely soaking their body, they're gasping for breath, and an hour later, a day later—in my case, a week later—you learn how to ride a bike.

And although we may make light of it, this is one of the more important experiences in a young person's life, because it's one of their first experiences where they begin to acquire some sense of confidence, of mastery of their own environment. This is particularly true of riding a bike because it is not a simple activity to learn.

And you're feeling great. So the next day, you go to Mother or Father and say, "I'm going to ride over to Tina's house today."

Naturally, every parent's response to this is the same—"No way!"

They say, "We're so proud of you, but that's five or six blocks away, and there's traffic, and you've just learned, so I think you need a little more practice. So today, I'm going to walk beside you. I don't need to hold the seat or the framus,* and let's see how you do today, and tomorrow, if you continue to make Mommy and Daddy proud, maybe early next week you can ride to Tina's house."

This, in a nutshell, is the Law of Competency-Based Coaching. Just as parents would never let their child ride in traffic before they were assured of their kid's cycling capability, a leader has the same responsibility to prepare his or her subordinates for the challenges they'll face. If leaders feel they don't have the time to coach their subordinates, then the solution is brutally simple: They need to make the time. Otherwise, they're doing the equivalent of sending their kids into traffic without being sure they're ready. There's no

---

*Framus *n, pl* -es any object for which the speaker cannot immediately recall the correct name. It applies in particular to objects of a mechanical nature.

such thing as not having the time. High-Performance Leaders recognize that they have to constantly juggle and rejuggle priorities so that those subordinates who need their coaching receive it. Coaching subordinates must not be allowed to migrate to the bottom of a leader's priority list. Too often the same leaders—those who complain about not having the time—want to know why they find it necessary to replace a subordinate, whose performance has been unsatisfactory, after only a year on the job.

But this law is not only about the importance of coaching per se, but about the importance of matching your teaching to the skill level of your subordinate. Most of us instinctively understand how to do this when a subordinate is new to a task and needs intensive coaching; High-Performance Leaders know how to provide a lighter touch with more experienced staff. When they have great people, High-Performance Leaders don't micromanage, disempower, or get in the way through intrusive coaching, unless there's a specific problem and a need for their direct involvement. There's a connection here with the Law of Expectations: coaching good people too closely sends a signal that you have low expectations, and so ultimately retards performance. Coaching less skilled subordinates, however (assuming they're aware of their shortcomings), sends a signal that you expect them to improve (else why bother coaching?), thereby raising the ceiling on performance.

A corollary to the sending-your-subordinate-into-traffic scenario involves training. Often, a leader feels proud that he or she has astutely assessed a subordinate's development needs. While this is an important role for a leader, frequently the assessment gets translated into sending the subordinate to a training program. Now, I believe in training. I've run large training organizations during my career, I teach MBAs today because I feel my course is helpful to their career success, and I participate in many of Columbia Business School's executive programs. I've seen that classroom experiences for aspiring and existing leaders can be valuable. But at least ninety percent of learning takes place on the job. It's the daily interactions that a subordinate has with his or her boss that present the best opportunity for skill development. Some of these teaching moments don't even take extra time. I often took young managers with me to meetings with other senior leaders so they could see firsthand how people interacted. But however they do it, High-Performance Leaders understand that they have the primary responsibility, not only for hiring talented people, but for teaching and coaching and grooming them. Before sending a subordinate to training, leaders should first ask what they can do to enhance a subordinate's skill. In the final analysis, leaders are teachers—they know this and assume this role willingly, no matter how busy they are.

8. THE LAW OF ACCOUNTABILITY

The previous seven laws address how to motivate and inspire subordinates. People respond when leaders practice these laws, and the difference is noticeable. But there is one last piece to the Laws of Leading Subordinates. If you want your entire organization to practice these laws, if you want your subordinates to practice these laws with their own staffs, you need to do more than encourage or exhort them. That may work with a few people, but *if you want all the leaders in your organization to feel accountable for living these laws, you have to measure performance against them.* Giving speeches to your organization about applying these laws won't work. It won't work because too many leaders in your organization will believe they don't have the time. Too many leaders will place some of the other priorities we've discussed ahead of teaching, coaching, and enabling subordinates, and too many leaders will feel that subordinates shouldn't be coddled, that they need to learn to fend for themselves. This Darwinian mind-set is simplistic, misguided, and alarmingly widespread. It explains why employee turnover of 3.3 percent per month[3] is so high in this country, and it explains why speeches alone seldom make a difference.

Measuring performance includes mechanisms such as 360-degree feedback, which can give a useful picture of whether these laws are being practiced in an organization. But there is a more straightforward way to know if your staff is practicing the laws. It's vital that leaders establish a Performance Contract with each of their subordinates. A Performance Contract is simply a clearly articulated and documented understanding of what you and your subordinate agree are his or her key accountabilities for the coming year. As a result of one or two conversations, a leader and subordinate can agree on key priorities and milestones for the subordinate. Importantly, a Performance Contract should include explicit performance metrics—that is, it will define what success looks like. I use the term "contract" because, along with a leader and subordinate agreeing on expected end results for the subordinate, the process should also clarify what the subordinate needs from the leader—what the leader can do and what support he or she can provide to enhance the likelihood of the subordinate's successfully meeting the performance targets. Implicit is that the leader and subordinate are both accountable for ensuring the subordinate's success. The value of a Performance Contract is that it satisfies the need for high clarity of expectations that both a leader and a subordinate must have for a successful relationship.

And Performance Contracts can be used in a wide variety of settings. Beyond the leader-subordinate context that we've discussed, I've also seen them used between peers, between consultants and their clients, and in the classroom. I make such a contract with every class of MBAs I teach. On the very first day of a term, I begin the class by explaining to students what they have a right to expect of me. I'm explicit in suggesting what they should hold me accountable for: that the course will be relevant and its content practical and usable when they graduate; that the course's design will be stimulating and enjoyable; that I'll bring enormous passion and energy to the subject of leadership; that I'll be prepared and primed for each class; that I'll be at every class—even if I have the flu or there's a foot of snow on the ground; and that I—not my teaching assistant—will grade their written assignments and provide each student with extensive written feedback.

I let this sink in for a minute and, after a pause, I tell the students that, in consideration for what I just committed to, I have some expectations of them. And then I tell them what I will hold them accountable for: that they invest heavily in the course by becoming co-owners, along with me, of the learning process. This means, I say, coming to class well prepared, actively participating in class discussions, and attending each class and arriving on time.

At this point I suggest it's a choice each student should make, whether he or she can uphold this contractual arrangement. I offer students the option of a free pass out of class, with no hard feelings on either side, if they don't feel this is something they can commit to. I ask, "Do we have a Performance Contract?" Nearly every student nods in the affirmative. I conclude by explaining I will assume that students who do not go on to drop this course are fully prepared to live up to their end of the agreement.

Students respond to this in an amazing way. Unexcused absences from class are extremely rare, and assignments are handed in on time and are thoroughly written. And as each party continues to live up to the commitments made in the contract, so our collective pride in what we are achieving grows. If any of you are familiar with the general attitude of MBA students to nonquantitative courses, you'll appreciate the difference this represents.

A Performance Contract is one effective way to measure the use of Feiner's Laws. There are other ways, which may also be effective, but whichever one you use, the Law of Accountability reminds us that if you don't measure use of the laws—if you don't take ownership of your subordinates' development—you shouldn't expect your people to apply them. Measurement, more than encouragement, will make the difference.

Those are the eight Laws of Leading Subordinates. I'm often asked which of the eight is really the most important. It's a fair question, since, as I've acknowledged, leaders have tough jobs with a dizzying array of demands to satisfy and dragons to slay. So you'll be relieved to hear that there's a simple answer to this most important question of priority among the laws—only Laws 1, 2, 3, 4, 5, 6, 7, and 8 are critical.

In all seriousness, every one of these laws is vital. There's no fluff in the list. Each complements, intersects with, and builds on each of the others. If you don't follow the Law of Intimacy, you can't follow the Law of Competency-Based Coaching. To follow the Law of Tough Love, you have to be skilled at the Law of Personal Commitment. The Laws of Expectations, Feedback, and Accountability go hand in hand. And without the Law of Building a Cathedral, the other laws are drained of their full impact.

After reading these laws, you may conclude that being a leader is an overwhelming task. I disagree. High-Performance Leadership demands a colossal investment of your time and energy but it is not overwhelming, and the return on the investment is huge, in terms of the results you'll be able to achieve through your people. And the impact on your subordinates of practicing these laws will be extraordinary. I know this because I've experienced it as a leader when, after years of mistakes, I saw my people become as energized and motivated as I had ever seen them.

Feiner's Laws of Leading Subordinates are not only directed at leaders of large numbers of people. These laws focus on interactions between two people—a leader and a subordinate—and are thus useful for an executive and his or her assistant as much as they are for a leader of a thousand-strong division. Indeed, practicing the laws with an assistant is how many leaders have come to appreciate their value.

There is a story about two famous British Prime Ministers of the nineteenth century that gives some sense of the power of these laws. It was said that after having dinner with Gladstone, you would leave thinking that he was the smartest, wittiest, and most interesting person you had ever met. But it was said that after having dinner with Disraeli, you would leave thinking *you* were the smartest, the wittiest, and the most interesting. The point is that Disraeli was interested in what others had to say. He was attentive and a great listener. (Not like my former boss who read his mail during our meetings.) He made others feel that what they had to say was important and worth listening to.

Compare this with many of today's leaders who are so busy that they don't have time to give feedback. Or coaching. Or tough love. Who don't have time to get to know their people, or to clarify expectations. Who don't convey confidence in your ability to meet expectations. Who are committed to their own fame and fortune, not yours.

Imagine, on the other hand, working for a leader who does practice Feiner's Laws of Leading Subordinates. It would feel like the afterglow of a dinner with Disraeli. Subordinates would feel—inevitably—that they matter, they count, they're valued, they're special, they're important to the team. A leader who invests so much time and devotes so much share of mind to subordinates will achieve great results. Subordinates will feel liberated and ennobled by working for this leader, as opposed to feeling forgotten, overlooked, unappreciated, or taken for granted, feelings all too common in organizations today.

When it comes to subordinates, High-Performance Leaders see people in terms of their potential, and in terms of enabling, teaching, and coaching them to meet or exceed that potential. It's not enough for a leader to assess an underling's performance. While this assessment process is part of every leader's job, *High-Performance Leaders think as much about developing future potential as about evaluating present performance.*

And this is what you take with you at the end of a career. A retired leader in his or her rocking chair thinks not about wealth or positions held or titles earned, but about memories of people successfully mentored and developed. That's the ultimate legacy of a High-Performance Leader, and it's a legacy that can be built using these laws.

Summary: Feiner's Laws of Leading Subordinates

1. The Law of Expectations

People respond to the level of confidence you show in them—expectations are a ceiling on performance, not a floor.

2. The Law of Intimacy

To lead your people, you must know your people.

3. The Law of Building a Cathedral

Leaders convince their people that they're building a cathedral, not cutting stone.

4. The Law of Personal Commitment

If a leader wants a subordinate to be committed to the success of the leader and the leader's organization, then the leader must be committed to the subordinate.

5. The Law of Feedback

Feedback is a gift—but to be useful, it must be camera-lens feedback, and a leader must connect the dots between feedback and its impact on the subordinate's performance, the team's performance, and the subordinate's career. If a leader withholds feedback out of a desire not to de-motivate, that leader actually retards improvement in a subordinate's performance.

6. The Law of Tough Love

On those occasions where it is as difficult for the leader to speak out as it is for the subordinate to hear, High-Performance Leaders have the courage to say what needs to be said.

7. The Law of Competency-Based Coaching

The lower a subordinate's skill and experience level, the more coaching and teaching a leader must provide.

8. The Law of Accountability

If you want all the leaders in your organization to follow these laws, you have to hold them accountable for doing so.

4	## Leading Bosses
	NEVER . . . EVER . . . EVER . . . EVER TREAT YOUR BOSS LIKE A BUMBLING OLD FOOL (EVEN IF HE OR SHE IS ONE)

By far the most common complaints in organizational life—from new managers, from seasoned executives, and from everyone else in between—concern working for bad bosses. The frustrations of working for a bad boss figure prominently in the complaints that I hear from the subordinates of my consulting clients, and in the reasons my MBA students give for returning to school, just as they did in the lives of many people who sought my counsel at Pepsi. And of the fifty or so former students I hear from each year, fifty-one want advice about working for a difficult, cruel, or insensitive boss!

These complaints take many forms: "My boss is stupid," "My boss is lazy," "My boss is obsessed with his or her own success," "My boss is missing in action," "My boss is an unethical shark," "My boss is a slave driver," "My boss takes credit for my ideas," "My boss treats me as if I'm a piece of dirt," "My boss doesn't notice I exist." These comments, and others like them, suggest that satisfaction at work depends, in large part, on the quality of your relationship with your boss. Bosses set the ceiling on your career, and they have all the electoral votes—they control pay, assignments, creature comforts, and access to senior people. They're a part of corporate life for all of us, and an unpleasant relationship with a boss is demoralizing.

A story from early in my career at Pepsi illustrates my own problem with a boss. I'd been there for six months. My boss, with whom I had developed a great relationship, called me into his office one afternoon and said, "We need to talk. I'm concerned about your commitment."

I said, "Really, Doug? Wow, I mean, I'm at my desk at seven in the morning . . . I don't take lunch, I work until six-thirty or seven at night . . . and you told me recently that you're pretty positive about my performance"—I had quickly established a very good reputation there.

He said, "Well I'm concerned because I've had reports that you're leaving early on Monday nights."

And I said, "That's true—I am. I'm in a softball league, and I have a game at six-thirty every Monday, so I've got to leave around six o'clock to get to the game."

And he said, more quickly, "Listen, Mike, I don't know about this softball stuff, but this is the big leagues now, see, this is— you're an executive and this is a big, highly visible job, and softball . . . that's fine if you're in college, but it's time to grow up."

And I said, "Well you probably don't know this about me but when I was a kid I thought I was going to be a professional ballplayer, so this is really important to me, it's my way of allowing myself to live my dream for as long as I can—I never really got over not being a ballplayer, and, you know, it's important to me."

And he said, more loudly, "That's all very interesting—I thank you for sharing that. But you need to work that out with your therapist. I'm telling you right now, leaving Monday nights at six is not good for you and it's personally embarrassing for me. Some of my colleagues have seen you leaving."

And I said, "Well, is there a performance issue here, Doug?"

"No. Your performance is fine."

"Are you concerned about my commitment? I know they're concerned about it, but are *you* concerned?"

"Well, yeah. I mean, if you're leaving at six . . ."

"But it's one night a week I'm leaving at six . . . what's the big deal?"

He said, "Listen, Mike, I don't want to talk about it anymore. You know, you're a big boy, you're in a big job, and if you want to do something on weekends, play softball or any of that stuff, that's fine with me, but, you know, frankly it's embarrassing."

So I said to him, "I understand your concern, but this is really important to me. This is *really* important to me, and I probably should have told you about this ahead of time—that was my mistake. But this is a big deal for me. I really feel the need to play, and I made a commitment to this team."

And he said, "Very noble of you. Mike, I don't give a damn. And I'm telling you, okay, you need to knock it off."

So rather than evaluate my options, I spent about three nanoseconds considering what I felt and what I thought he was trying to do (my reasoning went, if I recall, "He's a jerk and a control freak, and no one tells me what to do"), and I gave him my somewhat inadequately thought out response:

"Fuck. You."

This is the wrong thing to do. This is not good. I lost it. (How interesting that this incident is the flip side of my Halloween story in Chapter 3. Perhaps I handled Dan's need to go trick-or-treating the way I did because of this softball saga seven years earlier.) Faced with an inflexible boss and what I felt was a deeply unfair situation,

I had little to resort to other than shouted profanity, which is hardly high on the list of career-enhancing tactics in these situations. My experience here, together with the myriad tales and complaints I hear every day, points to a need for tools to improve our relationships with those we work for. We need tools to address the crisis moments like this one, and to address the paucity of options most of us feel in these situations. But we also need tools to stop the crises from occurring in the first place. Because the issue here is not *if* you'll have a bad boss in your career, but how you'll deal with it *when* you do. Feiner's Laws of Leading Bosses aim to improve your relationship with your boss so that minutes of acute conflict are increasingly replaced by months of authentic collaboration.

1. THE LAW OF MAKE YOUR OWN BED

To have any chance of building a reasonable relationship with a boss, you must recognize that you're solely responsible for the quality of that relationship. This is a truth that isn't always easy to accept, especially if your boss is a total knucklehead. But this doesn't matter. The starting point is that everyone has the ability to influence the quality and effectiveness of their relationship with their boss—no matter how insufferable he or she is. Without this belief people quickly adopt the attitude of a victim, complaining about the problem instead of addressing it. Life is unfair, they tell themselves, and there's nothing that can be done about it. Wrong. It's the things *you* do, or don't do, that determine how your boss behaves toward you.[1] So for openers, to have any chance of forging an effective relationship with your boss, you must believe you are master of your own destiny.

2. THE LAW OF WHO IS THAT MASKED MAN OR WOMAN?

Just as you need to know your subordinates (The Law of Intimacy) to lead them effectively, you need to *know your boss*. Who he or she is, what motivates him or her, what his or her priorities and goals are: These are obvious questions that you need to be able to answer. Beyond these questions are many others. What are his hot buttons, fears, and ambitions? What makes her tick? What are his weaknesses (other than not treating you appropriately)? And, of course, what are her expectations of you—does she want lots of data, or just the big picture; does she want key questions, or options and a recommendation; does she want lots of updates or a check-in only when the project is completed?

Once I figured out that Pete, that former boss of mine, was a quintessential manager—Mr. Details—who loved to follow up on projects, I made sure I always beat his due dates. So when he'd ask me my progress on a project, usually several days before it was to be completed, I made sure I already had it finished. After a few months of this, Pete concluded that I was as buttoned-up as he was, and his confidence in me grew.

I worked for another boss for about ten years. I discovered early on that he was not good in the morning—meetings before noon were to be avoided at all costs. Once I figured this out, I avoided the early-day slots if at all possible. And when his secretary called and said "Steve needs to see you tomorrow at ten," I would reply, "If it's urgent I can but I'm really jammed up—I have this outsider to see"—which was a fib, but which was worth it to avoid a morning meeting.

Obviously, learning how your boss prefers to operate can take some time. But watching a boss and listening to a boss will give you some of these answers. Some answers will come from trial and error. Some answers can be learned from observing a boss's office and what he or she hangs on the wall or places on the desk. Your colleagues and your boss's other direct reports will often share the lay of the land with you. And answers can come from secretaries and your boss's former subordinates. What's important is that you subtly seek out information about your boss, that you're open to the information that comes your way, and that you treat your findings not as evidence of your boss's competence or incompetence, but as invaluable data that will enable you to perform better. High-Performance Leaders move beyond a mind-set of evaluation to one of increasing their own effectiveness.

One other point. While the table of organization may show you reporting to a single boss, that's an oversimplification. The fact is that you work for lots of people. It's essential to learn as much as possible about everyone senior to you in the organization. In one way or another they all have a say in your career, so effectively, *you work for all of them!*

3. THE LAW OF PROFESSIONAL COMMITMENT

While the first two laws might seem straightforward, the third is a little counterintuitive, and more difficult to practice. But with the Law of Professional Commitment, we begin to get to the meat of leading bosses.

Whether your boss gives a damn about you or not, as a leader *you must commit yourself to your boss's success.* This means committing yourself to making your boss look good, and having a sense of ownership for his or her effectiveness and success. Now, this isn't easy to feel if your boss is concerned only with his or her own success. That's why this law is about *professional* commitment, not *personal* commitment. It appeals to the notion of professionalism that most of us are familiar with—that to be professional means to choose the interests of the organization over our own feelings or short-term self-interest when the two are in conflict. Even if your boss treats you poorly, it's up to you to act professionally and ship for him or her, whatever your personal desires might be. The fact that you hate your boss doesn't give you a pass—leaders are still on the hook to make bosses look good.

I'm not naive. There are some bosses who behave like swamp scum. They don't deserve your best, you may think. It would be easy to let them hang themselves—and swing slowly in the wind (and if you don't feel this way at first, then after numerous attempts on your part to make your boss look good have been thwarted by his or her own idiocy, you will). Big mistake. Nothing will say more about a leader's character than his or her willingness to try to make a bad boss look good, and to persevere in the attempt whatever the results. Believe me, the rest of the organization will take note.

Besides, the other options in the bad-boss situation are much less appealing in the long run. You could quit, but even ignoring the personal and financial costs of that decision, there are only so many times in life you can afford to walk away before your reputation as a Serial Quitter catches up with you. Or, you could decide to go to your boss's boss and let him or her know what a scoundrel/sloth/ogre you work for. Unless your boss is asking you to do something that is either illegal or that violates your ethical standards, this is a high-risk approach, and I'd advise against it for several reasons. All too often, the senior boss ends up supporting your boss, and you get fired as a disloyal complainer. Or worse, the big boss takes your side, your boss is fired or moved aside, and you become labeled a Boss Killer in the organization (this kind of information *always* gets out). Even though your (now former) boss might have been unpopular, the problem with being a factor in his or her removal is that sympathies in organizations change with lightning speed—so that while people are generally quick to form negative judgments of someone whose competence is in doubt, they are equally quick to feel sympathy for that person when he or she gets fired. If you're associated with the demise of the fired person, you're in deep trouble. No one wants a Boss Killer on their team.

My advice is to do the best work you're capable of, and to follow the rest of the laws, which, in the end, will make the situation much better and more tolerable. Bottom line, *respect the office even if you don't respect who sits in it.*

4. THE LAW OF THE CAREER COVENANT

Just as you need to build a Performance Contract with your subordinates as discussed in Chapter 3, you need to build a Career Covenant with your boss. The idea of the Career Covenant is that, in consideration of your committing to your boss's success à la Law 3, you have a right to receive certain things. (While the performance contract should be a written document, the covenant with your boss should not—it's really an informal understanding of what you want your boss to give you.) Together, the four things to which you're entitled provide the critical elements you need to develop your career.

First, you need the benefit of your boss's *coaching on your skill development*, especially if you're early in your career.

Second, you have a right to expect *performance feedback* at intervals you would find helpful.

Third, you'll want *career counsel and sponsorship* on the kinds of opportunities and promotional tracks that are available in your organization.

Fourth, if you're new to the organization you'll need a heads-up from time to time on *how things work* in the culture—those unwritten tribal rituals and taboos that exist in every organization.

I'm not suggesting here that as soon as you're assigned to a new boss you sit down with him or her and set out this list of requests. Most bosses would find this approach unusual, and, besides, they will be happier to agree to these when they've seen some evidence that you will ship for them. No, my point here is that you should feel it's legitimate to expect these four things, that you should not, therefore, feel hesitant about asking for them as your relationship with your boss develops, and that if you ask in vain there are problems ahead.

Often the best approach is to frame the question in terms of your own development: "One of the things I'd find really helpful, if you have a moment, is some advice about how I could get better at client meetings." Or, "I think I'd be able to do a better job at storyboarding presentations if you could give me a few pointers." Or, "I'm interested in attending this seminar on framus development—do you think it would be a good step for me?" Requests such as these send a strong signal that you're focused on doing better for your boss, and position your development as an interest the two of you share. They're another way that leaders show commitment to their performance, and to their boss's performance.

Why is this boss-subordinate guidance important? Here's what happened to me when I didn't get inside information on how things really work.

It's my first trip on the company plane, and I'm really excited. This is a big deal. "Only the real movers and shakers get to fly on the plane," I tell myself. I get there early—there's no way I'm going to be late for this one. My boss is already on board, with a colleague of his. I look around. Steve (the CEO) isn't there yet. We're going to California for a market tour and then a heavy-duty succession-planning meeting. It's my day in the sun, and my first time on the plane (did I mention that?). And man, it's wood, and wood, and wood, and leather, and goddamn! I've arrived! I mean I have really made it! And I sit down—I'm so excited, I tell you, I wish my wife could see me now! Jeez, what a guy I am!

Steve comes on the plane. It's morning—eight o'clock wheels up—and Steve doesn't do well in the mornings. He doesn't look happy. And he stares at me for a few seconds and says: "Get the hell out of my chair." My boss didn't tell me you *never* sit in the front left seat—that's Steve's chair.

Knowing the tribal rituals definitely needs to be a part of your Career Covenant.

5. THE LAW OF THE EMPEROR'S WARDROBE

I'd like to think that this will be the most important book on leadership ever written, but sadly I know that won't be the case. That's because the most important story on leadership was written in 1837, by Hans Christian Andersen. It's called "The Emperor's New Clothes," and if you're not familiar with it, here's a summary.

Two scoundrels pay a visit to the Emperor. The Emperor is famous for his vanity, particularly as far as clothing is concerned. So the scoundrels pose as tailors, and tell the Emperor that they have a marvelous new cloth, which is so finely wrought that only those of royal pedigree can see it at all. They suggest that they make a suit of clothes for him to wear in the upcoming parade.

The Emperor, worried that he can't see the cloth at all, asks his courtiers for guidance, and they, not wishing to seem ill-bred, unanimously agree that it is very fine cloth indeed. The suit is made—the two tailors make great show of working night and day with looms, thread, and needles that no one else can see—and the Emperor dons his new clothes to take his place at the head of the parade. He strides proudly out, in front of the assembled crowds, and they too, assuming that the Emperor would do only what is proper, acclaim his outfit, while keeping their doubts to themselves, and wishing that they had the pedigree to be able to see the cloth.

It is only when a small child cries, "Why is the Emperor naked?" that the people, the courtiers, and the Emperor realize they've been deceived, by which time the scoundrels are far away.

It's a deliberately exaggerated story, but it goes directly to the

kernel of many flawed human interactions. We're often so intimidated by the power of others and the pressure to conform with the
opinions of our peers that we ignore or suppress what our own
senses are telling us. And if enough people fall into that trap,
sooner or later—well, if the leader isn't exactly striding naked
down the high street, he's certainly facing an angry board, an SEC
inquiry, or shareholder lawsuits, which, all in all, might make a
stroll in the buff seem the more appealing option. As a subordinate
of this leader, you may ultimately have to suffer your firm's reputation taking a dive, but before that point you have to live with the
knowledge that you kept quiet when your counsel might have
changed the course of events.

So if you don't want to be a victim of a bad boss— or of an otherwise good boss who is kept woefully in the dark—you must preserve your self-esteem and integrity by knowing how to push back,
by knowing *how to tell the Emperor that he or she is wearing no
clothes.* A key point here is that the Emperor in the fairy tale, like
so many bosses today, didn't realize his predicament until someone
else told him about it. More often than you might assume, bosses
are in the dark about what their people really feel about their leadership, or their agenda, or about key decisions (which is why the
really wise bosses solicit feedback from their subordinates). As
Hans Christian Andersen so delightfully illustrates, it's scary to tell
a superior that you don't agree with him, that his priorities may be
askew, that her actions are poorly timed, that her behavior is inappropriate. It's so much safer to tell the boss (the person with more
power than you, and power, moreover, that could affect your career) that you agree. After all, you reason (as did the Emperor's
subjects in the tale), the boss probably knows more about what is
going on, so any intervention would make me seem stupid. If
everyone else is in agreement, I must be wrong in some way. Better to sit tight and try to figure out why later on. And anyway, if
I'm following the Law of Professional Commitment, I should fall

dutifully into line however muddleheaded this latest proposal appears to be.

But if every subordinate thinks like this, who's going to tell an Emperor that he or she is naked? As a leader, *you are*. If you don't, you'll lose your self-respect. Or go home every night and kick your cat. Or yell at your kids. Or argue with your spouse or partner.

The hardest concept to get people to accept is that, as a leader, they're *obligated* to tell bosses when they're naked. Not allowed-to-tell-if-the-moment-is-right, not supposed-to-tell-unless-other-circumstances-intervene, not permitted-to-tell-if-the-boss-is-open-to-it, but *obligated-to-tell-however-painful-it-might-be*. To be able to do so, however, you need to *set the ground rules early and reestablish them often*. With every boss, early in the relationship, you must let him or her know that you intend to demonstrate intellectual integrity. The key here is to do it artfully and sensitively.

You need to use phrases such as, "I owe you the truth," or, "I assume you'll want my point of view, especially if it differs from yours," or, "I may disagree but it's because I'm concerned about our success, and our performance." (Saying "our success," rather than "your success," signals commitment and a sense of joint endeavor.) Rather than use phrases such as, "I don't agree," or, "I think you're making a mistake," it's generally better to begin with:

"Another option we might want to consider . . ."

Or:

"Before we move forward maybe we should talk about . . ."

Or:

"One of the things that concerns me about this approach is . . ."

If in doubt, ask questions that seek a broader understanding of your boss's motivations and reasoning rather than making direct statements of your concerns. As we'll see in Chapter 6, High-Performance Leaders lead as much by using pull (questioning) as they do by using push (asserting): In terms of the tactics required, push-back might better be termed pull-back. Knowing *how* and *when* to push back may take some practice—and you have to really know your boss (The Law of Who Is That Masked Man or Woman?)—but there should be no question in your boss's mind as to your willingness to do it, and no doubt as to the reasons why.

The interaction between this law and The Law of Professional Commitment is easily explained. Professional commitment requires that you commit yourself to your boss's *success*, no matter how incompetent he or she may appear to be. It does not ask that you commit yourself automatically to anything and everything that he or she might want to do. The Law of the Emperor's Wardrobe, in fact, can be seen as a logical implication of the Law of Professional Commitment—in order to show commitment to success, you have to be willing to voice your concerns when you think success is at risk. And if your boss senses this commitment, it's much more likely that he or she will accept your push-back.

And remember, we're not talking here about situations where it's difficult to figure out what you think is wrong. The point of the fairy tale is that no one had the courage to speak up, despite the fact that the Emperor's nakedness was *obvious*. Indeed, one of the flaws with the recent preoccupation with smart people (whether at McKinsey & Company, or Enron, or any top-tier business school)[2] is the assumption that intelligence is the single determinant of an employee's value to an organization. But so many of the recent corporate downfalls seem to be much less a result of employees' lack of brains (intelligence) than of their lack of smarts (wisdom). *Intelligence is necessary to be a High-Performance Leader, but it is not sufficient.* The courage and the wisdom to know when and how to push back are what distinguish great people from merely good ones.

One final point from what I think is a very rich story: The Emperor has no one to turn to for advice other than his subordinates. It's *lonely* being a leader, and feedback tends to flow down the organization, not up it, so the loneliness is augmented by a lack of much indication of how you're doing. High-Performance Leaders realize that more often than not they're in the dark about how their people really feel about their leadership. If push-back is positioned so that it is questioning rather than challenging, and so that it encourages rather than curtails further debate (and thus generates more information on which the leader can base a decision), wise leaders will welcome it. It makes the job easier.

A rather stunning example of pushing back against the Emperor happened early in my career, after I had just joined Pepsi. The setting was a meeting with Paul, PepsiCo's President, about the possibility of pathing high-potential executives between the international and domestic beverage units. The goal was to develop executives with both the operating disciplines found in our domestic business, and the global perspective that an international experience would offer. A number of executives from both units were in attendance, discussing how to facilitate the process.

Paul—who had a reputation as a very tough, no-nonsense boss—began the meeting by stating that he was tired of all the barriers and excuses each unit had historically put up to prevent the exchange of its top talent. It was a kind of "I'm fed up and I'm not going to take it anymore" opening. As an example, he pointed out how the international unit had inflated the evaluation of one of its managers, hoping to export what Paul called an average bear rather than relinquish one of its real stars instead.

Stuart, the international unit President, whose style was one of iconoclasm and irreverence, smiled as Paul concluded his opening salvo. Paul's last words had hardly passed his lips when Stuart responded, "Paul, with the good captain's permission, allow me to say that . . . you're full of shit!"

I stopped breathing for a few seconds, too nervous to look at anyone else's reaction. Paul hesitated for a moment or two, but then began to laugh. Not very many bosses would have received this push-back as well as Paul, nor would many leaders have been as intemperate as Stuart. But the exchange does illustrate what is possible when two leaders—in this case a boss and his subordinate—have an understanding about discussing the Emperor's wardrobe.

We'll talk much more about push-back in Chapter 11, but for the time being the essential point is that for the good of the boss, for the benefit of the business, and, most importantly, for their own sense of self-worth, High-Performance Leaders have the courage to tell bosses when they're naked.

6. The Law of Class vs. Style

This law is best explained by the story of how I got my job at Pepsi.

It's 1975, and I'm back for my final round of interviews. Job of my dreams. Six final candidates, down to the last two. I have to have this job. I absolutely have to have this job. This is the third time I'm back—I must have seen fifteen people already. This day I see the Chairman, the President, and other senior executives; it's exhausting. And then I see Chuck.

Chuck is about to retire, and is going to be replaced by my boss-to-be, Doug. Chuck is about sixty-two, and he is on the interview list. And I know the minute I go in to see Chuck that he is not like the rest of the folks. First of all, he is sixty-two, when everybody else I've met is thirty-five to forty. Second of all, he is sixty-two. He's tired and slow and not cool and not sharp. And this, I think, is a waste of time. Because I'm a shooter—I'm a hotshot. I want this job, and this guy's a frigging shoe clerk. What am I doing here? So at the end of the interview, he says, "Do you have any questions?" And this has been a softball interview. He's been tossing me softball questions, and I've been hitting them out of the park.

Now, when you interview well, you know it. I get home that night, and my bride says, "How did you do?"

I say, "It's mine. It's my job. You're looking at Pepsi's new VP of Employee Relations."

The next morning I get a call from Doug, and I'm saying, "This is it! This is the offer! Goddamn!"

"We'd like you to come in again."

I was confused. "Doug, I've been in three times . . ."

"We need to talk."

So I come in. And he says, "We're very impressed with you. The Chairman liked you, the President liked you, the seventy-five other people who saw you liked you. So we're very impressed. But we have some concerns."

"Really?"

"Yes."

"About what?"

And he says, "About your interview with Chuck."

And I say, "Chuck? Chuck who's about to retire? What . . ."

"Well, you didn't have any questions. Chuck asked you a few times if you had any questions, and you said no, and I think he said, finally, 'You have no questions for me?' and you said no. Let me tell you a couple of things about Chuck. He's a nice guy. And until I officially succeed him, he still heads this function. Yes, he's grown old in the service of the Queen. Someday you will, and someday I will. Chuck used to be a pretty sharp executive. And if he's not anymore, he's still a lovely person, and a good human being. And we're not sure what it says about you and your character, the way you treated him. But whatever the reason, it was wrong."

It was a seminal moment in my life. You know how you get a flash when people put up a mirror and you see what an idiot you are? Well, I got a very big flash. Chuck was a nice man—not sharp, not cool, not young, not energetic—but a nice man, and I had treated him shamefully. I thought the interview said a lot about what was wrong with my character. People might not be as competent, or as smart, or as gifted, or as pedigreed, as you are (or as you think you are), but they have to be treated with civility and dignity. *There's a critical difference between class and style*, and High-Performance Leaders know this difference. It's easy to act with style—the right schools, the right clothes, the right words—when it suits your interests and when it fits with your ambitions. Class, on the other hand, is something that comes from within—it's drawn from your inner core. You can't put it on when you get out of bed in the morning. It grows out of your fundamental conceptions of other people, and of how others should be treated. In my interview with Chuck, I'd shown plenty of style—I looked the part and I had my answers ready to go—but no class whatsoever.

And the corollary of this law is that you should *Never ... Ever ... Ever ... EVER Treat Your Boss Like a Bumbling Old Fool (Even if He or She Is)*. Two reasons here. First, it's the wrong thing to do—it's just that simple. People who know what class is just don't treat their boss (or anyone's boss, or anyone else at all, for that matter) like an idiot. But if that isn't enough for you, consider the second reason: Everyone in the organization will see you doing it and will judge your character accordingly as *lacking class*.

In the same vein, and for the same reasons, you should also *Never ... Ever ... Ever ... EVER Upstage Your Boss*. Among many high-profile casualties of this mistake is AT&T's John R. Walter, whose upstaging of outgoing chairman Robert E. Allen cost him the CEO's office. Allen had agreed, reluctantly, to bring forward his retirement so that Walter could join AT&T as heir apparent, with a defined timetable for his succession. But Walter did very little to anticipate or assuage his boss's fears while he was in the number two position—rather, he eagerly took the media spotlight and appeared to spend little time getting to know the industry or its regulatory environment. He didn't show any appreciation of the fact that his boss might feel eclipsed or intimidated by his arrival.

Allen's suspicions of Walter's disloyalty and ineffectiveness—fueled by a staggering lack of communication between the two men—led to the AT&T board informing Walter that he would not, in fact, take the reins as CEO.[3]

The way I treated Chuck almost cost me my dream job. Pepsi's leaders knew how important relationships were; they saw my arrogant disregard for a senior employee, and they seriously considered not hiring me. A leader who understood the importance of values would have behaved in a very different way, and would have avoided taking a huge gamble with his career.

7. THE LAW OF ACTING GROWN-UP

When I listened to colleagues complaining about their bosses, I always asked what they'd done about it. All too often their answers were the same—nothing. As if powerless, we frequently refrain from doing one of the most important things adults are assumed to be capable of: acting on our own initiative. When you're not getting what you want, ASK FOR IT! If your boss is not giving you feedback, *ask for it*. If your boss is not giving you career counsel, *ask for it*. If your boss is not giving you the support you require, *ask for it*.

The common rationalization of the passive, complaining approach is that people feel they shouldn't have to ask for things that good bosses should do anyway. This argument doesn't cut it. As self-righteous as it may make you feel, waiting for what you want translates into giving up all the power you have at your disposal. My advice—when dealing with a boss, or for that matter with a subordinate or peer—is to ask for what you want. You don't always get what you ask for, but at least you tried to address the situation.

These seven laws can definitely make a difference with bosses. But if you're still skeptical, perhaps because you've been burned by some real cluck bosses in your day, let me emphasize that these laws are predicated on Three Truths About Leading Bosses.

First, *in this world you don't get to pick your boss.* You can choose your spouse or partner but not your boss. The parents among you will know that sooner or later your child will come home and complain that they have the toughest teacher in the school for the coming term, and you will know that the parental response is always, "Get over it"—or words to that effect—"that's no excuse for not doing well this year." The same goes for bosses.

Second, *High-Performance Leaders aren't victims.* While they may not be happy with a boss's behavior, they quickly begin figuring out what they need to do to change their relationship, so they get more of what they need and less of what they don't want. As Margaret Thatcher once said, "*Life* isn't fair." Complaining about it won't get you anywhere. Instead, begin by recognizing that you can learn from everybody, especially bad bosses, so that you don't make the same mistakes they made with you.

Third, *people join good companies but leave bad bosses.* The research is clear: The quality of a relationship with a boss has the biggest impact on tenure—more than any other factor, including pay.[4]

We began this chapter with a story about softball and my boss. Here's how it ended.

After I told Doug to go jam it, I went back to my office, got my coat, and drove home. Lying in bed that night I replayed the conversation with him in my mind about a thousand times. And I thought, "Oh man. Now what?" The one thing I knew I wasn't going to do straight away was tell my wife what had happened. I'd wait until the next day, by which time there'd be some closure— I'd know if Doug had fired me or maybe even forgiven me.

I'm not afraid of a lot of things, but when I went into work the next day I was really scared. I was thinking, "My desk isn't going to be there, or my nameplate's off my door, I've become a nonperson, or I've got a note on my desk—'Please See Personnel.'" And this had been the job of my dreams. But it was the damndest thing: Nothing happened. My office still had furniture and there was not a note on my desk from Doug saying "See Me." And, after a while I thought, "Jeez, I gotta figure out a way to go into his office"—we were always going back and forth into each other's offices, as is often the case with your boss—"so I can get a sense of how he is today." So I went into his office and made up a question: "Hey, do you want to see that framus report? I just finished it." And he said nothing about the previous day, and I said nothing. Everything was fine, so I said to myself, "Well, at least I can go home and tell my wife what happened yesterday." And every day after that went smoothly; it was as if our altercation had never happened. We never spoke about the incident again—ever.

To connect the dots here to the Law of Professional Commitment: After things returned to normal I worked harder than ever to deliver the goods. I never gave Doug reason to doubt my loyalty to him, and I didn't try to steal the limelight. Over time he began to see that I was committed to him and to the department. The payoff to me was that he became a big supporter and actively backed me when I was up for promotion.

But the fact remains that I was extremely lucky not to be fired on the spot. I said earlier that Feiner's Laws of Leading Bosses will help you survive a confrontation like the one I had with Doug, and will help you avoid the confrontation in the first place. We'll conclude this chapter by looking at what I might have done differently, had I known the laws.

The Law of Make Your Own Bed would have prompted me to tell Doug about the softball commitment up front, *before* he became concerned. "By the way, Doug, you may see me leaving a little early on Monday evenings—it's because I've made a commitment to my softball team—but rest assured, if I feel it's affecting my ability to deliver for you and the team I'll take another look at it." Doug was embarrassed when he found out about my absence from somebody else, and his embarrassment fed his anger; my following this law would have prevented that.

The Law of Who Is That Masked Man or Woman? would have made me think harder about the impact on Doug of having an ambitious fast-tracker reporting to him. I might have been better aware of the way my burgeoning reputation was making him feel, given that we were of a similar age and that comparisons between us were therefore inescapable. Instead of being narrowly focused on my own performance, I might have paused to consider his sensitivity to the perceptions of his peer group, and his need to be kept informed of what his subordinates were up to—and I might have concluded that his hearing about my early departures from another manager was not going to build trust with him.

The Law of Professional Commitment led me to redouble my efforts for Doug after our argument, as I've already said. But it could also have led me to consider giving up my softball commitment. After all, I was being told, rather directly, that the Pepsi executive culture didn't view early evening departures as professional. The fact that I didn't give up softball, but chose instead to demonstrate my commitment through the quality of my work in the remaining fifty-nine hours of the working week, illustrates a critical point about Feiner's Laws. Each of us must figure out our own way of implementing the laws: Although the laws tell us where to go, each of us will make different choices and trade-offs in getting there. So in this case, there were at least two possible approaches open to me that would have followed this law. I could have said, "Doug, I'm really committed to the success of our team, so if it means that much to you I'll quit the softball." For me, that wasn't a trade-off I was prepared to make, but that doesn't mean it wouldn't have been the case for another employee. Alternately, I could have said something like, "Doug, I want you to understand that I'm passionately committed to the success of our team" (if you look back at our conversation, you'll notice that while I mentioned my commitment to the softball team many times, I never actually told my boss of my commitment to *him*), "but I need some time to think about your concerns. Can we talk about this again in a day or so?" Doug might not have agreed to the delay, but stating my commitment up front would surely have increased the chances of a successful outcome, and would certainly have diffused some of the heat in the room.

If I had followed the Law of the Career Covenant I might just have avoided the entire episode, as I would have asked Doug for advice on the tribal rituals at Pepsi earlier in our relationship, and he would doubtless have mentioned the face-time requirement. I would also have avoided my humiliation on the company plane, but that's beside the point here.

The Law of the Emperor's Wardrobe might have led me to raise the issue again with Doug, after he had had a little time to cool off. I might have said, "Doug, to be honest with you, I don't think that face-time is what Pepsi is all about," or, "Doug, I'm truly sorry that I embarrassed you, but I don't think that this sort of arbitrary rule is what you stand for." Better still, I could have used pull-back instead of push-back during the original conversation: "Is there a way I can demonstrate my commitment to you and at the same time fulfill the commitment I've made to the softball team?" The pulling, questioning-rather-than-asserting approach would have sent a very different, and very strong, psychological signal. If you look back over our interaction once more, you'll see that not for a moment did I pause to ask Doug what was motivating his concerns, or to involve him in finding a solution. I was so busy stating and defending my position over and over again that I never once thought to ask him for help.

If I had known the Law of Class vs. Style, I might perhaps have chosen two different words to end the conversation. If I had maintained my professional dignity we might have been able to continue the conversation and explore other options. Instead, I chose to descend to Doug's level (or, rather, somewhat below it), and ran the risk of burning my bridges.

Finally, the Law of Acting Grown-up would have told me to ask for what I wanted. Review our conversation one last time. Did I ever actually ask Doug for what I needed from him? You'll see that, although I was clear about the importance of softball to me personally, I never explicitly asked for what I wanted. The conversation might have ended very differently had I said something like, "Doug, I need you to let me finish the season. I'm sorry I embarrassed you, but this is really important to me. I need you to cut me some slack on this one." Never underestimate the power of a direct request.

As you can see, following these laws would have resulted in a very different outcome from my clash with Doug. Although it's not certain that any of the approaches here would have allowed me to get what I wanted, I certainly would have had more options to consider, beyond shouting expletives at him. But more importantly—and whether I got what I wanted or not—following the laws set out here would have transformed the encounter from one where I put my relationship with my boss (not to mention my job) in serious jeopardy to one where I *strengthened* that relationship. Managing relationships isn't easy, but it's the sine qua non of leadership. And the genius of leadership, in this case, lies in knowing, in a moment of high emotion, how to build a better relationship with your boss, rather than demolish one.

Summary: Feiner's Laws of Leading Bosses

1. The Law of Make Your Own Bed

You must recognize that you're solely responsible for the quality of your relationship with your boss.

2. The Law of Who Is That Masked Man or Woman?

You have to know your boss—and you work for everybody senior to you in an organization.

3. The Law of Professional Commitment

Whether your boss gives a damn about you or not, you must commit yourself to his or her success. Boss Killers don't last long.

4. The Law of the Career Covenant

Just as you need to build a Performance Contract with your subordinates, you need to build a Career Covenant with your boss.

5. The Law of the Emperor's Wardrobe

You must preserve your self-esteem and individuality by knowing how to push back—how to tell the Emperor that he or she has no clothes.

6. The Law of Class vs. Style

Never . . . Ever . . . Ever . . . EVER Treat Your Boss Like a Bumbling Old Fool (Even if He or She Is One).

7. The Law of Acting Grown-up

When you're not getting what you want, ASK FOR IT!

Three Truths About Leading Bosses:

- You don't pick your boss.
- High-Performance Leaders aren't victims.
- People join good companies, but leave bad bosses.

<table>
<tr><td rowspan="2">5</td><td>*Leading Teams*</td></tr>
<tr><td>FIRST AMONG EQUALS</td></tr>
</table>

Teamwork is an important but, for some of us, frustrating part of organizational life. Meetings drag on for hours while colleagues' real opinions remain unspoken. Teams bicker over seemingly trivial details, team members have differing degrees of commitment to the goals, and reaching a consensus is a drawn-out battle. And if all this weren't bad enough, meetings get in the way of getting our regular work done.

There's a significant overlap between teamwork and meetings, so the following discussion will move between both topics. But it's worth noting that not all meetings are meetings of peers—many involve bosses and subordinates as well—so the laws in Chapters 3 and 4 are important in addition to those we'll review here.

Most people hate meetings, and my colleagues at Pepsi were no exception. The senior executive team had a meeting—nearly a whole-day affair—every Monday. My office was across from the conference room where we'd meet. The meeting would break up, and invariably someone would follow me into my office and ask, "What did you think?"

I would say, "About what?" (As we'll see later, leaders ask more questions than they give answers.)

"Mike, that meeting was pure garbage. Number one, Charlie's got to get control of his temper. Number two, when Andrea talks I don't know what the hell she's talking about. Anyway, I've got work to do, I've wasted most of the day, see you later . . ."

Then a minute later another colleague would come in.

"Mike, please tell me why we keep discussing our priorities— didn't we resolve this months ago? Haven't we resolved all that by now?"

Sometimes as many as six or seven different people would drop by my office and criticize various elements of the meeting that had just concluded. This happened week after week, and it happens in most organizations. Lots of bitching and complaining—all unofficial and secretive, of course—and yet the pathology never gets surfaced and treated in ensuing meetings.

It might sound simplistic, but complaints like these need to be addressed and worked out *in the meeting*. If someone has a problem with how Charlie acts or what Andrea says in a meeting, they've got to figure out ways to deal with it—*in the meeting*. As the leader you've got to introduce a mechanism for encouraging people to disagree and air their points of view during your team meetings. Why? Because after team members leave the meeting, they go back to their own teams and begin to bad-mouth what happened. And the consequences of bad-mouthing are devastatingly toxic. Out of frustration a department head complains about the meeting to a trusted lieutenant. "The meeting was a waste of time," or, "Sometimes Andrea talks another language," or, "Charlie's asleep at the switch except when he loses his cool." That's all it takes. And within a day or so, the grapevine has it as a front-page story. It's what leads to the intramural rivalries and friction and bickering and mistrust that occur in every organization. In Pepsi's case it's what led to many in the organization talking about how screwed-up the senior team was.

These same kinds of issues can occur with the task forces that people frequently find themselves assigned to. These teams have a designated shelf life and are usually formed to address a particular issue or problem. Nevertheless, on these types of teams the same frustrations arise, the same difficulties occur, the same back-channel gossip percolates.

Yet it doesn't have to be this way. Meetings really do matter, and can be a powerful vehicle for diagnosing problems, establishing direction, and aligning team members with the goal. Meetings don't have to be boring, tedious, or painful. It's a leader's job to make sure teams and their meetings work the way they should.

Too often leaders focus on what they see as the hard stuff—strategy, competition, cost control, and the like. They see the team effectiveness issue as foo-foo. But when was the last time you saw an ineffective team come up with a first-rate solution? *High-Performance Leaders understand the inextricable link between team effectiveness and the success of the organization.* These leaders know how to get the team to pool its collective wisdom. Molding fractious, ambitious, even disloyal subordinates is an important part of what a leader must do.

Again, having said that High-Performance Leaders understand the link between team effectiveness and organizational performance, we still need to address *how* they do this. So whether you're heading up a three-month task force or running your established department, here are the six Laws of Leading Teams that give you the hows of this critical aspect of a leader's duties, and that can make teams a constructive and valuable force in achieving great results.

1. THE LAW OF FIRST AMONG EQUALS

Simply stated, *a team needs a leader*. Even limited-life task teams and task forces that are assembled to attack a specific issue need a leader. The only exception is small teams of fewer than four or five people, which can often operate reasonably well without someone in the lead role—but even these teams tend to use their time much more effectively when a leader is chosen. Sometimes the sponsors of such a team will designate a team leader. Sometimes a leader will volunteer, and be accepted by the group. Frequently, however, neither of these occurs. The result is that team members spend more time jockeying for power than addressing the issues—or that, conversely, individuals waste time trying to figure out how to make decisions without appearing to usurp the leadership role and offend their peers. Even worse, in a task force comprised of peers without a clearly agreed-upon leader, the result is often that several members each *assume* that he or she is (or should be) the leader—and then the sparks really fly.

So it's important to be crystal-clear about who the leader is. Even if the team is a task force composed entirely of people of equal rank, the team should designate a *First Among Equals*, a person who embodies *unity of command* for leading the team to meet its objectives. Note here that I don't mean to imply that this leader will *unilaterally* make decisions and represent the team's view to the rest of the organization—as we are beginning to see, leadership is much less about command-and-control direction than it is about engaging, harnessing, and pulling others. Rather, my point is that without a single person who can own the outcome, the team is in great danger of under-performing.

The second part of this law addresses another common peril with teams. Here's the scenario: A task force is formed and a young manager is put in charge. The young manager, while thrilled at the chance to lead the team, is a bit embarrassed—several members of the team are his (more experienced) peers. So the embarrassed leader apologizes to his colleagues. "Just want you to know I didn't ask for this," "I'm not sure why they chose me instead of you to head this up," or, "I'm probably less qualified that you to run this thing": These are common refrains. Big mistake. The second part of the Law of First Among Equals states that you should *never apologize for leading a group of peers*. You demean yourself by doing so, and you deprive the team of one of the most important things that it *needs* in a leader—a figure who is comfortable in her own skin.

I have my own story to prove it. It takes place early in my career at Trans World Airlines (which I joined after graduating from Columbia Business school) during the halcyon days of the airline business.

The Teamsters had targeted TWA's eight thousand passenger service and reservations agents as ripe for unionization. Needless to say, TWA senior management was apoplectic, and told my boss to do whatever it would take to defeat the organizing drive.

In turn my boss, Ed, asked me to head up a task force to take on the Teamsters. He made it clear that I could access the entire Human Resources organization, though at the time I had just a small piece of it as Director–Organization Planning. Ed announced this to the team at the end of one of our monthly staff meetings.

I was a bit surprised that I was asked to head up this effort. I was twenty-nine at the time and most of the field employee and labor relations people were ten to fifteen years older than me. But I was psyched. I hated the Teamsters—they had given me fits (and a front yard full of gravel) in Pittsburgh two years earlier when I had my first field labor assignment. And this would be great for my visibility. The thought that the Teamsters might be successful never occurred to me (oh, to be twenty-nine again).

I decided I needed to call a meeting of all the field HR executives. These six executives reported to my boss and would be responsible for implementing the strategy for defeating the Teamsters. I'd be the one who'd lead this team to craft the strategy. Naturally, I told my boss that I was scheduling the meeting, and he was fine with it.

Being ever so clever, I thought it would make sense prior to the meeting to have a conference call with the six field veterans. I figured they might be a bit annoyed that Hot Shot Mike was put in charge, even though we all were technically at the same organization level. I felt a conference call would be the best way to announce this all-day working session I was going to convene. It would be much more personal than a memo, especially since five of the six were not based in New York, where TWA was headquartered and where the meeting would take place.

The conference call was brief: It didn't need to be a song and dance.

"Listen, folks, I appreciate your taking a few minutes: This won't take more than that. I'm not quite sure why Ed asked me to head up this thing—you all have a lot more seasoning than I do—but this Teamster deal is one we need to get our arms around."

I paused, waiting for any reactions. Silence on the line.

"Would you look at your schedules? I'd like us to get going on this. How about next Tuesday here in New York? We can spend the whole day framing our strategy for beating these guys. Will that work for everybody?"

To my surprise, no one voiced a problem with the meeting date. "I'll see you guys next Tuesday morning," was my close. The call had taken less than five minutes. Naturally I followed up with a confirming memo.

Tuesday rolled around and I was ready. Plenty of ideas for demolishing the Teamsters and an agenda for the meeting that would get everyone involved. I'd reserved the best conference room, and made sure we had flip charts and markers. And, leaving nothing to chance, I'd ordered plentiful snacks and a primo lunch. I was taking care of details!

At TWA, meetings started at 8:00 A.M. but I was there at seven-thirty to check out the conference room and make sure the breakfast was delivered. Imagine, I thought, Mike Feiner leading the effort to beat the Teamsters. My exploits would be written about in every leading business publication.

By eight, no one had arrived, but five of the six team members were traveling from out of town, so I presumed there had been some delay en route. By eight-fifteen, however, I was concerned: There was still no one in the conference room but me. I called the only local guy—he was based at Kennedy Airport, always a hotbed of Teamster activity for us. He was probably on the way, but perhaps he was stuck in traffic and had called his secretary.

His phone rang once and, to my dismay, he was on the other end of the line.

"Howard, it's Mike—did you forget about our Teamster meeting?" I blurted out.

"No, but things are crazy here. We've got a slowdown going with the ramp agents and there's no way I could get away."

"I would have appreciated a call so I knew you weren't coming." I was really angry but tried to sound professional, though Howard had clearly dissed me.

"Sorry, Mike. Post me on the meeting."

By eight-thirty no one had arrived and I was beginning to get the sense that I was going to be meeting with myself. I took one more shot.

I called Jack, based in Kansas City, a grizzled and gruff veteran of union wars who had taken a liking to me despite my youth (and MBA).

My heart sank when Jack answered his phone.

"Jack, it's Mike. How come you're not coming to our meeting?"

He paused. "You want the truth or should I tell you the line you'll hear from the other guys, like we got a slowdown or they're sabotaging the baggage carts or some malarkey like that?"

I didn't know how to respond—my mouth was dry and I felt like someone had kicked me in the stomach.

"The truth would work, Jack."

"Well, I lost respect for you last week. You called and told us about the meeting and then apologized for being in charge. Remember?"

"Jack, I was just trying to be sensitive to you guys. I mean, you're probably not happy that Ed gave me this assignment. I was just trying to be sensitive."

"Listen, son, we weren't too thrilled either that Ed's fair-haired boy was leading this team. 'Cause you don't know shit about this stuff even though you're smart. And 'cause it makes us feel older than we want to admit, you being in your twenties. But in apologizing to us you were kinda puttin' us on. And you demeaned yourself."

I was stunned—but I understood instantly what Jack was saying. *Being angry with Ed for putting me in charge was their problem. Apologizing for it made it my problem.* They'd sensed immediately that my apology was given not because I regretted being in charge, but because I wanted to appear sensitive to their concerns, and they'd seen straight through me.

I'm not suggesting you should strut your stuff and act like a pompous jerk when you're put in charge. There's no percentage in rubbing people's noses in your newfound leadership role, no matter how happy you might be at being appointed. But apologizing for your leadership appointment damages your credibility, and signals a lack of commitment to the team, and High-Performance Leaders don't do it.

2. THE LAW OF WINNING CHAMPIONSHIPS

If you're going to ship, your first requirement must be to *choose the best athletes available*, regardless of their rank. You can't ignore politics completely but, if given a choice, you should construct teams on the basis of skills required. And competence here must include not only the technical capabilities but the complementarity of skills as well. It's all too easy to duck a sensitive issue by choosing a participant who wouldn't necessarily hurt the group but who might not make as big a contribution as one of his or her more qualified subordinates. It's also very common to see teams that quickly become bloated with representatives of any and all affected constituencies, and that as a result move too slowly and reach results too compromised to have any impact. Allowing external considerations to determine the size or composition of teams is a mistake. *Great teams in organizations, as in sports, need the best players to win championships.* In forming task forces, leaders select for the skills they need, not the constituencies they feel they need to represent; they take risks in choosing the best people, even if the choices may not always be politically safe.

Having assembled the best team, however, don't make the mistake of assuming that they share your agenda or your approach to delivering the goods.

Michael Jordan was NBA Rookie of the Year in 1985, and in 1986–87 he began to win a string of scoring titles that would last for seven seasons, until his temporary retirement in 1993. Yet the Chicago Bulls did not win their first NBA title until 1991. One of the team's assistant coaches told Michael that he didn't need to carry the whole team on his shoulders. By now the coach's line has become legendary: "Michael, there's no 'I' in the word 'team.'"

Jordan's reply was instant: "There is in the word 'win'!"

My point here is that people bring their own motives and needs to a team. Not everyone will respond solely to the challenge of building a cathedral, no matter how compelling it is. Team members have different agendas and a leader must know what they are, and how to respond to them. There's a relationship here with the Law of Intimacy from Chapter 3, which tells us that we need to know our subordinates. But this goes further. Leaders must understand not only the individuals on their team, but the dynamics of their interactions with one another (and this is a much more complex undertaking). By reading the table, by watching team members during meetings, by speaking to them between meetings, and, most importantly, by *asking*, a leader will come to learn when and how much feedback, recognition, and encouragement are required for each individual on his or her team, and what each team member needs from the team as a whole in order to perform at his or her best.

3. THE LAW OF BUILDING A CATHEDRAL—AGAIN

Teams are living organisms, just like individuals. So teams must understand their overarching objectives, their reason for being. They must know how critical their work is to building the cathedral. If jobs aren't enough for the soul, then teamwork certainly isn't. So teams need to see their role as more than completing tasks and activities. Sure, they need to worry about the details of controlling costs and generating revenue and launching new products and planning conferences. Yet in immersing themselves in the details of running an organization, teams can quickly lose sight of the higher order of purpose—beating Coke, setting a new standard for customer service, or making the planet more healthy. So while it's essential—as we'll see in a moment—for the team to get the scope of its work right, it's equally important to tie this work to the mission, and to do so *continually*. Otherwise, it's easy for the team to lose focus and feel like it's cutting stone, not building a cathedral.

This doesn't mean that the leader should begin the first meeting with an awkward speech that appeals to this higher calling. But it does mean that the substance of the team's work—the meeting agendas, the timeline, the deliverables, all of the separate stone-cutting activities—should be positioned in terms of building the cathedral. High-Performance Leaders create an environment in which everything connects to the overarching goal.

A great example of this: Leaders at Federal Express constantly remind their people that "You're delivering the most important commerce in the history of the world. You're not delivering sand and gravel. You're delivering someone's pacemaker, chemotherapy treatment for cancer drugs, the part that keeps the F-18s flying, or the legal brief that decides the case."[1] And within the HR organization that I headed, my rallying cry was for us to create a Distinctive Human Enterprise, known as much for its human qualities as for its business results. My people really responded to this—it was the hook that got them to understand that we were building a cathedral, not planning the corporate picnic or blood drive that many personnel managers feel characterize their work.

4. THE LAW OF THE NITTY-GRITTY

Okay, you've made clear who's in charge of the team, you've assembled the best players, and each understands just how important the team's work is to the organization. Isn't that enough? Sorry, but you're not even halfway there. While all this is essential, leaders still must immerse themselves in some crucial details—the *nitty-gritty* of leading teams.

Leaders must clarify the *rules of engagement*: how decisions will be made, who will have what responsibilities, and how differences will be resolved.

First, decision ground rules must be established. At the outset, your team should know whether discussion of an issue will lead to, say, a vote where the team will decide by majority vote. Or whether you as leader want their input after which you will make the decision. Or whether no decision will be made until consensus is reached. The point here is that the team must be clear about *the decision mandate*. This avoids surprises, and is essential if people are to feel that the decision process was fair. And fairness, in turn, is not simply an altruistic concern. A large body of research on decision-making processes strongly suggests that if people buy into a process—if they perceive it as fair, that is—then they are much more likely to buy into its outcome. It's generally easier to obtain support for a process up front than it is to obtain support for difficult decisions later on, so the value of establishing the decision ground rules as the first order of business can be huge.

And beware of attempting to reach consensus on every point. Too often leaders try to get the entire team to buy into a decision, and while it would, indeed, be great if every member of a team was on board with a course of action, that's highly unlikely. Instead, leaders must strive to create a *process* for reaching a decision whereby every team member was heard. If team members have had a chance to voice their point of view and engage in healthy debate and, yes, disagreements over a particular issue, they will generally feel the process has been a fair one. If the process is fair, team unity will follow. *Unity should be the objective. Unanimity is unrealistic.*

One more point here: As a leader, one of your responsibilities is to close the discussion when a decision has been made. There's a particularly effective way to do this, especially if the decision was difficult. Rather than saying, "So that's our decision, and I'm counting on you for your support going forward" (which confronts dissenting team members with the fact of a decision they may not agree with, and which informs them that they'll still have to support it), try, "I like this decision, but more importantly, I like how we got here. Can I count on you for your support?" (which gives a personal *opinion* of the decision that's easier to accept than an objective statement, and which *asks* for support instead of *assuming* it).

The second area where rules of engagement must be agreed upon concerns who does what. Your team must have clarity about the team's *roles and accountabilities*. This usually isn't an issue with established teams. But with task forces and task teams, these groups should know the *expected outcome of their work*—what the British call their *brief.* If a task force is convened to recommend cost reduction initiatives, what specifically is expected? Will the task force be expected to suggest general *areas* of potential reductions? Or does the sponsor of the task force expect detailed cost reduction recommendations, with specific *line item* reductions, including detailed headcount layoffs? Beyond this, will the task force be making recommendations for review (and potential revision) by senior management, or will the task force be making final decisions? Again, without clarity on these issues, team members are much less likely to participate fully and take ownership of the outcome.

This brings us to the third area: How will differences be resolved? More importantly, how will you encourage differences to be expressed? *Because if differences are not expressed overtly, the leader should presume that they exist under the table.* Getting differences out in the open is more a question of continuous leadership throughout the life span of the team than it is of agreeing, at the first meeting, to express differences when they arise. Many teams start out with the best intentions, and with wholehearted agreement to debate the contentious points in a positive fashion, only to slip back to their old ways of murmured asides and corridor conversations when confronted with disagreements where reputations and egos are felt to be at stake. So the leader must watch for warning signs (such as a team member who seems to have very little to say) and must use various strategies in order to surface hidden differences. Just as at the outset the team needs to collaboratively determine the *rules of procedure for processing differences*, so the leader must ensure that differences are expressed.

After the rules of engagement are agreed upon, two other steps are required before plunging into the central task. First, teams have tasks to get done and projects to complete, so it's pivotal to establish a tight work plan, with explicit timelines and milestones. In the best of all worlds (which means when time allows it) *the team should collaborate in developing this work plan.* A tight work plan is a form of discipline for the team, and disciplined teams are more likely to deliver, on time and on budget.

But things never happen exactly as planned. Stuff happens, crises develop, so the unexpected should always be expected. That's why good leaders recognize that *course corrections are the norm.* The team must be prepared to *replan the plan.* Without this mind-set, teams become stuck in quicksand and are at the mercy of an out-of-date plan. Worse, they get into the habit of ignoring the plan, as it's never current. Leaders must recognize that even the best plans must be revisited and reset, in order to adapt to unanticipated events, forces, and situations.

Second, each meeting needs an agenda. A classic problem here is the boss who sends around the agenda for *his or her* upcoming meeting, reflecting items *he or she* wants to talk about. It's no wonder that people have so little interest in attending meetings with agendas created like this—they feel it's not their meeting, *it's the boss's.* And when they feel it's not their meeting, they'll feel very little ownership over its outcome! It's mandatory, therefore, that the team see the meeting as *theirs.* This means that the team must *own* the agenda for the meeting, which means not that the leader tells them that they own it, but that everyone has a role in shaping it.

A common misconception is that if all team members are invited to submit agenda items, usually a couple of days in advance, this constitutes ownership. It doesn't. It results in a fifteen-item

agenda, when the team only has time to properly address five issues, and it results in fifteen items, moreover, each of which is
owned by an individual, but *none* of which is owned by the team.
Again, if you want people to own something, you have to let them
help create it. With our senior executive meetings, it wasn't until
we took thirty minutes at the end of every meeting to discuss and
debate and formulate the next week's agenda that our meetings became valuable. I felt it was my meeting as much as anyone else's.
After all, I'd played a role in deciding what we were going to talk
about.

All of this matters because *meetings matter*. A leader will recognize
that these nitty-gritty issues determine whether people will find
meetings painful or productive, and whether or not teams will
reach their full potential.

5. The Law of Communicating Up

Many leaders are strong-willed and independent-minded. They
like to not only *be* in charge—they like to *feel* in charge. So the tendency is to act as independent operatives. The reasoning goes
something like this: "I've got a good track record, I don't want to
be micromanaged, and I need to be able to run my own show."
There's nothing wrong with this logic except that it often prompts
leaders to act like isolated and detached archipelagos. This is a
huge mistake.

Principals should be kept in the loop about the team and its
progress, its challenges, and its struggles. Some bosses may not
want interim downloads on progress—"just let me know when
you've shipped" may be heard on occasion. But most bosses will
appreciate updates, even if they have not asked for them. Think of
it from a boss's perspective: The last thing you want to have to do,
when juggling ten or twenty issues at a time, is to ask for updates

from your teams. That's what makes a boss worry, and one of a leader's key priorities is to stay off his or her boss's worry-radar. *The more information you give bosses, the more reason you give them to trust you, and the more they will feel part of your world.* The less they think you're withholding, the more they'll feel invested in you and your career.

It's easy to keep a boss in the loop like this, yet few people do. Communicating up effectively is one way to distinguish yourself from your peers. (And one more hint: Choose frequency over length. A two-sentence e-mail every three days is much more valuable than a six-page memo every three weeks.)

High-Performance Leaders demonstrate their commitment to the mission when they deliberately overcommunicate in this way, and as we saw during our discussion of subordinate-boss relationships in Chapter 4, the Law of Professional Commitment is a key requirement for successful leadership.

6. THE LAW OF TEAM TOGETHER, TEAM APART

Team members don't always have to like one another. It would be great if they did but personal idiosyncrasies and personality conflicts are inevitable. Hence the need to follow the Law of Building a Cathedral and continually emphasize the greater goal.

Beyond this refrain, however, leaders must remind the team of how destructive these personal conflicts and differences are. They play themselves out in all organizations. A few team members return to their department after a meeting and begin to bad-mouth the competence or the behavior of other team members. Or they bad-mouth the leader's competence or behavior. These pronouncements are never done publicly—rather, it's a sidebar conversation—but nevertheless, within a day or two, the organizational grapevine is ripe with the story of a frustrating meeting and the ineptitude of the team. This happens because in any organization people spend a great deal of time looking *up*. They want to gauge the lay of the land with their bosses. They want to see which way the corporate winds are blowing. So seemingly private comments take on a life of their own—a destructive and corrosive life.

It follows that leaders must enforce the Law of Team Together, Team Apart, which states very simply that if a team member lacks the courage to say something in a meeting, it's not acceptable for him or her to say it outside the meeting. It's perfectly appropriate for team members to debate, disagree, and argue during meetings: Indeed, as we've seen, the leader should go out of his or her way to encourage this. But if the team wants to be a team, it must act like one. However impassioned the debate when the team is *together* inside the meeting room, once the session is over and the team is *apart*, all criticism and complaint must stop.

This does not give license for people to make speeches at meetings, constantly repeating themselves in response to a colleague's opposing opinion. In our senior executive meetings we introduced the 80/20 rule, which was based on the precept that eighty percent of the value of our opinions is expressed in the first twenty percent of our statement. The rule was that any team member had the right to yell out, "80/20," and if the speaker was simply repeating points he or she had already made in that statement, he or she had to stop talking. This really worked—team members moved quickly from espousing *what* they believed to *why* they did. We began to focus on the pros and cons of varying positions and were able to find some common ground.

Encouraging disagreement on the facts and issues before the group also means that the leader must surface and diffuse differences that are personality-driven. You'd be amazed how quickly personality conflicts recede in importance after a leader openly calls the parties on it. When the occasion demanded it, I'd say to team members during a meeting, "Are you two arguing about the issue or is there some personal dispute going on?" or, "I'm not sure what's driving the disagreement here—is the issue driving it or are you folks letting something else get in the way?" (Again, questions, not assertions.) Not only does this refocus the discussion, it sufficiently embarrasses the team members that they become much more aware of how *transparent* motives are to the rest of the team. Your goal here is not to explore the personality conflict, but simply to eliminate it from the discussion, and calling attention to it frequently has the desired effect.

We introduced one other tactic at Pepsi that goes directly to the heart of the Team Together, Team Apart idea. At the end of every meeting (once we'd agreed on the agenda for the next session) we would take a few minutes to craft an "elevator speech" summarizing the key points and decisions made. It's called an elevator speech because it needs to be sufficiently brief so that it can be communicated with a colleague in the time it takes for an elevator to get to the next floor. This reflected another truism of organizational life: that whenever there's a meeting involving more than a couple of people that lasts more than a couple of hours, anyone remotely associated with the people in the meeting knows that it's going on, knows what's on the agenda, and is keen to find out what has been decided. If participants emerge from the meeting with differing views of what took place, these differences are seized upon by the eager spectators, and are very quickly magnified a hundred times. So our team would create a thirty-second verbal summary of the meeting that any of us could pass on to our subordinates, and that would be entirely *consistent* across the team. It wasn't always a positive summary—this is not a Pollyannaish prescription, and besides, most people can tell the difference between spin and truth—but over time the consistency of the messages stopped the rumor mill at its source, and both the senior team and the entire organization benefited.

*   *   *

With regard to my TWA fiasco of calling a meeting that no one attended because I apologized for being the leader, I scrambled to regroup. Rather than hold another conference call, I talked to each team member individually. As I recall, the conversations went something like this:

"Howard, I want to jump-start our assignment to defeat the Teamster drive. Obviously, you and all the field VPs will carry the burden here in executing our counteroffensive day to day. But we need to figure out a national strategy and coordinate its implementation centrally. That's my job, though I can't do it without your help."

There was a slight pause, after which every team member responded in basically the same way: "When's the next meeting?"

I never again apologized for leading a group of peers.

Summary: Feiner's Laws of Leading Teams

1. The Law of First Among Equals

A team needs a leader who embodies *unity of command* for leading the team to meet its objectives. Never apologize for leading a group of peers.

2. The Law of Winning Championships

You can't ignore politics, but your first goal must be to choose the best athletes available, regardless of rank. Team members have different agendas, and a High-Performance Leader knows what they are.

3. The Law of Building a Cathedral—Again

Teams need to understand the overarching objectives.

4. The Law of the Nitty-Gritty

You have to clarify the rules of engagement: how decisions will be made, who does what, and how differences will be resolved. Achieve unity through a fair process, not unanimity through a protracted fight. The team, not the leader, must own the agenda. And establish a tight work plan—with timelines and milestones—because course corrections are the norm, and a tight plan is easier to reset.

5. The Law of Communicating Up

Keep your principals in the loop: Give them a reason to trust you, and find out about course corrections early.

6. The Law of Team Together, Team Apart

Keep the disagreement behind closed doors by encouraging the conflict of ideas, and addressing openly the conflict of personalities. Create an elevator speech to quell the rumors at the source.

6

Leading Peers

TELLING YOUR CAT AND THE BETTER MOUSETRAP

Leadership is about managing relationships, and power is often a crucial factor in these relationships. A boss, for example, has a significant amount of power inherent in his or her relationship with subordinates. But it's dangerous to overrely on this power. A leader whose only tactic is to assert and direct (think of my troubles getting my team over the wall on Hurricane Island) will have subordinates who simply *comply* with, rather than *commit* to, his or her direction. That's why successful leaders understand that over the long haul they need to pull people rather than push them; they need to take people with them rather than herd them ahead.

This idea is especially important in peer relationships. While power remains an important factor in boss-subordinate relationships, and the task of the leader is to achieve a *balance* between push and pull that enables the team to ship, with your peers the situation is different. By definition, there is no variation in formal power and authority in a peer relationship. So colleagueship, to work, must be based on a currency of trust and mutual respect. Without trust, peer relationships degenerate into backbiting, gamesmanship, sabotage, bad-mouthing, and political intramurals, not just between individuals, but between the entire organizations that these leaders run.

A real-life example will dramatize what I mean.

I was responsible for giving bonus recommendations to my boss, Derek, for the top fifty executives at Pepsi. I also wrote the bonus appraisals, to justify the awards. I'd give the recommendations and appraisals to Derek, and he'd approve them. It was a simple process.

One day I get a call. "Derek's on the phone."

"Yeah, Derek, I'm in a meeting, what's up?"

"Hey, I just got Chris's bonus recommendations—I don't know why they came to me, but I thought they were fine, and I signed off on them."

"What do you mean, you got Chris's bonus recommendations?"

"I don't know, they came to me . . . I guess they got misrouted or something . . . and I signed off on them."

I said, "Well, why don't you send them down to me—I want to take a look at them."

I got off the phone and walked directly to Chris's office. Chris was the Executive VP of Marketing, and he reported to my boss.

I said to his secretary, "He in?"

"Yes, he's in a—"

"Good."

I opened the door to his office. Chris and another person I didn't recognize were sitting opposite each other. "Chris?"

"Hey, Mike, I'm interviewing."

I looked at the other person. "Would you excuse us for a moment?" I was incredibly rude.

The candidate left. I stepped into Chris's office and said, "Don't you ever, ever, pull that stunt again. Am I being clear?"

"What are you talking about?"

"I'm talking about the bonus recommendations. For four years you've been handling the bonus recommendations by routing them to me. I'm the bonus guy. Right? In fact, I decide your bonus."

I didn't bother asking Chris anything or, for that matter, asking myself anything. It was cut-and-dry: This was my turf, he was pulling an end run, this was an ambush, I was going to kick his butt. This was an affront to my position, an insult to my role.

"Don't you ever pull that shit again, Chris. You know damn well that bonuses are supposed to go through me, right?"

"Right."

"So what the hell are you doing? It's dishonest and it's duplicitous and it's cheap and it's underhanded."

I was being as direct as ever that day. Chris knew the process. The process was Feiner Does Bonuses. Don't Mess With Feiner When It Comes To Bonuses. It was my turf, my role. And I wasn't about to give it up.

What Chris said to me, when I finally let him get a word in edgeways, was: "Well, I'm sorry, Mike, but I know darn well that every time I send you these bonuses you lower them. You've lowered them for the past four years. And you think you're right, you always have to be right, we talk about these bonuses every year, and every year I'm never able to get a big award for any of my stars. In the end it's always your call. And you know what? I probably shouldn't have gone direct to Derek, it was probably underhanded like you say, but it was the only way I had a shot at getting some rewards for my people that I think are well deserved. Because the fact is, you never listen. Once you decide, that's it. You never listen."

Which is a nice way of saying, "You're completely insufferable."

Or, "I don't trust you." This is too often the way people privately feel about a peer. It's easy to find fault with a colleague's competence or intentions or quirks, or with all of these. Too often our colleagues don't behave the way we think they should—the way we would have handled it. We may feel that their people aren't as competent or as hardworking as ours. Perhaps they can't be depended on to ship as productively as we can. Whatever the reason, colleagues make life so difficult for us perfect people!

These are the tapes about many of our colleagues that we hold in cerebral storage, and replay to ourselves from time to time. As soon as I found out that Chris had taken me out of the loop on the bonus recommendations, I sought out my mental Chris-Is-a-Treacherous-Schemer tape, reviewed its key points, and, convinced of the essential rightness of my position and the wrongness of his, set out to put him straight on the realities of the world. That was certainly the path of least resistance for me: I didn't have to think too hard about what his motives might have been, or pause to ask him about them. But of course I was wrong, and—not for the first time in my career—finished up making myself look like an idiot.

High-Performance Leaders are adept at erasing these mental tapes, or at least controlling the urge to play them every time something doesn't go their way. Because they're committed to those they work with, they resist the urge to leap to conclusions, and build trust by trying to understand reasons instead of attributing blame.

You don't have to like everyone you work with—you're not paid to like people. But you are paid to work with them effectively. That involves treating your peers with respect, slowing your rush to judgment, and building colleagues' trust. The Laws of Leading Peers that follow explore these requirements and others in more detail.

1. THE LAW OF EQUALITY

Some peers will have more clout or stroke than others if their position is more central to the function of the organization. In a consumer products company, for example, the marketing officer will likely have more electoral votes on a team than the HR executive or the Systems executive. In a pharmaceutical company the R&D executive will have more unofficial power, perhaps even more than the CFO or Manufacturing head. Regardless of centrality, however, a peer relationship will only be successful *if neither party feels he or she is boss of the other*. You must adopt a *partnership* mentality. People understand the concept of centrality—they recognize that some team members, by virtue of their positions or seniority or talent, have more influence with the team and its leader. But when a colleague's centrality morphs into swagger and hubris, people don't feel equal, and the foundation for a productive relationship is removed. A peer will not accept inferior treatment from you simply because you have more unofficial power. High-Performance Leaders respect values, and these values lead them to treat colleagues with equal respect and professionalism, regardless of their centrality.

There's another important reason to treat peers with dignity. In organizational life you're dependent on peers to do their jobs so that you can complete yours. And they, in turn, are dependent on you. This sort of dynamic is a key component in every social system, and the business organization is no exception. Values aside, peers need one another's help and support in order to ship. *Everybody's effort is equally important*.

2. THE LAW OF PULL VS. PUSH

The key to convincing others that you see them as partners, and that you recognize the interdependence of your relationship, is to understand the difference between *push* and *pull*. As should be obvious by now, understanding this difference is absolutely critical to all the other relationships we're concerned with as leaders. In fact, it might well be the most important leadership concept of all—it's a key tool in leading your boss, in telling the Emperor that he or she is naked, in leading conflict and difference, and in many other areas. But I address it here because in a peer-to-peer relationship the possibilities for push (asserting and directing) are distinctly limited, so if you have nothing else to fall back on, you have no tools with which to lead.

In organizational life, being competent isn't enough. It sounds obvious that if you build a better mousetrap people will beat a path to your door. After all, the saying has been around for a long time. But with peer relationships, this is simply not the case. A colleague wants it to be *fun* and *enjoyable* to transact business with a peer. The process of dealing with a colleague must be satisfying. *Not just because your advice or competence is impeccable, but because the interaction itself is as optimal as the solution you're offering.* This doesn't mean that you need to be able to transform yourself into a Jerry Seinfeld—this isn't about being a stand-up comedian. Rather, I'm talking about the need for people to find you civil, respectful, and positive when they interact with you. It means listening to what your peer has to say, and giving his or her points of view your genuine consideration.

I had one of the great fastballs in the annals of the corporate diamond. I'd rear back and throw my argument with lightning speed, force, and clarity—like I did with Chris over the bonus issue. My arguments would be *persuasive* and *assertive*. My logic would be clear, my reasoning *emphatic*. I was the master of the *push* technique.

One problem with this approach is that, after a while, people know you have only one pitch. So they're ready for it—and hit it out of the park when you throw it. They know how you will go about communicating your position, and they get good at blunting or countering it, or in the worst case, ignoring it.

The main problem with *push*, however, is that while it might elicit *compliance*, it's much less good at encouraging *commitment*. My one-pitch approach made people feel that I was always the seller of a point of view and they were always the buyer. The result was that they rarely enjoyed buying my mousetrap, however great it might have been, and that when they went along with me they did so without feeling any ownership of my solution.

It took quite a while before I figured out I needed more pitches in my repertoire. I began to notice that successful leaders use the *pull* approach as well as the push approach. Leaders using pull often start by *asking* peers for their point of view or for an explanation of their behavior. I wonder how different my transaction with Chris would have been if, after entering his office, I had asked, "Hey, Chris, help me understand why you sent your bonus recommendations to Derek directly." The pull approach consists of *involving, questioning, listening*, and *discussing*, in order to find the common ground. It's quite different from the push technique of *declaring, proposing*, and *asserting* a point of view.

Think back to the comparison of Gladstone and Disraeli with which we concluded Chapter 3. After dinner with Gladstone, you'll recall, you would leave thinking that he was the smartest, wittiest, and most interesting person you had ever met. But after dinner with Disraeli, you would leave thinking *you* were the smartest, the wittiest, and the most interesting. Gladstone was a master at expounding and expanding on any issue—he was a virtuoso at the push technique. Disraeli, on the other hand, sent the message that the opinions of his dining companion truly mattered to him—he was a maestro of pull.

Or think back to my experiences on Hurricane Island that we discussed in Chapter 1. Prompted by Anita's suggestion, I figured out that the push approach wasn't producing results, and found that switching to pull transformed the performance of the team. My Outward Bound experience taught me that sometimes pull is needed because the leader doesn't know what to do!

There's another reason to use pull in a team situation. On occasions High-Performance Leaders choose not to push their solution because it makes sense to let the team discuss, debate, and resolve a problem. Out of collaborative problem-solving and giving the team the right to be wrong comes the likelihood that the group will *own* the solution because each team member feels he or she had a role in crafting it.

Both approaches can be effective depending on the person involved and the situation at hand. It generally takes more time to use pull (and when a leader takes this time, that is in itself a signal of commitment), so at moments of crisis, or when the time to ship has arrived, push can be entirely appropriate. *The point, however, is that High-Performance Leaders use pull on some occasions and push on others, never relying on just one pitch to advance their argument.* Because their colleagues know these leaders can use pull effectively, they recognize push, when they see it, as necessitated by circumstances, not as a signal of arrogance. And when High-Performance Leaders do use pull, they display commitment to their peer or their team, and to the potential contributions of either, and they increase the likelihood that they will find common ground with their colleagues on those sticky issues where compromise may be most difficult to reach. On the other hand, leaders who overrely on the push technique send a very different signal about the value of their peers' contributions—and believe me, peers will look for reasons *not* to buy your mousetrap if they think the process will be too painful or unsatisfying.

3. THE LAW OF THE GOOD SAMARITAN

It's easy to watch a peer make a fool of himself or herself, with the boss, for example, or with a customer. And in the highly competitive corporate world, their waning power or stature will mean that you gain in centrality or have one fewer internal competitor to worry about. But peer relationships are all about building partnerships, and this in turn requires a leader to tell a partner honestly how he or she is doing. Beyond that, it means fighting hard to prevent a peer from making a mistake.

This is a good time to talk about Nicholas, a peer on the senior team. While Nicholas was technically competent, attending team meetings with him was painful. He had a way of expressing his views that was nearly impossible to follow. During heated debates he would weigh in with his opinion, and when he did, it wouldn't take long before people would begin to roll their eyes. Sometimes his comments got so obtuse that team members would try to hide their smirks by staring at the floor. On occasion I'd lock eyes with a peer and we'd each try to stop ourselves from giggling.

Someone needed to do something, even though it would have been easy to duck the issue and let our boss address the problem as he saw fit. I decided to talk with Nicholas about the problem. When I told him, after a senior team meeting, what I thought he had communicated—based on the notes I took of his comments—he was shocked. When I informed him that the team often couldn't follow what in the world he was talking about, he was flabbergasted. Even though his peers thought Nicholas was smart and highly competent, I told him that at times it seemed like he talked another language. Our discussion prompted Nicholas to get an outside coach, who helped him to really improve his communication skills. Too often we assume that the boss will provide this feedback. And all too often it never happens. In this case Nicholas appreciated my feedback, unpleasant as it was for him to hear.

The Law of the Good Samaritan takes the concept that *feedback is a gift* from the context of subordinates (where we first encountered it), to the context of peers—and we've also seen it in the boss context under the guise of the Law of the Emperor's Wardrobe. The power of camera-lens feedback in all aspects of relational leadership is one of the most important lessons of this book. This power is difficult to access, as giving constructive feedback is often one of the most difficult tasks a leader faces. But because of its importance, *and* because of its difficulty, feedback is absolutely central to High-Performance Leadership.

One other comment here. It may seem from this story and the others told so far that leaders must behave like Gandhi or Mother Teresa. That's not at all what I'm trying to say. Each of us, to varying degrees, will exhibit impatience, pettiness, insensitivity, rudeness, and worse, throughout our careers. The stories I've told already and my travails described in the remaining chapters certainly confirm my capability to make plenty of mistakes. We're all human and it's unlikely that any of us are headed for sainthood. However, the laws recognize the frailties and imperfections in each of us. Their purpose is to dramatically increase the chances that we'll take the high road in managing relationships, thereby minimizing the number of occasions we screw up and behave badly. Because we're human, the operative word here is minimize, not eliminate.

4. The Law of the Mirror

As a starting point, a leader must assume a partner's basic competence. So if you're having a problem with a colleague, it follows that you must assume you're the cause and you're the source. This isn't easy, since most of us fall into the blame game trap. We externalize the cause of the problem, and reflexively look for its sources outside of what we did and who we are. It never, ever occurred to

me to ask myself *why* Chris may have sent those bonus recommendations to Derek, and it didn't occur to me to ask because my
first assumption was that he'd done it because he was the idiot!

Don't assume evil intent unless you're sure of it, unless you see
it. Instead, begin by looking in the mirror and asking what *you've*
done or said—or not done or said—that has contributed to the
problem. *And if your automatic response is nothing, keep looking in
the mirror.* Each of us always contributes in some way to a problem
with a peer. It's so much more productive to move from blaming
another to thinking how each of you has contributed to the problem. *For openers, assume that both of you are at fault, and that neither of you meant to cause the problem.*

Use the pull technique to check out behavior by a colleague
when you're not sure. "Help me understand why you did that" is
the best question to ask of a peer, before you draw any conclusions
about his or her motives. Recall that I didn't ask any questions before I started dismantling Chris over his bonus gambit. I just assumed his motives were evil. Had I given Chris a chance to explain
his actions, I might have understood that my prior actions in handling his bonus recommendations had, in fact, contributed to his
behavior.

5. THE LAW OF FEEDBACK—AGAIN

While the Law of the Good Samaritan tells us not to stand by
while a peer heads toward failure, there are also situations where, if
a problem is not fixed, we will suffer ourselves. If a leader fails to
bring these problems and concerns to a partner's attention
promptly, the problem festers, and becomes a bigger problem for
both parties. It's therefore essential to acknowledge your concerns
and worries to your peers, and not to hide them. Too often a leader
will complain to a subordinate or another peer about a problem
with a colleague. Yet it's the peer who's the last to know—or who

never knows. For partners to work well together and trust one another, it's essential to be open with feedback, to display commitment to the team's success by voicing it, and to demonstrate courage by raising what could be a sensitive issue.

A story here may help illustrate what I mean.

In my first job with Pepsi—the job of my dreams—I was head of Employee Relations for the firm's company-owned bottling operations. In the interests of efficiencies and cost control, the same Human Resources staff functions that I relied on also provided support to Pepsi's franchise organization. It didn't take long for me to discover that the franchise business was getting more attention from the HR staff than mine. I was new and didn't want to come across as an ax murderer (that would happen soon enough), so I tried to resolve the problems with the staff managers of compensation, labor relations, training, and so on. They promised to be more responsive but whenever I needed their timely support, it was clear that the franchise business's needs got higher priority. Every week was a struggle in getting my assignments and projects completed on time. Finally, I decided to speak directly to the head of the HR staff—a peer who reported, along with me, to the Vice President of Human Resources. The conversation went something like this:

"Ann, if you have a few minutes, I need your help."

"Sure, come on in. So how are things going? You're a veteran now that you've been here a few months."

"Actually, it's almost six months."

"Really—wow."

I wanted to proceed gently. "Listen, Ann, I know you're busy so I won't take up a lot of your time. It's just that I'm concerned about the pressures your team is under."

"What do you mean?"

"Well, I'm trying to establish credibility with my clients. Obviously I want to be more responsive than Mark [my predecessor who had been fired]. Clearly he didn't provide heroic support to the bottling group. And I'm finding that your people are having difficulty balancing my priorities with those in the franchise group."

"Mike, this is not a new problem. And I'm not surprised you're finding it a bit of a challenge not having your own staff."

"Ann, I knew I had to rely on your staff to get my work done when I took this job. We even talked about it when you and I met during the interview process. My concern is that I get the impression that my work is almost always given a lower priority than the franchise business. Let me give you some examples." I proceeded to review with Ann a list of projects I had requested that were not completed on time.

"This list is longer than I had imagined," she responded. "I knew of a few occasions where we were late but this is more of a problem than I realized."

"Don't misunderstand me. I know there'll be many times when a franchise project has a higher priority than mine. But when there's more work than your staff can handle, I think we need to talk so you have a better sense of the bottling group's needs vis-à-vis franchise. Then you and I can sort out how to prioritize the projects."

"And my staff will feel a lot less conflicted about serving two business units. Have you talked to the boss about this?"

"No, I thought we ought to try to figure this out first. But it might make sense to get him involved when you and I are unable to sort out the priority of projects."

"I'm glad we talked about this. And I'm glad you saw fit to talk with me directly. I'll talk to my staff and make sure we're more evenhanded in getting your work done."

The discussion led Ann to design a simple process that allowed her to learn quickly when her staff was overloaded—and allowed the two of us to resolve the conflicting priorities. Now this isn't a particularly exciting story on the face of it. But this was no slam-dunk. Ann was a seasoned leader with tons of credibility through-out Pepsi—and I was the new guy on the block. Yet I was in a bind, unhappy with the work of Ann's staff, which was causing me problems with my own constituents. So I decided to tell Ann my concerns and give her the feedback she probably didn't want to hear.

The lesson here is that if you've got a problem with a peer, you must step up and speak up, confronting the issue directly with him or her. Remember—feedback is a gift!

6. THE LAW OF TRUST

As we've already discussed, trust is the single most important ele-ment of peer-to-peer relationships. It's the foundation for produc-tive feedback being given and received, it's the antidote to reflexive and destructive assumptions of a partner's incompetence, and it's what enables push and pull to be used in the right balance. So how do leaders develop trust in a relationship? The answer is simple—being trustworthy builds trust. *Demonstrating trust elicits trust.* Talking behind a peer's back destroys trust—since the peer will al-ways find out what you said. And trust, like reputations and like stock markets, can lose ninety percent of its value overnight. Or as a former student once told me, trust is like virginity: You only lose it once! A leader—or anyone else—can't be trustworthy only some of the time. Building trust is nothing less than a 24/7/365 com-mitment to oneself, the partner, the organization, and the planet!

A rather unusual incident illustrates this point.

When I started at Pepsi, I had to spend much of my time work-ing with Alex, the Manufacturing VP, addressing a variety of peo-ple issues, from union problems in some of our factories to weak managerial capability in his regional offices. Within a matter of a few months I had gained considerable credibility with him; he had come to trust my judgment and felt I was helping him make progress in fixing the problems in his department. At the end of one of our meetings, I was surprised when he took an unusual tack.

"You know, Mike, I'm damn pleased Doug [my boss] finally put someone competent in your job. Once it was clear he couldn't be very helpful himself, I pushed him for months to get someone who could help me resolve these issues."

What an odd comment, I thought to myself. Where is he going with this? I gave a cautious reply.

"Well I'm glad I got the job—there's lots to do and I think I can add value here."

"Mike, you don't need to be polite with me—you and I both know that Doug couldn't have made the progress you already have. Doug—let's face it—Doug has no real interest or skill in handling these kinds of operational problems."

I was taken aback by Alex's comments, yet flattered at the same time. Still, what he had said made me very uncomfortable. Even if I had the edge over Doug in this stuff, he was still my boss. For a split second I was tempted to pile on and agree with Alex, but something told me not to do it—it was the kind of stab in the back that a boss does not deserve.

"Alex, you've worked with Doug for a lot longer than I have, so you have your opinion of him. But he's been very supportive to me in my first few months here and, in fact, he's encouraged me to focus most of my time on your group. So I think you're being hard on him. Whatever—I can tell you he's sensitive to Manufacturing's issues and wants me to help you resolve them."

Alex began to smile—broadly.

"You know, I was hoping you'd respond that way. I don't know what you really think about Doug and I don't really care. What I do care about is whether I can trust you—because if you talk about

Doug in front of me, then you'll probably talk about me in front of Charlotte, or Lee. Or Doug! Well done."

Right after that the word went out from Alex to the rest of the bottling operations unit: "You can trust Mike Feiner—his integrity is unimpeachable!"

Now you should understand that this Doug was the same Doug who, only a few weeks previously, had told me that playing softball on Monday evenings was unacceptable, and that I had to quit the team. The same Doug who, as I'm sure you'll remember, had received my eloquent advice on what he should do with himself. So I could easily have succumbed to the temptation to join with Alex in criticizing him—and I might well have worked off some of my simmering anger over the softball episode by doing so. But something about Alex's questioning didn't smell right, and (thankfully) I chose to do the right thing. Being trustworthy is the only way to build trust.

7. THE LAW OF TELL YOUR CAT!

Gossip, backbiting, and rumor mongering are insidious and destructive. You've seen the game. Someone comes to your office and asks if you can keep a secret because they've got a corporate bombshell to drop, so they have to tell the one person they trust. This doesn't cut it—it violates the first rule of confidentiality: *If everyone tells the one person they trust, in no time at all the entire firm knows. Do the math!*

My advice here is simple, obvious, and extremely hard to follow. Don't ever traffic in gossip about peers (or anyone else). Keep the gossip until you get home and then tell your cat. *If you're not willing to see it on the bulletin board or in an e-mail, don't say it and don't write it.*

The inevitable question is, won't you look like a do-gooder if you don't engage in this kind of small talk while everyone else does? Or won't it seem like you're not part of the crowd?

Not necessarily. One script might go like this:

"Hey, this kind of talk isn't productive. We all have our gripes—just as people gripe about us. Let's stick to finding solutions to the problem instead of always personalizing their source."

If that's not to your liking, you might try this approach:

"How is it that we always gravitate to character assassination? The speeches usually differ from one person to another but it still sounds like the same kind of soap opera. We'd be less frustrated if we focused on what we can do to address business issues—and left the other stuff to the gossip columnists."

Again, if leaders don't uphold values, then no one will.

To finish the story of Chris and the bonuses, I was speechless when he told me that I behaved as though I was always right, and always had to be right. And I'm rarely speechless. I had no quick retort. My mouth was open but no words came out. Was I that difficult to deal with? It was clear that Chris thought so. He waited for my reaction, becoming visibly more nervous the longer my silence lasted.

Finally, I said, "Maybe you're right. Maybe I don't listen when you argue for your people. But that's because I think your standards are too low."

"Mike, maybe my standards are too low. Or maybe they're just different from yours. But if you start out thinking my standards are too low, then you'll never hear what I'm saying about some of my people—you've made up your mind before we ever begin talking."

Again, I was silent. Chris was right. Deciding ahead of time made our past bonus discussions superfluous. No wonder he didn't trust me to be evenhanded in judging his bonus recommendations. So I said, after a long pause, "Chris, let's start again. Tell me why you think these three stars deserve to max out at one hundred and fifty percent." This was a pull approach I rarely used. Chris went on to talk passionately about why his three stars deserved maximum bonus awards. Interestingly, it was obvious that he appreciated the chance to state his case. To him the process of deciding bonuses for his people seemed fairer when he got to share his opinions with me. And I realized I hadn't listened in the past to his point of view. I don't recall what the final outcome was for his three people. I do recall that I approved higher awards for his people than I had initially—and was happy to do so. Although it took us a while (and an unpleasant confrontation) to get to it, the pull approach allowed us to find a common ground that each of us owned, since both of us helped find it.

These laws seem simple enough. Nothing I've said here is conceptually difficult, counterintuitive, or a blazing insight into humankind. As with many things in business, however, what's difficult—and where most people trip up—is the execution. Putting these laws into practice is incredibly challenging. They require us to change assumptions we might have held for a long time. Assumptions that tell us not to trust someone until *they* show they can be trusted. Or not to judge someone as competent until *they* demonstrate it. The Laws of Leading Peers require a whole new mind-set, require us to reorient our thinking about organizational life. I'm not naive, and this book isn't meant to be the Boy Scout manual of doing good. So yes, there are some untrustworthy people in organizations who don't care about you. And there are probably even a few who wish your career harm. But my focus here is improving the quality of your career, and improving the organization you work for. My experience has taught me that my negative attitudes elicited the very kind of responses I didn't want. They became a kind of self-fulfilling prophecy, a Pygmalion experiment in reverse. The incident with Chris over the bonus is a great example—I signaled that I didn't trust him, so he behaved deceitfully by going behind my back. You could argue that he should have had the courage to confront me directly, but given how insufferable I was being, it's hardly surprising that he didn't.

However difficult it might be in practice, do what you can to stem the tide of negativity. You'll be amazed how differently peers will respond to your more open, trusting, and positive behavior—they'll be more open, trusting, and positive toward you!

Summary: Feiner's Laws of Leading Peers

1. The Law of Equality

Neither of you is the boss of the other, so you need a partnership mentality. It's important to understand the interdependence inherent in peer relationships.

2. The Law of Pull vs. Push

Sometimes you need to push to get people moving in the right directions, and sometimes you need to pull. But if you want to exercise influence over the long run, you have to use pull more than push. You won't make the sale simply through having the better mousetrap. Your peers have to enjoy buying it from you.

3. The Law of the Good Samaritan

Fight hard to prevent a peer from making a mistake—don't let him or her fail.

4. The Law of the Mirror

Start with the assumption that you're the problem, and don't assume evil intent unless you see it.

5. The Law of Feedback—Again

Acknowledge your concerns and worries to your peers—don't hide them.

6. The Law of Trust

Being trustworthy builds trust. And trust, like reputations and like stock markets, can lose most of its value overnight.

7. The Law of Tell Your Cat!

Don't traffic in gossip about your peers. If everyone tells the one person they trust, in no time at all the entire firm knows. Keep the gossip for your cat.

7	*Leadership Style*
	THE HADLEY PARADOX

In 1993, Leonard Hadley, a fifty-eight-year-old accountant and thirty-six-year veteran of the Maytag Corporation, was appointed as its CEO after the untimely death of its chairman. Expectations for his performance were uniformly low. If the nicest thing that commentators can say about you is that you're "loyal," you know you're falling behind in the charisma stakes. Hadley was considered both "loyal" and "unimaginative," maybe even "dull," which further relegated him to the ranks of the evangelically challenged.[1] His performance as the firm's number two officer had only served to mark him as one of the grayer spots on a gray wall, and early predictions of a lackluster tenure seemed to be borne out by a distinct absence of media and analyst coverage, slim attendance at industry speaking engagements, and waning participation in quarterly conference calls.

Yet Leonard Hadley transformed Maytag. He cleaned house in the management ranks, he divested the firm's overseas operations in a dramatic reversal of a globalization strategy, and he invested in new technology, including the widely successful Neptune washer. When Hadley took control, Maytag's stock traded at $14. Five years later, it was in the $50 range. One director acknowledged that the board was surprised at how well Hadley had taken the reins. "Len Hadley has—quietly, softly—done a spectacular job," he observed.

How can this be explained? How in the world could this "quiet" executive have turned around Maytag? In Chapter 1, we reviewed the recent attempts to rewrite the Great Man Myth of leadership, and we concluded that if there's anything heroic about leadership, it has much less to do with individual star qualities, and much more to do with extraordinary skill at *managing the details of relationships*. The story of Leonard Hadley demonstrates that this thesis extends to *leadership style* as well. If leaders are not lone superheroes, then neither do they need to adopt the style of lone superheroes to succeed. Again, the reason for much misunderstanding here is that we only see leaders who maintain a high profile, so we assume that leadership demands a high profile. We fail to notice the many effective leaders in our organizations who achieve results in a very different style. These quiet leaders evince their own brand of High-Performance Leadership.

In Part II, we've examined the laws of leading subordinates, bosses, peers, and teams. The laws have set out the details—the hows—of effective leadership through managing relationships. To understand what we mean by leadership style, it might help to think of these laws as products that must reach our followers—and if that's the case, then leadership style is the distribution channel for these products. You will remember that at the end of Chapter 4, we looked at how I might have behaved differently with my boss, Doug, over my commitment to play softball, and we noted that each of us will choose to implement the laws in different ways. The notion of leadership style expands on this idea. *The laws re-*

main unchanged, irrespective of the style of the leader implementing them, in the same way that a product sold through one channel is substantially identical to the same product sold through a different channel. But just as distribution channels must be carefully selected and tailored to take account of the nature of the product and the need to reach a particular customer segment, so leadership style must take account of the personality of the leader, and the characteristics of each target audience.

Early on in my Pepsi tenure, I had a dual reporting relationship with two bosses. Initially, I behaved in a similar way with both of these bosses. I was buttoned-up, I beat deadlines, and I kept them both posted on what was going on.

But after a short while, I began to realize how differently they were responding to me. The first boss, if I was working on a project for him, would ask me for a progress update a week and a half *before* the deadline. The second boss generally forgot that he made a deadline—he was only interested in knowing when the project was done, so posting him ahead of time on progress was more irritating to him than helpful. I eventually figured out that I had to vary my style in order to work best with my two bosses. Although the things that I was doing—displaying commitment to each boss's success and owning the outcome of each project—were the same in each case, I began to understand that the *style* in which I did these things had to change for each boss.

I'm not saying, however, that you should attempt to be all things to all people. There is a tension between varying your style to suit the situation, and yet remaining true to yourself. This tension is important because although successful leaders know how to flex their style to take account of changing situations, it's equally true that people will not follow a leader who they perceive to be false or artificial. You can flex your style, but not your values.

I recall telling Leo, one of my primary clients at Pepsi and a very senior executive, that he needed to improve his wardrobe. I was following the Law of the Good Samaritan by speaking to him—a number of his peers had commented to me that his appearance was drawing negative comments. Leo had, in fact, been identified as potential CEO material, but one of the senior team had asked rather pointedly at a talent review if we couldn't dress him up so he looked like an executive. I went to see Leo and gingerly explained to him that he looked like "Doubleknit Dan" in a company where sartorial style counted, and where almost everyone followed the lead of the CEO and dressed in expensive, pin-striped suits.

He listened to my spiel for a few minutes before politely interrupting me.

"Mike, I know you care about me and my success, and that's why you're telling me this. But I've never been too interested in looking studly: It's never been that important to me. Maybe I'll ask Delores [his wife] to pick out some new ties—I guess these ones are a little dated. But the suits are okay by me, so I'll stay with them. Thanks for bringing this up, though. I know it can't have been easy."

Leo went on to become a very successful executive, much admired by his people and his bosses for his talents and accomplishments. Sometime after our conversation, I went on to another assignment and no longer had much contact with him, but when I looked back I realized that Leo was one of the best executives I ever worked for. The important point here is this: Leo succeeded neither in spite of nor because of his penchant for inexpensive suits and loud ties. Rather he succeeded, in large measure, because he was entirely comfortable with who he was, with his own personal style. *His charisma* (and he had plenty of that) *came from his being real and down-to-earth.* His colleagues might not have liked his *style of dress*, but they sure liked his *style of authenticity.*

So there are two important ideas when we consider leadership style. First, as my experience with my two bosses taught me, High-

Performance Leaders *flex their style* to take account of the person they're working with. Second, as both Leonard Hadley and Leo illustrate, *there is no single correct style*. Leo was willing to flex certain elements of his style, but not others—he used a different style of interaction with our boss than he did with me, but he insisted on maintaining his idiosyncratic dress sense, because that element of his style worked for him. Hadley chose to maintain the authenticity of his "dull" style, rather than attempt to be something that he wasn't.

I observed a great many successful leaders throughout my career, and their range and diversity of style was remarkably wide. High-Performance Leaders come in all shapes and sizes. Some dress for success, some don't. Some are short, some are tall. Some are great communicators; many are not particularly eloquent or articulate. Some are outgoing and affiliative; others are shy and introverted. Some, like Hadley, can seem dull and boring and accountant-like; others, like Leo, wear wide ties. All of them, however, know their own style and strengths, and are comfortable with that. They flex their style as needed in order to connect with their colleagues, but they never compromise their integrity in doing so. They are genuine, and willing to be themselves. The tension that successful leaders manage is to remain true to their essential character while adapting, within that, to what their partners and bosses and subordinates need in order to ship.

We have all been to sales rallies and off-site conferences where senior leaders pump up the audience with emotional exhortations about the company's growth opportunities. And we've all heard a leader articulate key opportunities that the organization must seize to deliver on its promise. Since I occasionally helped write some parts of those speeches for leaders I worked for, I'd sometimes randomly ask conference participants a day or two later what they thought about the leader's talk. They often responded positively, commenting approvingly at what a moving, compelling, and powerful talk it had been. When I then asked if they were in agreement with the key initiatives that, say, Trevor outlined, I usually got an uncomfortable stare.

"Sure, absolutely, those are the challenges," would be the response.

I'd probe further: "Well, in terms of prioritizing them, what do you think?" And here's where I was amazed. Most of the time people had only a vague and fuzzy recollection of the initiatives—and often they could remember only one.

I said at the beginning of this book that leadership has very little to do with oratory, even though the list that many of us generate when asked to think of stellar leaders generally contains famous orators. I argued that this misconception was largely the result of a visibility problem—that we associate successful leadership with what we see successful leaders doing, which, for the most part, is speechmaking. (It's also the result of a problem with our historical viewpoint. Great speeches are like fossils: They're the imprint that's left behind when the person of the leader has long since departed. But just as fossils give us only the external picture, so speeches, remembered long into posterity, give only the external face of the leader, not the hand-to-hand combat that constitutes the essence of the leadership role.)

But the subject of oratory deserves a brief examination here. Even though the main focus of this book is the ninety percent of the leadership iceberg that is hidden from view, speechmaking is certainly a factor in the ten percent we see above the surface, so it's appropriate to look at its role more closely. And the appropriate question for us to ask is this: If, as the story above suggests, we remember so little of the content of many speeches, what, precisely, is their role in leadership? I'll argue that effective oral and written communications (a larger group of activities, which includes oratory) are effective for the same family of reasons that personal styles are effective. We'll see that this has relatively little to do with what we might consider the hard content of a speech, and much more to do with the qualities of the leader that are communicated through the style of the speech. Although the following isn't intended as a history lesson, it might help explain what I mean.

After the assassination of John F. Kennedy in 1963, Lyndon Baines Johnson became the thirty-sixth President of the United States. Five days later he addressed a joint session of Congress. In a speech of only 1,633 words (compare the 9,298 words of President Clinton's final State of the Union address), Johnson succeeded in providing new purpose to a nation shocked at the terrible events that had taken place in Dallas, and mourning both the death of a man and the apparent death of a dream. But more importantly, he succeeded in establishing himself as the new leader of the country. After paying tribute to the deceased President, and pledging that his ideas and dreams would be translated into reality, Johnson moved on to the most critical section of his speech:

> For thirty-two years Capitol Hill has been my home. I have shared many moments of pride with you, pride in the ability of the Congress of the United States to act, to meet any crisis, to distill from our difference strong programs of national action.
>
> An assassin's bullet has thrust upon me the awesome burden of the Presidency. I am here today to say I need your help; I cannot bear this burden alone. . . . It is our duty, yours and mine . . . to do away with uncertainty and doubt and delay, and to show that we are capable of decisive action; that from the brutal loss of our leader we will derive not weakness, but strength; that we can and will act and act now. . . .
>
> This is our challenge—not to hesitate, not to pause, not to turn about and linger over this evil moment, but to continue on our course so that we may fulfill the destiny that history has set for us.

The first phrase of this excerpt ("For thirty-two years . . .") was added by the new President to a late draft of the speech.[2] In a stroke, it signals Johnson's humility (he shares the experiences of his immediate audience) and his dedication (in equating Congress with home, he equates it with what is closest to the heart)—the phrase is a glimpse of his authenticity. He continues by asking for support in direct terms ("I need your help; I cannot bear this burden alone"), by appealing to shared duty, and by invoking the notion of historical destiny as an overarching mission. The message here is simple: We are in this together, I am one of you, and I need your help if we are to realize our goal.

There are two elements of this speech that are important here. First, Johnson articulates a vision (and although we've said that vision is far from the top of the list of leadership priorities, in speechmaking it assumes much greater significance). He gives his audience something to *aspire* to, something bigger than they are, that can only be won through joint endeavor. Second, he does this in words that are authentic, heartfelt, genuine, and personal. He needs to establish his own leadership in Kennedy's shadow—he is speaking only two days after JFK's funeral—and he does this by showing his humanity—and humility. "For thirty-two years, Capitol Hill has been my home" roots his presidency in the human dimension. This speech was hailed as just what the country needed; no one seemed to mind that Johnson's speaking skills paled in comparison to Kennedy's.

Eighteen years earlier, Harry S Truman had stood in the same room, in a very similar situation. As the United States finally approached victory in World War II, its President of twelve years, Franklin Delano Roosevelt, had died suddenly of a cerebral hemorrhage. In his subsequent address to a joint session of Congress, Truman had to unite a grieving nation and establish his own leadership (and whereas Johnson had been a prominent political leader for many years prior to his vice presidency, Truman had had a much lesser leadership role in the Senate). There are striking similarities between his words and those that Johnson would use two decades later:

> With great humility I call upon all Americans to help me keep our nation united in defense of those ideals which have been so eloquently proclaimed by Franklin Roosevelt. I want in turn to assure my fellow Americans and all of those who love peace and liberty throughout the world that I will support and defend those ideals with all my strength and all my heart. That is my duty and I shall not shirk it. . . .
>
> You, the Members of the Congress, surely know how I feel. Only with your help can I hope to complete one of the greatest tasks ever assigned to a public servant. With Divine guidance, and your help, we will find the new passage to a far better world, a kindly and friendly world, with just and lasting peace. . . .
>
> At this moment, I have in my heart a prayer. As I have assumed my heavy duties, I humbly pray Almighty God, in the words of King Solomon: "Give therefore thy servant an understanding heart to judge thy people, that I may discern between good and bad; for who is able to judge this thy so great a people?"
>
> I ask only to be a good and faithful servant of my Lord and my people.

Just as Johnson would do after him, Truman establishes his own humility, asks for help, and appeals to the ideals of his predecessor, which, by repeating, he makes his own. In his wonderful biography of Truman, David McCullough has this to say about the address: "People everywhere felt relief, even hope, as they listened. *He seemed a good man, so straightforward, so determined to do his job.* The voice and accent would take some getting used to—he pronounced 'United States' as 'U-nited States,' said 'nation' almost as though it rhymed with 'session,' at times 'I' came close to 'Ah'—but *he sounded as though he meant every word* [emphasis added]."[3] In other words, Truman established his authenticity, his comfort with who he was and how he sounded. And like Johnson, Truman was in the difficult position of following a President who had raised speechmaking to an art form.

This notion of authenticity was critical for both Johnson and Truman, because neither of them had been elected to the office of President. Neither had a mandate from the people to lead, yet both were forced to assume leadership. And both were astute enough to realize that *authenticity establishes leadership*. People want to follow a human being, not a stuffed suit, so they need to see the human side of their leader. And humans are fallible and gloriously varied, so signals of humility (awareness of one's own fallibility) and comfort with one's own characteristics (Harry Truman's nonestablishment accent) go a long way toward establishing this human dimension. To take a more recent presidential example, many (but not all) Americans find the malapropism-laden remarks of George W. Bush, complete with references to "malfeance"[4] and "embetterment,"[5] significantly more appealing than they found the polished and erudite words of Bill Clinton. This is precisely because Bush shows his own fallibility (and hence commonality with those he leads) where Clinton showed perfection and polish (and a measured style of delivery) that some (but again, not all) found increasingly patronizing—and disingenuous. In rational terms, this might make little sense—why prefer a leader who often seems tongue-tied to one who appears consummately well prepared and a master of his material?—but in emotional terms it rings true.

Neither LBJ nor Truman is remembered as a great orator—certainly when compared with their immediate predecessors. Truman rarely attained the poetry of "a date which will live in infamy";[6]

likewise LBJ, the Great Society notwithstanding, seldom rose to the vivid metaphor of "the torch has been passed to a new generation of Americans."[7] But both of them recognized that, in oratorical terms, they could not compete with their predecessors, and so neither tried to do so. There were other similarities in the situations they faced: They were both speaking at a time of national crisis, and both had to establish their leadership quickly. They did this not by banging the table or issuing directions left, right, and center, but by asking for help and acknowledging the difficulty of the task ahead, by embracing ideals and a vision of the future, and by leaving no one in any doubt of their emotional grounding, and their comfort with who they were. They demonstrated humility, vision, and authenticity.

But neither authenticity nor vision demands lofty words. Neither of these demands what we think of as great oratory. Of course, it's a bonus to be an articulate speaker—I'm not arguing that great oratory isn't effective at moving people. (Although I will argue that inspirational oratory has a remarkably short half-life: Its emotional effects fade quickly from the collective memory, and it's only when it is reinforced by the hand-to-hand combat of leadership that its effects on followership are at all lasting. Moreover, hand-to-hand combat without great oratory is just as effective in most cases.) But I've found that successful speakers—who aren't necessarily successful *orators* (polished prose does not pour from their lips)—succeed much more because of their ability to access and convey their authenticity than because of any great verbal fluency. Did the great orators of history move people with their great words? Of course they did. But in most cases they were also sending a strong signal of their ultimate authenticity—either through their text, like Johnson did, or through their delivery, like Truman did.

If you're writing a memo or preparing a speech, remember, then, that not only is it okay to be merely human, but in many cases it's the most effective approach. You can't fake authenticity in your spoken or written communications, just as you can't fake the Law of Commitment to your subordinates. But if your words are characterized by a sincere willingness to show your humanity, and stem from a profound understanding of your own humility, then however tongue-tied or inarticulate you might think you are, you'll find your communications to be surprisingly effective.

We'll conclude Part II with a closer look at the interaction between the laws and leadership style by reviewing the laws in action. We'll take a (hypothetical) scenario—involving a boss who's dissatisfied with a subordinate's performance—and show how a difficult, real-time, one-on-one interaction is improved by a number of Feiner's Laws. The scenario will also show the laws implemented in widely varying styles.

Before we do so, however, there's an important point to be made about the laws presented in Part II. Because Feiner's Laws are intended to be immediately useful in the organizations we work in, and because leadership is predominantly about managing relationships, the laws we've seen are grouped according to these relationships—with a boss, with a subordinate, with a peer, or with a team. If you face a difficult situation with a subordinate, your first reference is Chapter 3; if the problem is with a team you lead, you turn first to Chapter 5. But this is not to suggest that the laws presented in the context of one relationship won't be enormously useful in another. The laws are grouped as they are because collectively they define a philosophical approach to each type of relationship (with a subordinate, "You count"; with a boss, "I'm committed to you"; with a team, "We're in this together"; with peers, "I'm here to earn your trust"). But the Law of Feedback, for example, is important to *all* the relationships here. The Law of Pull vs. Push is important to *all* the relationships here. The Law of Building a Cathedral is important to *all* the relationships here. While we might construct our organizations in terms of boss-peer-subordinate hierarchies, the fundamentals of human relationships pay little heed to these artificial distinctions. So even though the dialogues that follow illustrate a boss-subordinate interaction, you'll see laws from other sections of the book in use, in addition to those from Chapter 3.

Here's the scenario: Bob and Meredith work for Onepitch, Inc., a leading roofing materials manufacturer. Bob, the boss, has decided to meet with Meredith, the subordinate, to discuss Meredith's performance. Meredith has been reporting to Bob for six months, and Bob has become increasingly annoyed and concerned with her behavior. Meredith's responsibilities include marketing and customer relationship building for a key market, and she's also been tasked with implementing a revised marketing strategy that was developed by Bob before Meredith's arrival. For reasons that Bob can't explain, the marketing strategy, which calls for close interaction with and support of clients, has had little discernible impact on the behavior of Meredith's group, who maintain a distance from their customers that Bob finds bewildering. As far as Bob can see, Meredith seems to have checked out. On a couple of occasions Bob has had to step in at the last moment to avert disaster when Meredith should have acted. At other times important deadlines have been missed. To Bob it seems that Meredith prefers a formal, distant, and analytical management style in marked contrast to the intimate, involved, and convivial style that Bob has found to be most successful.

Bob has reached the conclusion that the situation with Meredith, which has been festering for some time, must be resolved before more damage is done, and so he's arranged a one-on-one meeting with her. He's well aware that Meredith's departure, either voluntarily or involuntarily, will be seen by Dick, Bob's boss, as a sign of failure—Dick will undoubtedly judge Bob on how well he is able to motivate Meredith. So Bob has to either solve the problem of Meredith's performance, or figure out a way to manage the team around Meredith's shortcomings.

Because this type of situation is so common in organizational life, I frequently ask my audiences to role-play the Bob and Meredith interaction. More often than not, a smart, well-educated young manager assuming the role of Bob will approach the difficult conversation with Meredith something like this:

BOB: Meredith, I want to thank you for making time to see me today. I really hope we can come up with some ways to turn things around.

MEREDITH: Okay.

BOB: I'm sure you're aware that your performance has been a great concern to me over the last few months. We simply must address your interactions with your team and with your customers. I want to give you all the help I can so that you can lift your game.

MEREDITH: Okay.

BOB: Yes, so it strikes me that you've got to become more hands-on with your constituents, both inside and outside the firm. Your style is perceived as aloof and removed, and that's a big problem.

MEREDITH: So you're saying I have to do things your way? We've had this conversation before.

BOB: *(Quickly)* No, that's not what I mean.

MEREDITH: But you're a hands-on guy, and you're asking me to be more hands-on. So you really *are* asking me to do things your way.

BOB: It's not my way—it's just the way that works, and the way that will support the marketing strategy best. Now, I realize you've had some difficulty with this in the past, so I want to help. I've devoted quite a lot of thought to this recently, and I think there are some specific, concrete steps we can take which you'll find to be very positive. First, I've investigated the training opportunities we have available here at Onepitch, and you'll be glad to hear that there's a one-day seminar available on Improving Client Networking Skills. I'd like to sign you up for that, perhaps early next week. Second, I'd like you to develop a relationship with Rebecca, who as you know has been with us for a number of years. I think she'd make a great mentor for you, and she'll help you develop your relationship skills further. And finally, I know I'm partially at fault in all of this, because I haven't given you enough feedback recently. So I'd like us to arrange a series of lunches, perhaps every two weeks or so, so that I can post you on how you're doing, and you can let me know more about your progress.

I think that if we can do all of this, we can really get things moving in the right direction. I'm sorry it's taken me so long to get around to speaking with you, but I hope we can accentuate the positive as we go forward together!

MEREDITH: *(Unsmiling silence)*

In this dialogue, Bob has recognized the problem, presented his analysis of its causes, and laid out his action plan to get to a solution. And Meredith is furious. Why?

First, Meredith hasn't been able to get a word in edgewise. Bob knows that the tension between the two of them is palpable, and he's wary lest the situation deteriorate any further. So he makes sure that, by talking almost continuously, he retains control of the conversation. Second, Bob has done what many of us do when faced with an emotionally challenging situation: He has taken refuge in the control and predictability of management activity. He's developed an analysis and an action plan—straightforward, emotionally "safe" steps that don't take him close to the dangerous ground of how Meredith might actually feel about all this. Third, Bob has resorted to that great, outsource-able panacea for employee problems—training. Let's be clear here: Training does not, will not, and cannot solve interpersonal problems unless a boss first tries to take ownership for coaching the subordinate. It's an excuse for ducking the issue, not a way of resolving it. Finally, like me in the early days of my career, *Bob has only one pitch*—he's all *push*. His directives might, if he's lucky, gain Meredith's compliance, but they'll never gain her commitment.

Bob's approach might be very different if he brought some of Feiner's Laws into play. To show the interplay between the laws and varying leadership styles, we'll look at the laws implemented in three distinct styles. First, we'll see Bob using a *direct, to-the-point style*. Then, we'll see how the laws work with a more *wordy, less direct style*. Finally, we'll see the use of a *data-driven, factually analytical style*. This is not to say that these are the only styles that leaders use—there are nearly as many distinct styles as there are leaders—but these are perhaps more common than others.

So let's run the tape again, but this time with a Bob who has been freshly brainwashed at the Feiner Academy of Leadership. In this example, we'll see Bob use the concept of authenticity from this chapter, the Law of Pull vs. Push, and the Law of the Mirror (both from Chapter 6). As we've said, here he uses a fairly *direct* style. He doesn't mince words, or use more than are absolutely necessary to get his point across. He succinctly identifies what's on his mind at each moment in the conversation, and communicates it in a highly condensed manner:

*(First, Bob has the courage to acknowledge the diffi-
culty of the situation—and thereby enhance his authenticity—even though this immediately puts the
conversation on "dangerous" emotional ground.)*

BOB: Meredith, look, this is a difficult conversation for
                me, and I'm not entirely certain where to begin. I
                want to be clear about one thing, though—I want
                to help.

MEREDITH: I'm not sure what you mean.

*(Now, Bob uses the Law of Pull vs. Push and asks a
question rather than presenting his diagnosis.)*

BOB: You and I are not clicking. The marketing strategy
                is at risk, so we have to fix this. What's going on
                here?

*(A long pause. Bob, resisting the acute temptation to
fill silence with words, remains quiet.)*

MEREDITH: I can't figure out how to give you what you want.

BOB: *(Using the Law of the Mirror)* Is it something that
                I'm doing, or failing to do?

(Another pause)

MEREDITH: Frankly, Bob, I'm ticked off.

BOB: *(Using pull again)* How come?

MEREDITH: You keep jumping in and taking over whenever
                you think I'm not doing things as you would. You
                seem to have no faith in my ability to execute. And
                you want me to become a clone of you. That's just

not in my DNA. Why won't you leave me alone to
do my job?

This is a radically different opening from the first one. The focus
of the conversation has shifted from Bob, and his concerns and
need for resolution, to Meredith and what's bothering her. Importantly, Bob, through using pull and then waiting for answers, has
succeeded in getting Meredith to begin to air her frustrations with
the relationship. Meredith might still be angry, but she's getting
less angry, not more. Bob has begun to get to the root of the problem—Meredith feels micromanaged—and is already much closer
to a joint solution than he was in our first dialogue.

Before we look at how the conversation might continue, let's
see how Bob might use the same laws, but in a rather different, *in-
direct*, style. Here, he uses more words to express himself, and approaches issues from the side rather than head-on:

BOB: Meredith, look, thanks for juggling your schedule
              so we could meet. I know you're pretty busy right
              now, so I appreciate your coming by. It sure has
              been crazy around here lately, what with budgets
              and capital plans due. And next week I have to
              present our annual operating plan to Dick and the
              board.

MEREDITH: I know.

BOB: Anyway, I just want to say that, well, I'm not sure
              how to get this conversation going. *(Long pause)*
              Frankly, I've been avoiding speaking with you. I've
              been worrying about our relationship for quite a
              while now, and to be honest with you I don't think
              we're on the same track.

              (Using push) I'm worried that, if the two of us
              aren't able to come up with some better way of

working together, then the marketing strategy might be at risk. The strategy is, after all, intended to resonate with our customers. Don't you agree?

MEREDITH: I'm not sure.

BOB: Well, it depends on building close relationships inside and outside the firm, and I'm not sure that we're moving in that direction. But more importantly, it doesn't seem that either of us is having any fun here. *(Now the switch to pull)* Can you help me to understand the problem we're having? Maybe you can help me see it from your perspective?

(A long pause. Bob, resisting the acute temptation to fill silence with words, remains quiet.)

MEREDITH: The bottom line is I can't figure out how to give you what you want.

BOB: *(Law of the Mirror)* Why—am I part of the problem here? I mean, if I'm getting in the way, I'd like to understand why and how. If I'm not being clear with what I need, I'd like to understand how to be more clear.

MEREDITH: I'd say that, yes, you are part of the problem. Frankly, Bob, I'm ticked off.

BOB: *(Using pull again)* I'm sorry you feel that way. Are we not spending enough time together?

MEREDITH: That's not the problem.

BOB: I've given you plenty of feedback, I think. And I've tried to be clear in setting out your responsibilities and my expectations. So connect the dots for me. How come you feel the way you do?

MEREDITH: Well, you keep jumping in and taking over when-

ever you think I'm not doing things as you would.
You seem to have no faith in my ability to execute.
And you want me to become a clone of you. That's
just not in my DNA. Why won't you give me the
space to do my job?

Bob's style here is less direct, more tentative, and less to the point.
He dances around touchy issues, and takes much longer to get to
the root causes (perhaps because he's more sensitive to the emotions at stake). But the conversation follows the same contours, irrespective of this difference in style. Again, Bob establishes his
authentic concern and trepidation, and uses push, pull, and the
Law of the Mirror to get Meredith talking.

   Now we'll follow the interaction through to the end, this time
with a Bob who's more *data- and fact-driven* in his approach, and
whose tendency is to present an *analysis* rather than make an assertion:

BOB: So if I follow you, you're angry because my inter-
                  vening with your team signals a lack of trust in
                  your ability to get the job done?
MEREDITH: That's about it.
BOB: *(Giving camera-lens feedback)* If I'm honest with
                  you, Meredith, my confidence in your abilities *has*
                  diminished recently. When I stepped in last time,
                  it was because I'd had a phone call from Larry
                  Tubbs—who as you know accounts for about eight
                  percent of our domestic materials orders—and
                  who'd expressed some surprise that he hadn't heard
                  from us in a couple of months. And that's not the
                  first time this has happened. It appears to me that
                  there's a pattern here: You only contact clients
                  when there's a pressing need to do so. But we've

been successful in the past partly through treating our clients as partners, and by trying to maintain a constant dialogue with them. In fact, our results have improved because of our customer partnerships. Our sales growth is up six points in the last quarter over the previous year, and that correlates directly with an increase in customer satisfaction scores of thirteen percent over last year. It's clear to me that enhanced customer contact is leading to enhanced results. But you don't seem comfortable with that approach.

MEREDITH: You're right—that's just not my way of doing things. I don't want to come across as a slick salesperson. I'd rather the clients know we're here when they need us, but that we don't intend to get under their feet.

BOB: But I'd argue that we'll never find out what they need, and when they need us, if we don't maintain regular contact. That's a conclusion that's well supported by the market data. Indeed, it's the whole foundation of the marketing strategy, and it's your job to implement it.

MEREDITH: But Bob, I didn't create the damn strategy. You simply presented it to me and told me to go to it. There's more than one way to skin a cat, you know, and I'd just be more comfortable doing this my way. It also would have been nice to be asked first.

BOB: (Push) You didn't say anything when you came on board, if I remember correctly . . .

MEREDITH: Well I didn't want to rock the boat on day one. But if I'm honest with you, I've had reservations about this from the get-go, and I've never felt that this approach fit my style.

BOB: *(Pull again)* What kind of reservations?

MEREDITH: Bob, if you must know, the more I've looked at what you put together, the more I've concluded that it's wrong for the business, and fundamentally wrong for the team we've got. If you really want to know what I think, I think we should take a whole new look at the strategy.

BOB: *(Back to push)* Wait a second—the strategy has been in place, with implementation pending, for a long time now. If you want my read here, that train has left the station.

MEREDITH: And that's my problem. You tell me the train's left the station, you tell me it's my job to implement the strategy, and yet I can't convince myself it's the right strategy. I wasn't part of it, and I'm still not part of it. And it drives me nuts that you don't see this, that you don't listen to my viewpoint, that you treat me as just a squeaky wheel to be tolerated or ignored. Bob, if you give the order, I guess I'll try to respond. But this isn't the way to get my best stuff.

BOB: *(A moment of silence)* How—precisely—can I get your best stuff?

MEREDITH: Take the time to review the strategy with me. Let me give you my input. Give me a vote!

BOB: I'm not sure we have the time. Dick has been expecting the implementation plan for a while now, and he's been pressuring me to deliver—and that's why I've been leaning on you.

MEREDITH: Look—this is really important to me. If the strategy could reflect my input, I'm sure you'd find you need to micromanage me much less.

BOB: *(Switching to the Law of Personal Commitment)*

Okay, I hear you. You want to feel some ownership for this. I'm not sure what changes we can make, and I'm not sure how it will help you, but I think I understand where you're coming from. How would it sound if I take it upon myself to get Dick to cut us some slack, and you and I take another week or so to go over this thing together, and look at what we might change so that you can put your signature on the bottom line?

MEREDITH: I have to say, I'd really appreciate that—and I know that Dick can be pretty open with his opinions when his deadlines get pushed back, so thanks for putting yourself in the firing line. I have a bunch of ideas that I think could really improve our effectiveness in the field—without our coming across as phony schmoozers.

BOB: Well, maybe we have a deal. But at the same time, I need you to get more on board with the customers. That's been a problem for a while now, and developing your skills there would position you for much greater success in this industry. *(Law of Accountability)* If I'm willing to take the time to review our strategy with you, then I need you to commit to getting closer to our clients—and I'm going to hold you to task on that. In fact, we really should continue this conversation to figure out exactly what our performance contract should look like.

MEREDITH: That's only fair. When can we pick this up again?

And the two ride off into the sunset together. Granted, this dialogue is a little contrived, but it demonstrates how the leader's approach to the details of a difficult interaction can make the difference between a positive outcome—and enhanced perform-ance from a subordinate—and a less happy ending. The most im-portant tactics when sitting down with a difficult subordinate are to recognize the difficulty of the conversation up front, and to avoid giving a long and well-intentioned, but completely counter-productive, one-sided speech at the outset. The key is to get as quickly as possible to the point where you can ask a question, and then to bite your lip until you get the complete answer. I'll say that again—it's important. Bite your lip until you get the complete an-swer. Refrain from problem solving or attempting to move the conversation on until you're sure that your subordinate has told you everything on his or her mind.

A brief note about the final outcome: You might argue that in accepting a further delay to the implementation plan so as to get Meredith on board, Bob has moved even further away from his im-mediate goal—to ship. It might therefore seem that I'm suggesting that his best approach in this case is to give in to what his subor-dinate wants. *The reality is quite the opposite.* Meredith has not de-livered on the implementation for a long time (because of the reasons that Bob has now discovered), and without some change in the relationship, *Meredith will never deliver.* So Bob's choice isn't between now or later, *it's between later or never.* Forcing the issue with Meredith will get him nowhere. In following the laws, Bob begins to address not what Meredith *wants*, but what she *needs*: The laws allow him to restore the relationship to a point where the delivery of the plan becomes much more likely.

In this example, we've seen a leader relying on authenticity (by acknowledging difficulty, and by confessing to a lack of solutions), and then using the Law of Pull vs. Push and the Law of the Mirror to understand the problem in more depth, using the Law of Per-sonal Commitment to signal the importance of finding a joint so-lution, and using the Law of Accountability to clarify the need for reciprocity and to begin the process of developing a Performance

Contract. We saw that these laws can be used by a leader in three different styles: one whose natural style is *direct and to-the-point*; one who uses more words, and tends to approach issues *indirectly*; and one who is fact- and data-driven and who approaches issues *analytically. All three of these styles can be effective, as can many others.* If a leader really knows his or her people—if he or she practices the Law of Intimacy—then that leader will understand how to flex his or her style to best fit the subordinate. *But the essence of the laws— their core rationale—doesn't change between one style and another.*

You might suggest that in a case such as this one, where an element of the underlying problem is a difference in style between a boss and an employee, part of the solution would be to seek out subordinates who have a style similar to your own. Perhaps opposites attract in connection with choosing a spouse, you might say, but in organizational life this is not the case. Look at most enterprises and the range of styles is remarkably narrow, you'd point out—it's natural for leaders to prefer people with whom they feel compatible. But I'd argue that this thinking is dangerous. Choosing people on the basis of fit is one criterion, but it shouldn't be the only one. Leaders must hear different views and perspectives to deliver consistently great results. While consensus may be harder to achieve, organizations with people of different styles are more innovative and adaptive. I'm not suggesting that an organization composed entirely of mavericks is sensible. It is sensible, however, for leaders to fight the tendency to pick people solely on the basis of style compatibility. Employees who are intuitive and achieve results through their abilities as relationship builders are invaluable, as are employees who take a quantitative, analytical approach to decision making. Employees who encourage participation and share power (which research has shown to be a predominantly female style) are invaluable, as are employees who rely on their organizational position and formal authority to do their jobs (a predominantly male style). Leaders need to listen to others who see problems and challenges through a different lens. Yet many organizations are comprised of people who look and sound frighteningly similar. It's this sameness that leads to insularity and the risk of group-think. High-Performance Leaders build great teams by hiring and growing great people. But more than this, these leaders recognize that teams don't make great decisions unless there are *diverse* people pushing the boundaries of ideas, by offering a variety of perspectives. It follows that teams with a variety of styles tend to achieve better results, and therefore that it's incumbent on leaders to be able to lead across differences in style.

We all know there are few Martin Luther Kings, JFKs, Gandhis, or Churchills in organizational life. For every magnetic Jack Welch, there are thousands of leaders who never show up on the radar screen, who have lots of strengths and their share of weaknesses, who are as "dull" as a Leonard Hadley—and who are High-Performance Leaders!

But the final point in this chapter is this: People look to a leader's substance, not style, to validate their leadership value. Al Dunlap was, by all accounts, very charismatic. His self-assured, ex-Marine toughness electrified Sunbeam's board, and won him rave reviews on Wall Street. Yet inside accounts of his tenure at Sunbeam indicate that his behavior cost him virtually all his credibility within his organization.

Conversely, the best boss I ever had (Leo, the man of the hellacious ties) was an outstanding leader, whose down-to-earth style made him seem real and approachable to his team—and to the entire organization. He was someone who didn't knock your socks off with his eloquence or palpable toughness. Make no mistake, he was smart, very able, and had high standards. He just never wore this on his sleeve. He treated everyone with warmth and respect, was up front in communicating his concerns, and was comfortable in his own skin. He never tried to be tough; he never tried to be anything other than who he was. He didn't have to, because people responded to his decency and authenticity. People wanted to do a good job for him out of respect—and in consideration for the respect he showed them. In fact, it was his down-to-earth approachability that made him charismatic, because his authenticity was so appealingly real and human to people.

It's substance and character, not style, that determine followership.

That's why charisma can't *sustain* followership in the long run. Authenticity can. A leader's willingness to be real and genuine, to be himself or herself, is what ultimately engages and hooks people. The late Israeli Prime Minister Yitzak Rabin is an example of this. Rabin was comfortable with being himself—quiet, reserved, and laconic—and it was his reliance on earnestly espousing his convictions that galvanized his country and led to the Oslo Peace Accords in 1993. Jack Welch is another example of someone who, because he openly acknowledged his speech impediment, people found appealing, despite his tough and direct transactional style. If you are real, and have the courage to allow people to see who you are, warts and all, the organization is more likely to see you as human—and you're much more likely to build the sort of followership that outlasts the glow of a great speech.

Summary: Leadership Style

- The Laws of High-Performance Leadership remain unchanged, regardless of the style of the leader implementing them.
- Leaders flex their style to suit varying situations, yet they don't attempt to be all things to all people. You can flex your style, but not your values.
- Leaders recognize that authenticity, and hence charisma, come from being true to yourself, not necessarily from telling your audience what it wants to hear.

• In speechmaking, humility, authenticity, and vision are key—and none of these demands lofty words.

• It's substance and character, not style, that build followership.

PART III

Situation-Specific Leadership

Even if one understands how to lead subordinates, bosses, teams, and peers, more tools and skills are required to be a High-Performance Leader. Part III builds on the laws of Part II in moving from relationships to situations. While relational issues are omnipresent in every leader's organizational life, situation-specific issues—such as handling conflict, implementing change, and leading difference—can be just as challenging. The following chapters discuss these situations and provide laws for each. You will see that certain laws and themes from Part II appear again in Part III: This reflects the fact that the fundamentals of relational leadership apply in the situations we're looking at. In this part, however, we will view leadership through a situation-specific lens.

8	*Leading Conflict*
	THE ART OF THE PRODUCTIVE DISAGREEMENT

Let me tell you the story of a meeting early in my career at Pepsi. Pepsi did not have one of those caste-system cultures, which dictates that meetings can only occur between executives fairly close in level. To the contrary, when you went to a meeting there as a junior executive, the President might be there, or the CFO—if you had a reason to be at a meeting you could be there with people from three or four levels above you. There were maybe eight or nine people from a variety of functions at this particular meeting, then, from up and down the firm. As I was new to the company, I expected the discussion to give me a good cross section of how executives at the various levels thought and behaved.

While I don't remember what we were discussing, I do remember it was an absolutely dreadful meeting. The executive running it was bullying and dominating—not listening, not asking questions, but cutting people off—and no one had the guts to tell him to shut up. No one advanced an alternate point of view by saying something like, "You may be right but let me give you another per-spective on that." It struck me that the team did not do a good job of analyzing the issues, or dissecting the problem, or getting to its root causes. I thought they were trying to solve for symptoms, and I thought the meeting—which had taken an hour or more—was pretty pathetic. The boss was a loudmouth, everybody else at the table behaved like sheep, they weren't good at problem solving or brainstorming, and because they failed to identify the root of the problem their solution didn't make any sense.

As we left the conference room my boss—who had arrived late and had attended only part of the session—took me to one side and said, "Well, what did you think of the meeting?"

I said, "Do you really want to know?"

He said, "Sure."

And I said, "This was one of the worst meetings I've ever been to in my life. This was pretty sad. For the following reasons . . ." And I recounted the long list of dysfunctional behaviors I had ob-served. I was, as you might expect having read this far, fairly forth-right in my assessment.

And my boss said, "Well, yeah, that's true. And if I think about it I can understand why you feel that way. But what did you do?"

I said, "What do you mean? I'm new, I'm—"

He said, "You're at the meeting, you're an executive, and if you were there to observe, I would have told the group that you were there to take notes. You were there to be part of the meeting. Lead-ers affect the outcome of meetings, and around here, reporting on what's wrong with the meeting without taking any personal re-sponsibility for the outcome suggests you exercise zero leadership. So do you want to report on the problem, or do you want to take personal responsibility for fixing the problem? Because if you want to do the former, you're in the wrong place. I could care less about the other people in the meeting, but I hired you because I thought you had what it takes to be a leader. Leadership is not about identifying problems, nor reporting them, nor tabling them, but being a party to fixing them. I'd give you an A for analysis, but you just flunked your first leadership test."

In other words, my boss was telling me that leaders take ownership of outcomes. One of the ways that they do this—and this would have greatly improved the ill-tempered meeting we'd both just attended—is by leading conflict.

Now, conflict is a lot like cholesterol. There's the good kind and the bad kind, and just as people have both types of cholesterol, so organizations have both types of conflict. Most health-conscious people know that not all cholesterol is bad, and that the goal is to increase HDL while minimizing LDL. When it comes to organizational conflict, however, we often assume it's all bad. This is not the case. Organizations need conflict—the good kind—to grow and prosper. High-Performance Leaders, in fact, seek to *create* healthy conflict, because it is from debate and the exchange of ideas that the best decisions get made, innovation occurs, and needed change is produced. These are all essential to organizational growth. In the case of my first meeting at Pepsi, a good dose of healthy conflict would have gone a long way toward preventing the kind of group-think that occurred as well as improving the analysis of the issues. It also would have helped pressure-test the solution. The boss, however, failed to create an environment where this kind of conflict could occur. Instead, by continuously cutting people off and stifling debate, he created the bad kind of conflict.

We've seen the bad kind of conflict on a couple of occasions in Part II. We saw conflict over work-life balance (the softball and trick-or-treat stories), and conflict in peer relationships (the Chris-and-the-bonuses story), and we saw how the relational leadership laws could address these instances within the relationships that sparked them. But even if a leader practices the relational leadership laws in Part II, situations still develop where all kinds of unhealthy conflict arise. And while the relational leadership laws address conflict between you and a boss, peer, or subordinate, there are numerous instances where leaders must address unhealthy conflict within their teams, or between their team and another team.

These might include personality conflict, where people clash because they simply don't like one another. Or conflict over treatment, where a person feels his or her wages, hours, or working conditions are unfair. Or conflict due to jealousy, where a manager covets what a colleague has. Or conflict where someone feels their ethics or values system is threatened by a decision. Or conflict when people are asked to go along with a major organizational change they don't agree with. Or conflict over power and position, where two leaders (and the businesses they run) may be vying for the same brass ring, like the John Mack, Phil Purcell power struggle at Morgan Stanley, which led to Mack's resignation in January 2001. When unhealthy conflict between two leaders metastasizes to entire divisions of an organization, its effects are especially damaging—people working in those groups spend much too much of their time worrying about the internal enemy, the conflict quickly becomes focused on personalities rather than objective viewpoints, and while this is going on the competition vanishes into the distance.

This chapter, then, presents Feiner's Laws of Leading Conflict, which give you the hows of containing or avoiding the bad kind of conflict and encouraging the good kind.

1. THE LAW OF INTERDEPENDENCE

Leaders can never rely solely on the power of their position, on their formal authority. They are in a continuous state of interdependence with bosses, peers, and subordinates—especially with subordinates, as they depend on their subordinates to ship on their behalf. The Law of Interdependence reminds us that overreliance on power *generates* conflict, as people feel bullied into following a leader. Leaders need people to *commit* to, rather than *comply* with, their expectations; they need to pull people more than they push people; they need to take people with them. If they overrely on their formal authority, and fail to respect the interdependence inherent in most working relationships, people are likely to pretend in public that they're with the program, but check out in private, as I observed at the meeting I just described.

But isn't this obvious to any leader? Doesn't everyone know this today? You'd be surprised how common this kind of top-down, "my way or the highway" mentality is.

That's exactly what I found with a new client fairly recently. I was retained to help a CEO and COO clarify their roles and accountabilities. They were, in a sense, tripping over each other, and creating real tension in the process. In the course of interviewing their subordinates to learn how they saw the problem, it became clear that the CEO had his own set of issues. People found him brilliant but abusive, often railing at his team for what he saw as their mistakes or incompetence in carrying out his agenda. The source of much of the unhealthy conflict in the organization, in other words, was the CEO himself and his overreliance on power.

Realizing that this situation was as crucial to the organization's success as was the CEO-COO relationship, I met with the CEO to surface this issue. Because he was a highly emotional guy, I knew I needed to proceed with care.

"Mitch, before we meet with Jack to talk about your roles, I wanted to download some general observations about the organization that I picked up in my interviews."

"Go ahead—I'm interested in what my team had to say."

"Well, there's no question that people are committed to the organization—they want to win. I didn't find anyone who wasn't passionate about making Olympia the number one player in the industry." (Olympia is a fictitious name; at the time of our meeting it was a $4 billion company.)

"Hell, I would hope they feel this way—I've been telling them we should be number one for more than a year. But by now you've figured out that this is the gang that can't shoot straight. They're incapable of following through on my directives."

This was going to be as tricky as I had anticipated.

"Mitch, this is basically a sound team. I'm sure you'd like more Hall of Fame players but the ones you have can deliver what you want to get done. It's just going to take your galvanizing their commitment around some key priorities. Right now my sense is that they're running all over the place, trying to attack too many issues. It seems like a bit of a fire drill."

"Listen, Mike, I've pointed out a thousand times to these bozos what needs to get done. And they've got a million excuses when things don't happen. I'm tired of it. And I'm tired of being the one that has to kick their ass—I think Jack could be more help to me on this instead of being MIA the whole time."

"Mitch, there are a number of ways to get this team headed in the right direction. And Jack can do it one way and you may do it another. But if all you're doing is kicking them and yelling at them and pushing them, you'll demoralize them and strip them of their self-confidence. The team feels your disdain. They need to feel your leadership."

"Did Jack or someone on the team put you up to this?"

"Mitch, no one put me up to this. I'm telling you that this team has the capability to meet your objectives. They need to be pulled as well as pushed. You need to sell them on your priorities. You can't order people to buy into your agenda. They need to own it as much as you do."

"What are you telling me here? Are you saying that it's my problem, that I'm at fault?"

"Look, Mitch, it would have been easy for me to duck this issue and to have confined my work to sorting out your role vis-à-vis Jack's. But I decided this is a huge organizational issue for you and

Olympia. And your team is going to continue disappointing you until you change the way you're trying to groove it. I know you're frustrated. But what you're doing to get their act together is a losing strategy. I've put on a sheet of paper a summary of what I'm saying."

I handed the sheet to Mitch and he began to read it—the actual content of the sheet is reprinted below:

YOUR LEADERSHIP CHALLENGE IS TO:

Take People With You...

- You must *sell* your ideals/agenda/vision/priorities.
- You must influence, not command, their buy-in.
- You must pull the team to commit vs. push the team to comply.
- You must decide to own your team:

  - Leverage their strengths.
  - Stop railing at their incompetence.
  - Acknowledge their value/contributions.
  - Demonstrate your appreciation (continually).
  - Catch people doing things right.
  - Stop "public assassinations."
  - Build their self-esteem.

TO ENHANCE YOUR *LEADERSHIP*, YOU MUST GROW THEIR *FOLLOWERSHIP!*

"Mitch," I continued, as he read, "you should look at this as a kind of reference guide you can use. A leadership template. If it makes sense to you, we can develop very specific tactics to implement what I'm suggesting."

Mitch looked up from the sheet—his face was beet red. "I get it. You heard my people complain that I'm too hard on them, that I tell them when they screw up and when they don't deliver. So they co-opted you and now you're doing their bidding. Well, let me tell you I'm not going to go soft, I'm not going to let up, I'm not going to stop pushing these dolts. This sophomoric, candy-ass approach to leadership you're suggesting is not what will work in Olympia. And I thought you were supposed to be a tough, no-nonsense executive. Anyway, we'll have to cut this short—I'm already ten minutes late for my next meeting. But thanks for your point of view."

A few days later Mitch's secretary called and told me that my meeting on roles with Mitch and Jack had to be rescheduled and she'd call me with some new dates. I knew instantly that this was code for "my consulting services were no longer needed."

I'd suggest that not only is top-down, command-and-control direction all too common in today's organizations, but its ability to generate unhealthy conflict is as strong as ever.

By the way, since my conversation with Mitch, turnover in Olympia's senior team has been damagingly high. Nearly every position on the team has turned over at least once—and in some cases twice—either through voluntary or involuntary departures. And Olympia's stock has significantly lagged the market over the last five years, declining some forty percent during a period where the S&P 500 has declined twenty percent.

What makes a leader isn't a title, but his or her ability to *convince and persuade* people with different views that his or her approach makes the most sense. That's why High-Performance Leaders, rather than simply relying on the power of their office, are constantly *selling* their ideas and priorities rather than *commanding* people to accept them. By doing this, they show that their people and their opinions matter to them, and they pull their people along, rather than pushing them. That's how these leaders build followership, and it's a good way to minimize unhealthy conflict.

2. The Law of Building a Cathedral—Again

To keep people focused on the prize rather than on their differences with one another, leaders must continually remind their people that they're building a cathedral, not cutting stone. When bickering, gamesmanship, intramurals, and other conflicts begin to dominate a team, the antidote is often a shared goal in place of individual opinions. Cathedral building works as a vaccine too— used as a regular part of the leadership toolkit, it can inoculate a group against much low-intensity interpersonal conflict. At Pepsi, it was our noble quest to beat Coke—a mantra that our leaders often invoked—that helped move our petty differences to the back burner.

3. The Law of Options

Many of us think of dealing with conflict in a binary way. Either we duck it completely until it subsides or we confront it head-on. But part of the genius of leadership is knowing what the options are in a crisis—and knowing how to implement those options. Leaders know that there are many gradations of action for dealing with conflict—and so complete is their ownership of the end result that they will leave no stone unturned in getting there.

Knowing which of these options to use on which occasions is a judgment call: There are no hard-and-fast rules. For most people, however, the hard part is realizing that in almost every situation there *are* options. Once they figure out that the first response to occur to them isn't the only possible response, they don't have much trouble finding a good approach.

The first two options are the two that occur to most of us when we think of a conflict situation. They could be summarized as doing nothing, or doing everything, and there are occasions when they're a strong choice.

Option 1: Avoiding

A leader may choose to avoid (that is, ignore) the conflict if involved directly, or might choose to separate the dueling parties on his or her team, if necessary. The presumption here is that *"this too shall pass,"* especially if the exigencies of time are not an issue.

Option 2: Confronting

Believing in his or her position, the leader might choose to *push* for his or her objectives, using the powers of persuasion to win the case. As we've seen, I was a champ at using the push approach!

While there are times when this option makes sense, we've also seen that overusing this approach, after a while, can get a little wearing on your colleagues, and can ultimately prove counterproductive.

The third option is often the next to come to mind:

Option 3: Compromising

Here a leader can try to find a fair solution that may satisfy both parties. The mind-set is one of splitting the difference. A simple example would be where a marketing executive wants to roll out a new product on September 1, but the manufacturing executive believes November 1 is a more conservative goal—so the two agree on October 1 as a reasonable compromise. There is a caveat here, however. If the substance of the conflict is not personality-based, but issues-based, a compromise solution may not successfully get all the important facts out in the open. The marketing executive might be aware of a competing product launch scheduled for September 10, whereas the manufacturing executive might be making time to schedule maintenance—these additional facts could well have a bearing on the final decision. In this type of situation, it may be better to use an alternative method to quell any interpersonal conflict, and then (if the issue is an important one) seek to generate *more* issues-based conflict in order to fully unearth the facts.

The fourth option is a close cousin of the first, avoiding. It was often used by my bosses:

Option 4: Delegating

Here, the leader asks a subordinate to resolve the conflict on his or her behalf. I became known as something of a "fix-it" guy, and so my bosses would often deputize me to resolve conflict between two other executives. If you have a subordinate who has a good track record of conflict resolution, this can be an effective way to fully utilize the strengths of your team. It's also useful in that it sends a signal that not every piece of conflict should be escalated to the boss.

The last two options are the most difficult. They require a degree of emotional separation from the conflict that is hard to achieve. Without these options, however, a leader's conflict-resolution arsenal is dangerously incomplete. Again, the challenge of leadership here is not in figuring out what to do—neither of these options is that complex—but rather in summoning the courage to do what's required. Wisdom, not brains, is the critical requirement here.

Option 5: Collaborating

The approach here is to try to openly discuss disagreements and *jointly* determine a solution. While this sounds simple enough, it requires that people *not* be emotionally invested in their original position. This is rarely the case, since these situations are often reduced to win-lose outcomes in the minds of the protagonists. One of the keys to collaboration is to openly acknowledge that difference in points of view exist, with a phrase such as:

"We obviously feel differently about this issue—tell me again why you read the situation this way."

This uses the *pull* technique, which can help get the conversation going. Continuing this opening with a *fact-based* approach often works well, as facts are emotionally neutral, and can help get past any personality issues:

"We obviously see this problem differently—are there any more facts or data we can bring in that would help us make the best judgment?"

This approach extends to the situation where two departments are in conflict, as can be the case with sales and credit departments, or between marketing and manufacturing. In this kind of conflict, being open about the damage being done and the implications for the organization is a good starting point:

"Our differences have filtered down to our entire organizations—it's like a civil war. How can we find a way to resolve this dispute for our own good and the good of the organization?"

Collaborating might not be the quickest of the options here, but it produces the best, most enduring results.

Option 6: Accommodating

Sometimes a leader may decide that giving in to "keep the peace" is the best option, particularly if maintaining the relationship is the overarching objective and the contentious issue doesn't jeopardize the organization.

This last option is one that we perfect people find especially difficult to stomach. It certainly didn't seem a palatable choice to me when, as Chief People Officer for Pepsi worldwide, I found myself in frequent conflict with my HR colleagues in PepsiCo's corporate office. I found them second-guessing the programs my team developed, or suggesting modifications that were trivial or unnecessary.

But I was still surprised when, at the end of a conversation about a thorny organizational problem, Trevor, Pepsi's CEO and my boss, turned the conversation in a new direction. The exchange went something like this:

"Mike, one other thing. What's going on with Spencer and the folks at Corporate?"

"Hell, I don't know. What I do know is they're a pain in the butt."

"Yeah, I bet they are. And they know you feel that way."

"Okay, Trevor—what's this about?"

"I walked by Spencer's office when I was at Corporate the other day. He talked for some time about how difficult it is to deal with you."

"Spencer and his dwarfs are droolers." I was annoyed. "First of all, they don't have the imagination to come up with the world-class programs we're introducing here. But—I send over the stuff we've developed because they can use it in the other divisions. So what happens? Spencer or his idiots want us to change the name of the program or some other inane, trivial suggestion. It's all small-minded drivel."

"Mike, slow down. Don't you think I know how terrific these programs are that you and your people are creating? Give me more credit than that. You just need to recognize that Spencer wants some input—especially since he and his team weren't able to come up with the programs in the first place."

"But Trevor, Spencer's suggestions are stupid. He's wrong in what he suggests we change."

"Mike, are there any occasions when he may be right?"

"No!"

"No—he's never right?" Trevor began to smile.

"I know it sounds bad when I say it—but I'm right on these issues."

"Well, then you need to give in on a few of his suggestions and tell him he's right—he's got a good idea."

"But he doesn't have good ideas and he's not right—so how can I tell him he's right?"

Now Trevor was beginning to chuckle. "Mike, the folks at Corporate are important to us—to our division. And to you. So let 'em be right once in a while. They hate it that you're always right."

"But Trevor, I *am* always right with them."

Now Trevor was in a full-scale fit of laughter. "Listen, Mike, my hunch is they know you're usually right. And deep down, they know you and your people outshine them in terms of talent and capability. That's what drives them crazy. So be wrong once in a while. That way they can feel better about themselves."

"Trevor, let me get this straight. You want me to pretend I'm wrong even when I'm right?" This just wasn't how I was wired.

"That's exactly what I'm suggesting. Especially when it's not really going to compromise your program. We're not talking here about mortgaging the business."

I was dumbfounded—this was a totally foreign concept to me.

Trevor was patient with me that day. He had introduced me to the option of accommodating, an option certainly not in my transactional repertoire up to that point in my career. Looking back, I'm not even sure that Trevor believed I was right on every single occasion—this may well have prompted his laughter during our conversation. If that's the case, then what he was doing was itself accommodating—he was accommodating my need to believe I was right one hundred percent of the time, even though, privately, he might have felt otherwise.

Now, many of you will say, in response to this, that it's intellectually dishonest to stifle your opinion when you know you're in the right. And you'll point out that the Law of the Emperor's Wardrobe *requires* leaders to speak up when their colleagues are heading in the wrong direction. Well, both of those points are valid—and on critical issues, the Law of the Emperor's Wardrobe can make the difference between success and failure. But the point here is that there are some battles you can afford to lose in the context of the relationship—and that in a conflict situation, both parties *always* believe they're *always* right, even though this is logically impossible. Many of the secrets of managing relationships lie in understanding when to choose pragmatism over realism.

After Trevor's intervention, I worked hard at developing my options for handling conflict. On occasion, I even asked my team to collaborate with Spencer's staff on some of our projects. While it wasn't always easy for me to share pride of authorship with the corporate group, co-authorship guaranteed their buy-in and eliminated the second-guessing and meddling that I'd been dealing with up to that point—in other words, it made it easier for me to ship.

And even though I finally got Trevor's message, on an intellectual level it wasn't easy for me to use these options. Yet I got better at it over time—and as I did so, my relationship with Spencer and his people improved. And the level of unhealthy conflict and resentment shrank dramatically.

4. THE LAW OF THE CONSCIENTIOUS OBJECTOR

It's easy to get caught up in interdepartmental rivalries and squabbles. Your boss is in a real donnybrook with his or her colleague and you, naturally, are rooting for your boss to win. However, beyond wanting your boss, whom you like and respect, to come out on top, you should *resist taking up arms in someone else's fight*—even if he or she is the person you work for. Too often a disciple gets wounded when he or she comes to the aid of a dueling boss or peer. It's no surprise that once Phil Purcell, originally head of Dean Witter, ousted John Mack from Morgan Stanley Dean Witter, many of Mack's people were pushed out as the Dean Witter executives began to take over. They'd fought too vigorously on Mack's behalf to be considered team players once the power struggle was over.

It's important to clarify the difference between this law and the Law of Professional Commitment from Chapter 4. The Law of Professional Commitment, if you remember, states that whether your boss gives a damn about you or not, as a leader *you must commit yourself to his or her success.* Why doesn't this extend to supporting your boss in an intramural conflict? The answer is that in order to offer your boss the sort of support that this requires, you very often have to criticize others in the organization. The trusted lieutenants, in this situation, can quickly become the shock troops. We see this behavior all the time in political campaigns—think of James Carville or Karl Rove—but there's a key difference between running for public office and struggling for control of a company: The losing party in a political contest expects to have to find other jobs, whereas contesting factions inside an organization expect to remain there after the dust has settled. So the Law of the Conscientious Objector sets an important ceiling on the extent to which you should demonstrate *professional commitment.* Display commitment to your boss, certainly: *But do it through the quality of your work, not by criticizing others.* The best way to be loyal and supportive is to do excellent work and ship, not to become cannon fodder.

5. THE LAW OF THE LAST CHANCE SALOON

Even if you practice the preceding laws, the reality is that unhealthy conflict is unavoidable. It's bound to happen—two people who work in your organization will be locked in a tussle of one kind or another.

It's possible that your playing the mediator can work in these situations. In this role, you try to build on the positives each of these players may feel about the other. There are always skills or attributes a person respects in another, no matter how intense the overall conflict. Sometimes working individually and sometimes working with both parties present, you may be able to reduce the friction and restore relative harmony.

But this approach doesn't always work, and you will find that *there are times when a leader must ask people in conflict to resolve it themselves—or live with the resolution the leader chooses and imposes.* It's amazing how often two of my people set aside their differences after I sat them down and said, "Last chance, folks—if you don't fix this, I will. And then you live with my solution, not yours."

6. THE LAW OF HEALTHY CONFLICT

Healthy conflict—*the conflict of ideas*—must be encouraged. Just as the good kind of cholesterol can reduce the risk of heart attack, the conflict of ideas is what keeps organizations healthy. *Debate, discussion, disagreement, and dialogue are the lifeblood of vibrant and adaptive organizations.* For this reason High-Performance Leaders establish the conflict of ideas as a cultural value.

This does not mean that meetings ought to be turned into forums where people get on their soapboxes and unilaterally espouse their differing positions. We've all been in a meeting where a colleague differs with our position by making another speech, reiterating his or her original position, and reprising the same arguments, only more vociferously. As we saw in Chapter 5, a leader must get his or her team members to move from expressing *what* they think on a particular issue to *why* they think the way they do.

There are many techniques a leader can use to make this transition. At Pepsi we used a technique in some of our senior meetings that we called the Diverge/Converge Method. It's really much less complicated than it sounds. Basically, the CEO would tee up an important decision facing the business. The CEO might have asked our CFO to briefly present some financial data on the cost of the decision. At that point the CEO would ask us to take fifteen minutes to think about the issue privately and write on some sticky notes what each team member thought were the three key issues in making this decision. We'd then array these notes on the conference room wall to see the *divergence* of views on the issue. Very quickly the team could see where there was consensus and where there was dissent. We'd then spend the next hour or two debating the issue and trying to get a fuller understanding of all the views that had been expressed. From this debate and discussion a *convergence* of opinion was sought. If the decision was a major one, many meetings would be involved and this method would be used at each one.

What's so special about this technique? Well, without it, it would have been typical for a few team members to be the most vocal about the subject. The CFO and senior marketing officer would have weighed in with all the arguments—both pro and con—for making a particular decision. And the rest of the team, including the heads of Manufacturing, HR, IT, and Sales would likely have withheld their views or presented them tentatively. But there was a lot of history and insight on our team—and the Diverge/Converge Method made it easy to access all this knowledge. This technique eliminates a lot of the intimidation that can occur when functional heads leverage their authority to win support for their recommendations.

One other note here. If you reverse the process to a Converge/Diverge sequence, you effectively protect the team against group-think. Occasionally the CEO might present an issue that seemed to gain consensus after only a brief, thirty-minute discussion. If that occurred, the CEO might ask us to take fifteen minutes to identify the downsides and risks to such a decision. Through the process of writing on stickies our leader wanted to make sure that the quick consensus reached earlier hadn't dissuaded anyone from expressing any lingering doubts.

Another series of approaches, again aimed at increasing the healthy conflict of ideas, relies on the explicit design of the decision-making process. Common to these approaches is the technique of assigning one person or group to advocate a particular position. Sometimes, a leader will designate a devil's advocate, whose job it is to come up with an opposing position to that favored by the group. On other occasions, the leader will divide the team into two groups, each of which is assigned the task of advocating a particular option. With both of these approaches, the healthy conflict of ideas is hardwired into the organization of the team, and as such is depersonalized—those disagreeing with a position are doing so because that's their role, not because they dislike the people they're opposing.

As we noted in Chapter 5, it's important that the team agree up front how the final decision will be made, so that the decision becomes (as much as possible) an emotionally neutral part of the process. Whenever a process is used that explicitly creates conflicting views and judgments, it's critical to set out in advance how much of that conflict will be resolved in the final decision. In either the devil's advocate or the opposing groups approach, the leader can wait until one approach has the support of the majority, or even until consensus emerges, thereby allowing the conflict to resolve itself. Conversely, he or she can announce that, having heard the arguments for and against, he or she will make the final choice alone, leaving, by definition, some conflict unresolved. The concern here is one of implementation—if the group debating the various pros and cons, and enthusiastically immersing itself in healthy conflict, will ultimately be responsible for implementing the final decision, then the degree of support for the various options can determine the ease with which these can be implemented.

A final concern in selecting a process of conflict generation is to ensure that the process fits the situation. The intent of explicitly surfacing differing views is to ensure that the final decision takes into account as much data as possible, and has been thoroughly pressure-tested. Ironically, this type of approach is more important when the future is less certain, and when the decision carries with it a higher degree of risk. When time is plentiful, when the competitive environment is clear, when the decision is not of the bet-the-firm variety—this is when healthy conflict is less important. But as the importance and risk of the decision increases, so—perhaps counterintuitively—does the importance of vigorous debate. The more important the choice, the greater the need for conflict.

There is a classic example of this type of conflict generation in action. Robert Kennedy's 1967 memoir, *Thirteen Days*,[1] is a remarkable firsthand account of the Cuban Missile Crisis, and it is the decision-making process at the heart of this crisis, adopted by the so-called Ex Comm, or Executive Committee of the National Security Council, that has become the benchmark in the use of healthy conflict to improve decision making.

The outlines of the crisis are familiar to most of us: A U-2 flight over Cuba on October 14, 1962, provided evidence that the

USSR had begun to install nuclear missiles on the island—missiles that would place much of the United States under the threat of nuclear attack. Over the ensuing days, two schools of thought emerged among President Kennedy's advisers as they weighed the options available. One was a series of air strikes leading to a full-scale invasion of Cuba, the other was a blockade, to prevent supply ships from delivering further missiles and components. The Ex Comm debated these two alternatives and variants on them back and forth for hours, without reaching a consensus on one approach or the other. Robert Kennedy records this conflict with approval:

> They were men of the highest intelligence, industrious, coura-
> geous, and dedicated to their country's well-being. It is no re-
> flection on them that none was consistent in his opinion from
> the very beginning to the end. That kind of open, unfettered
> mind was essential. . . .[2]
>
> At our meeting at the State Department, there were sharp
> disagreements again. The strain and the hours without sleep
> were beginning to take their toll. . . . For every position there
> were inherent weaknesses; and those opposed would point
> them out, often with devastating effects.[3]

Struggling to respond fully to the President's request that he be presented with one or more fully developed courses of action, the Ex Comm attempted a new process. It divided into two groups, one in favor of the blockade, the other in favor of immediate military action. The two groups separated, and each prepared a paper in support of its recommendation, covering in detail every proposed step from the announcement of the policy through its implementation, and attempting to anticipate all possible responses and contingencies. The groups then reconvened, reviewed, and criticized each other's papers, and then divided again to make changes in response to these criticisms. It was from this process that the final options presented to the President emerged. RFK comments:

> During all these deliberations, we all spoke as equals. There was no rank, and, in fact, we did not even have a chairman. . . . As a result . . . the conversations were completely uninhibited and unrestricted. Everyone had an equal opportunity to express himself and to be heard directly. It was a tremendously advantageous procedure that does not frequently occur within the executive branch of government, where rank is often so important.[4]

The Ex Comm, critically, gave up trying to *resolve* the conflict of ideas over the best course of action, and instead adopted a process that *acknowledged and confirmed* that conflict. As a result, both options were discussed at length during briefings with the President, and the factual basis for each was more fully explored than might have been the case had one option been discarded earlier. Most importantly, it was the repeated attempts by each group to justify its approach and to prevail over the alternate proposal that generated ever more detailed analyses and hypotheses. It was the healthy conflict between the groups that contributed directly to the richness and quality of the final decision.

The President, as we know, selected the blockade or quarantine approach, and the crisis was ultimately defused without a nuclear exchange. In the context of the discussion above regarding the importance of resolving the conflict of ideas once a decision has been made, it is interesting to note JFK's remarks to the Chairman of the Joint Chiefs of Staff, General Maxwell Taylor, who had, on behalf of the Chiefs, been a strong proponent of direct military action. Taylor reports that Kennedy had said to him, "I know you and your colleagues are unhappy with the decision, but I trust that you will support me in this decision."[5] The general assured the

President that he was, indeed, opposed to the decision, but would back him completely. Rather than simply hoping for compliance from those who would have to implement the blockade, Kennedy was wise enough to explicitly seek their commitment. It seems likely that the process of arriving at the decision influenced Taylor's commitment.

Don't misunderstand the purpose of the laws of leading conflict. Unhealthy conflict can never be eliminated from organizational life (or from any other part of life, for that matter). Rather, the objective for any leader is to minimize as much as possible the bad conflict while encouraging the good, so that healthy debate and dialogue far outweigh unhealthy disagreements and clashes. If the good kind of cholesterol reduces your chances of suffering a heart attack, then the good sort of conflict can dramatically reduce your chances of a corporate coronary.

Summary: Feiner's Laws of Leading Conflict

1. The Law of Interdependence

Leaders can never rely on power alone. High-Performance Leaders recognize they are in positions of interdependence with bosses, peers, and subordinates, and that the more senior they become, the less unilaterally they can rely on naked power. Overreliance on power *generates* conflict.

2. The Law of Building a Cathedral—Again

Keeping people focused on building a cathedral, not cutting stone, reduces the likelihood that unhealthy conflict will arise.

3. The Law of Options

Leaders need to know their options for managing conflict, and to understand the value of being wrong once in a while.

4. The Law of the Conscientious Objector

Never take up arms in someone else's fight—even if he or she is your boss. The way to be loyal and supportive is to deliver the goods, not to become cannon fodder.

5. The Law of the Last Chance Saloon

There are times when a leader must ask people in conflict to resolve it themselves—or live with the resolution the leader chooses.

6. The Law of Healthy Conflict

High-Performance Leaders encourage conflict of ideas—the healthy kind of conflict.

9	*Leading Change*
	THE BURNING PLATFORM

Leading change is one of the cardinal objectives of a leader. Indeed, as we saw in Chapter 2, it is one of the key differences between leadership and management. If you seek to lead, rather than manage, then almost by definition you seek to produce change. High-Performance Leaders recognize the need to make their organizations adaptive to forces such as fierce competition, new products, new regulation, and new technology. Without the capability to evolve in this way, organizations get stuck doing the same things in the same ways they've always been done. Enterprises like these become ensnared in controls, process, and procedures—and ultimately become myopic, insular, and slow-moving. While the refrains of "today's fast-paced business environment" or "the ever-increasing rate of change" have been used to suggest that in recent years something has changed about change itself, the simple reality is that the ability to adapt has always characterized successful organizations. As renowned quality guru W. Edwards Deming wryly observed, "It is not necessary to change. Survival is not mandatory."

It's equally true, however, that people in organizations are resistant to major change, even positive change. Change disrupts our expectations of how things will work and how people will behave. It raises the specter of the unknown over our comfortable and predictable lives. Even when we understand what the new reality will be, we don't know what it will feel like to live in until we get there. And when change is first announced, before we even know what the new reality will look like, our fears are exponentially increased. For these reasons, people have a hard time adapting to change, even when they know intellectually that change is necessary or in their best interests. *For most of us, the certainty of misery is more desirable than the misery of uncertainty.*[1] To lead change, therefore, a leader must understand how to cut through organizational resistance. And paradoxically, in order to do this leaders must leverage their management skills. Without attention to detail, planning, and process, any major organizational change effort is doomed.

The history of business is littered with examples of otherwise talented leaders who failed to successfully lead change efforts. Jacques Nasser, for example, lost his battle at Ford to get independent dealers to accept the idea that the company would operate its own dealerships. The ensuing dealer mutiny was one of the major factors in his dismissal as CEO in 2001. Richard Thoman, a former IBM executive who became CEO at Xerox in April 1999, saw clearly the need for a change in the firm's business strategy, but failed to get the support of the senior executive team for the changes he was pushing for, and was fired thirteen months later.

But it's not just CEOs who face the challenge of leading a change initiative. Every day leaders at all levels of an organization are engaged in introducing change. A manufacturing executive may try to implement total quality systems in his factories. A franchise executive decides to launch a new menu offering among her franchised restaurants. A retail store manager wants her salespeople to get behind a new clothing line. A marketing manager directs his team to focus more on sales margins than sales volume. A systems executive plans to reorganize her department. A general manager sees the need to initiate cost reduction measures.

All these efforts, big and small, require a detailed understanding of the tactics of leading change. Hundreds—if not thousands—of books and articles have been written about change, and I'm not trying to eclipse any of these. Yet my personal involvement in a number of change efforts during my career has taught me a few key dos and don'ts about leading change. This book would be incomplete without a discussion of these learnings, central as they are to a leader's role as an agent of change.

Consistently used, the following four laws can determine whether a change effort succeeds, or alternately becomes just another flavor of the month.

1. The Law of the Burning Platform

To end right, change has to start right.

In July 1988, the worst oil rig disaster in history occurred in the North Sea. Late in the evening, there was a violent explosion. Most of the rig was destroyed in the first few minutes, and 167 of the 229 men on board lost their lives. Three days after the explosion, *Nightline's* Ted Koppel interviewed one of the survivors. By chance, I happened to watch the show that evening. The interview, if I recall, went something like this:

Ted began, "So, Clem [I don't recall the survivor's real name], let me just reprise for the viewers what you were facing the other night. Ten o'clock at night, you're fifteen stories high, a huge explosion rocks you out of your sleeping bunk, you're dazed and confused, partially in shock, most of the upper platform has been destroyed, and you look over the edge of what's left of this platform and see debris and burning oil one hundred and fifty feet below you, and you jump. Is that right?"

"Yes, sir."

"And you were one hundred and fifty feet high?"

"Yes, sir."

Ted, now struggling to get the interviewee to be a little more expressive, asked, "So what was it like?"

"Dark."

"It was pitch dark, wasn't it?"

"Yes, sir."

"Well, tell me, one hundred and fifty feet up, fifteen stories, pitch black smoke, you're partially dazed, you look down and see burning debris, burning oil—Clem, what prompted you to jump?"

And Clem said, "Well if I didn't, Mr. Koppel, my ass was gonna fry."

The Law of the Burning Platform is irrefutable: If you want to successfully lead a major change effort—in a department, in a sector, a division, in a subsidiary, or in a company—you had better convince people that there is a Burning Platform Decision. That is, *without change, a painful end awaits.* A platform can be burning at present or it can face the threat of a future conflagration. Either way, if you fail to get this message across, the change can't hope to succeed. People who will be impacted by the change need to see their adaptation to it as a "must do," not a "nice to do."

This metaphor of the burning platform is not new news—but then again, neither is it broadly used. Despite the colossal amount of literature on change, and the legions of consultants who offer change-related services, change efforts still derail with predictable regularity, and frequently this is because of the lack of a burning platform, or because the burning platform is not clearly communicated.

As an example, often senior leaders decide that they want to change the culture in their organizations. Perhaps high turnover gets them to realize that the culture is too unforgiving or too brittle, or feedback from customers tells them that they're not sensitive to customer needs. But when it's time to communicate the intended change, leaders tell employees in general terms that it's necessary to change the culture, without connecting the dots to their future survival. "We need to build a new culture at Rippers, Inc.," say the voice-mails and e-mails, "to address employee and customer concerns." It's unlikely that this approach will prompt people to buy into the change. People must see the need to change the culture as a make-or-break business issue—crucial to the health and success and long-term survival of the business. For instance, a High-Performance Leader will communicate that turnover is crippling the organization's need to attract and retain talent; further, that this churn of new people having to learn new jobs is damaging its ability to operate effectively and retain customers. And his or her words and actions will make it clear that, without this change, the future of the business is in doubt.

But the burning platform is only a start. It's impossible to over-communicate the importance of the desired change to achieving the overarching mission, to the task of building a cathedral. Explaining to people how a lack of customer focus imperils the organization is a good first step, but only a first step. And indicating that customer focus will lead to increased profitability won't do it either. Linking customer focus with this organization's quest to be, say, the number one consumer products company in the world is what will prompt people to see their role in the change effort as part of an effort to build a cathedral, not just cut stone. At Pepsi, the effort to become more customer-focused—which we'll discuss shortly—was positioned, not as a trendy initiative, but as an absolute necessity in our quest to win the Cola Wars.

The Law of the Burning Platform, however, is not about fabricating reasons, just as the Law of Building a Cathedral is not about inventing a mission. It's about deliberately thinking through the reasons for the change, and linking them to the fundamentals of the business, and through those fundamentals to the best interests of the employees. (If it's impossible to make these links, by the way, you should expect some tough questions about the reasons for the change effort in the first place.) The Law of the Burning Platform is about making the consequences of failure to change explicit and tangible.

2. The Law of Cascading Sponsorship

Leaders cannot delegate responsibility for implementing change. Frequently, leaders recognize the need for taking their organization in a new direction and think, once they've rationally explained the reasons, their staffs can handle the rollout and implementation. Not so.

I recall working at TWA in Pittsburgh in my first front-line union relations position. For several years relations with the Machinists Union had been extremely acrimonious throughout TWA's system. In some locations the Machinists were resorting to violence and sabotage to fight local management's efforts to run the operations more efficiently. They made their views on my role clear, shortly after the beginning of my assignment, by dumping three tons of gravel on my front lawn one night.

Then an edict came down from headquarters, in the form of a letter to all management personnel. The letter explained that senior management and Machinist leaders had been meeting for some time and had reached consensus on the need for a new approach. "We need to change the state of our labor-management relations in this company," it said. "We need to move from an adversarial and hostile relationship to one where we collaborate in a spirit of partnership, in an effort to build better relationships with our employees at all levels." The letter concluded by urging all local managers to begin developing relationships with local union officials based on cooperation and respect.

This struck me as a pretty good idea. Tired of threatening phone calls at 2:00 A.M. and repeated sabotage of my car in the employee parking lot, I thought things could only get better in Pittsburgh if we followed this new approach.

My optimism was short-lived. The local GM—my boss—walked into my office later that day, his face flushed. "Have you read this letter?" he asked, brandishing it at me.

I said, "I have."

"What do you think?"

I said, "Well under the circumstances I think it's probably a good idea, because there's no more room for gravel in the front yard, and if these lunatic Machinist fanatics start dumping it in the backyard, my wife's going to move back to New York."

He said, "Let me tell you what I think about this letter." His voice rose, rapidly. "It's a complete fraud. It's a waste of my time and a waste of paper." Balling up the letter in his hand, he threw it on the office floor. By now he was shouting. "Forget this letter—I'm telling you it's still war with these thugs! Don't even think of waving the white flag, not for one minute, whatever those lily-livered idiots in New York have to say about it. Okay?"

Needless to say, union relations did not improve in Pittsburgh, or anywhere else throughout TWA's system.

This incident involved a desired change in labor-management relationships. But it could be about a new computer system or a new marketing program, or any organization-wide change. *Directives from on high get sucked into a black hole of resistance if executives think their job is done when the memo is written.*

A change process requires the involvement and support of many. High-Performance Leaders recognize that they must win this support from every level of the organization. *So these leaders win this support, one organization level at a time.* Once a High-

Performance Leader gets his or her direct reports on board, this group then works together to get the next organization stratum committed to the change. This *cascading sponsorship* is essential to the successful implementation of change. High-Performance Leaders understand they must stay continually and intimately involved from start to finish.

There's a great story about W. Edwards Deming, who in 1981 was asked by the CEO of a major automobile company to address his top two hundred executives on the requirements of implementing a total quality program—what would become the basis of this company's quality focus throughout the 1980s. Deming was introduced to the executives by the CEO himself, who extolled Deming's credentials with great conviction. As Deming approached the podium to enthusiastic applause, he noticed the CEO walking toward the exit of the auditorium. The octogenarian Deming, in his famous basso-profundo voice, remarked for all to hear, "If this isn't important to you, it's not important to me." The CEO, startled, returned to his seat and remained for the rest of the discussion.

Deming understood not only how to build a quality program but how it had to be successfully implemented. If you think sponsorship doesn't require active, continued involvement, you don't understand change. *You can't delegate sponsorship*—people need to see you, as the leader, intimately involved in the process.

3. THE LAW OF NUTS AND BOLTS

There are six million parts in a Boeing 747-400 jumbo jet.[2] Pretty much all of them have to work to get the thing off the ground and safely to its destination. A change campaign is a similar proposition, and requires a similar degree of precision engineering if it is to succeed.

Leaders generally begin the change process with a speech or other message to their people. Though speeches per se aren't enough to make change stick, they're an important part of the change toolkit. But a speech is only a small part of an effective change process. A leader who delivers a speech about the need for change, assuming people will accept his or her compelling explanation, rarely elicits full buy-in. Even when a leader articulates the burning platform and links this danger to the overarching mission (the cathedral) it threatens, much more needs to be done.

Long before the first communication, then, a leader must begin the process of striving to understand what it will take to achieve successful change in his or her organization. And this is no walk in the park. Careful thought and discussion with key advisers needs to answer the following questions (and more) before any communications are drafted: How much time will it take? What are the key milestones along the way? Who are the key supporters required to introduce the change? How will these supporters be won over? Where should I expect resistance? What role will the key supporters have in assisting the change sponsor? How will the need for the change be convincingly communicated? How will communications change for each audience within the firm? What's the best way to communicate the positive impact of the change on people's individual role and job in the organization? What input do I want from employees at each level? What's my role at each stage of the journey? How will we go about continually reinforcing the need for the change? A leader must analyze every step of the process, must determine exactly what is required for success, and must take responsibility for the successful implementation of the change.

We've already examined the hows of communicating the need for change in our discussion of the Law of the Burning Platform, and later in this chapter the Law of Ownership will take a look at the need for input from employees. The question of the time required for change, though, merits further discussion here. High-Performance Leaders recognize that change is *not* an event. Leaders need to learn to approach it as a highly fluid and dynamic *process*, demanding continual adjustment and refinement. As leaders observe how the organization responds to the change being implemented, plans may be revised. At first people are often naively optimistic about the change. After a short time, however, people begin to understand how difficult change is to fully embrace and operationalize. This period of frustration is followed by a more realistic sense of how much discipline and rigor are required to adopt new skills or drop old ways of doing things. *Throughout this journey the organization adapts because High-Performance Leaders remain involved, revisiting and revising implementation plans as required.*

Planning for resistance is also critical. No matter how obvious the need for change, resistance to it is unavoidable. It doesn't matter whether the fire on the burning platform is visible or not. Some people will resist, so leaders must carefully identify those individuals or groups who will most likely fight the change, and must spearhead efforts to overcome their resistance. This resistance can be overt or, more likely, covert. When I asked my boss in Pittsburgh what he was going to say to his boss about the letter from headquarters, he smiled for a second and replied, "What do you think I'm going to say—I'm gonna tell him it's a great approach and pretend to salute like a good soldier."

Leaders should overcome resistance by working hard at allowing, even encouraging, people to express their doubts and concerns. This is yet another instance where the power of the pull approach is invaluable. The signal sent by this approach—"your opinions matter to me"—goes a long way to counteract the fear of change that can underlie much resistance, by giving back a measure of control.

These are just some of the questions leaders must think about. No matter how obvious the need for change, High-Performance Leaders recognize that *managing the nuts and bolts is essential to suc-*

cessfully introducing change. Just as the Law of the Nitty-Gritty in our discussion of leading teams emphasizes activities that are as much management as leadership, so the Law of Nuts and Bolts reminds us that High-Performance Leaders have both strong leadership and strong management skills. The mastery of the six million nuts and bolts in any change effort is a litmus test of management skill, and it's critical: Ready-fire-aim doesn't work with change. *The devil is in the details of implementation.*

4. THE LAW OF OWNERSHIP

One of the reasons people hate change is because it's imposed on them. So even if they understand the reason for the change, *it still feels that they're at the mercy of what someone else decided.* For this reason, people need to have a vote along the way. Otherwise, they won't own the outcome of the change process.

This doesn't mean leaders are obliged to offer change referenda to their organizations. *It does mean, however, that during the process of cascading the change, people at each level of the organization should have a chance to offer their reactions and questions.* When their input makes sense, leaders need to incorporate it into the change process as it proceeds through the department or division or sector or company. And the *process* of giving people a chance to respond and provide feedback and input makes people feel heard. *That's why they own the change—they had a chance to affect it.*

When the senior leadership team decided we needed to make Pepsi less inward-looking and more customer-focused, we embarked on a journey to explain the need for our new philosophy to every employee. Why the need for change? Well, the financial data was beginning to tell us that our margins were getting tighter. We had no room for maneuver on pricing, as Coke and Pepsi were locked into a competitive battle that allowed no possibility of price increases without a catastrophic loss of market share. Costs had already been cut to the bone. And so we concluded that we had to compete more effectively through our front-line people. Customer data was telling us that we were seen as insensitive and arrogant, by everyone from large supermarket chains to convenience stores to mom-and-pop store owners. And employee surveys we had been conducting were setting off alarm bells: Our front-line employees were so taken for granted that they felt they'd fallen off the org chart altogether.

It took a while for the senior team to digest all this alarming information. As we did we realized the need to transform the way we did business—from top to bottom. We might have had a great trademark, great brands, and great advertising, but that wasn't enough. We needed to put front-line employees—who interfaced with customers every day—at the *top* of the organization. We needed to redesign our core processes in order to support our front-line employees as our secret weapon in the Cola Wars. Thus the birth of what we called the Right Side Up Company, with front-line employees at the top of the pyramid.

We launched a cascading implementation approach that sought to reach and enroll each level in the organization in turn. First, the senior team of eight executives argued and debated until there was consensus as to how we needed to transform ourselves as a company. Sixty days later, after some careful meeting planning, the senior team met for several days with the next stratum—about seventy senior managers. With more debate and input and eventual buy-in, ninety days later the original eight plus the seventy enrolled the next three hundred managers, using the same off-site meeting protocol, where lots of interaction and two-way communication took place. After another three months these three hundred enrolled managers convened the next fifteen hundred, explaining the reasons we needed to transform the way we did business and getting reactions and ideas for improving our approach. At that point, all five thousand management personnel met in Dallas to explain the burning platform facing Pepsi. Importantly, at each of these meetings all enrolled managers had a role in running the agenda—so that first-time attendees would see this effort as having the full commitment and involvement of their bosses. But we weren't done yet. We then had to explain and educate our remaining twenty-five thousand employees as to what this change was all about and what impact it would have on them.

So over a forty-five-day period regional meetings were held so that all front-line employees had a chance to learn about what we wanted to do differently as an organization, and why. A cross section of regional managers ran these meetings, again to demonstrate management buy-in (and to do so much more effectively than a sterile memo would have done). The most critical element of the design of this process was that it allowed employees to let us know, during these meetings, what they thought. We asked for comments on what concerns they had about the change, what tweaks we needed to consider in the future rollout process, what processes or systems we needed to revise, and what new initiatives in support of the change we should consider.

The result of all this? Because every employee had a chance to influence the change process, and saw that the leadership team was committed to the change itself, and to their thoughts and their reactions, the chances of their accepting the change were significantly increased. But positive business results were not instantaneous. Far from it. The Right Side Up transformation involved a new field structure with lots of redesigned jobs. New accounting and billing procedures were instituted that were more customer-friendly. Route sales personnel began to receive sales training—some for the first time. And many other systems and processes were introduced, all with the purpose of building a world-class operating company. This wasn't something that could take place overnight, and indeed, Right Side Up did not lead to immediate success (most major change efforts don't!). All these changes took time to incubate. Yet the heavy lifting and toil and hand-to-hand combat involved in implementing Right Side Up eventually led to sixteen straight quarters of on- or above-plan profit performance.

Two further stories from my corporate experience illustrate just how challenging it is for organizations to introduce major change. In the early eighties Frito-Lay, Pepsi's sister division and the dominant player in the salty snack business, decided to introduce a line of sweet snacks. After all, the thinking went, the sweet snack category is huge—it had about $4 billion in retail sales in 1982. Within the sweet snack category cookies accounted for almost $2.5 billion in retail sales. To put this in perspective, Frito-Lay's total sales had passed the $2 billion mark in 1982. Leveraging its phalanx-like store door delivery system, Frito believed it could come to dominate sweet snacks in the same way that it had a commanding share in the salty snack category. Frito developed a line of cookies that blew away the competition in laboratory tests, focus groups, and home use tests. In test markets, the real measure of consumer reaction, the product did extraordinarily well against those of the main competitors.

Frito developed world-class packaging and advertising and went national with a full line of Grandma's Cookies in 1983.

And the business failed. By 1985 Frito-Lay had decided to exit the cookie business in supermarkets. Why? Certainly, the fierce competitive reaction from Procter and Gamble's Duncan Hines brand was a significant factor. But one of the major reasons was that Frito's route salespeople, and their managers, never really understood the importance of this initiative to Frito's long-term vision. The burning platform was missing. Nor did Frito's management understand the magnitude or complexity of getting into the cookie business. The nuts and bolts were missing. Frito executives assumed that it was axiomatic, given their dominance in the salty snack category, that the company could use its marketing expertise and powerful delivery system for the new product line. But Frito never totally understood that their salespeople weren't motivated to deliver a new product to a different section of the supermarket. After all, the salesforce didn't know the store personnel who handled this kind of product—they had up to this point gotten to know only the salty snack folks. And delivering both cookies and chips meant they'd have to spend more time in each store, requiring either longer days or a restructuring of their routes—two *changes* that no route salesperson would be wild about! Importantly, route sales personnel never felt that their cookie sales would match the supermarket volume of their chip business (their commission was based on sales volume)—meaning pushing the new product was a low priority. They hadn't been asked how they felt about the changes, or been given the opportunity to suggest implementation solutions: The Law of Ownership was missing. A more in-depth planning effort before the product launch would have discovered these key structural resistance points. A properly designed change effort would have resolved them. Frito did neither. So, from the get-go, the Frito people on the front lines of this new product introduction were not on board.

Despite enormous effort by the R&D people to develop a great product, despite enormous effort in manufacturing to produce a quality cookie, and despite terrific marketing and advertising support, the effort failed. It failed because one of the key components of the change effort—the delivery organization—was not given the same attention and focus as other parts of the change initiative. The failed venture probably cost Frito between $50 million and $75 million; that's between $75 million and $115 million in today's dollars. Worse still, Frito's dream of entering a new line of business and growing Grandma's Cookies to mega-brand status—with perhaps as much as $500 million in revenue—went down the tubes.

* * *

Ten years later Pepsi faced another change challenge. It was clear we needed to introduce open-date coding on our diet colas, as artificial sweeteners degraded within six months of production and caused an off taste that was increasingly damaging our brand's credibility with consumers. The codes would facilitate the removal of out-of-date product from shelves. It was the best solution to a problem that was threatening the brand—and yet for the many constituencies affected, the status quo seemed preferable. Franchise bottlers wanted to be compensated if they had to replace stale product already on shelves in their territories. Route salespeople were unexcited about having to rotate stock and remove stale product—both of which would take more of their time and add more record-keeping burden to their job. Vending machine delivery people would have the same reaction. To top it off, a number of PepsiCo executives were concerned about the one-time charge to the bottom line that would result from such a change.

Remembering what had happened at Frito a decade earlier, Pepsi approached this change effort with the kind of obsessive attention to detail that you would find in a military campaign. This was the Law of Nuts and Bolts on steroids.

All the stakeholders involved in the change were carefully mapped. And there were plenty of them: route salespeople and their supervisors, merchandisers, sales management, the sales training staff, quality control technicians, warehouse employees, union business agents, and company-owned and franchise bottlers, to name just some. For each stakeholder group, key tasks and action steps were identified and leaders were assigned accountability for directing these activities. This massive implementation centered around the importance of engaging the *Head, Heart* and *Hands* of each employee touched by the change. *Head* meant that people knew *what* to do to pull off the change; *Heart* meant people knew *why* they were doing it; and *Hands* meant they knew *how* to do it—they possessed the required skills. I still have the planning materials from this effort in my files: They fill several hundred pages, contained in two large binders. The change effort took more than two thousand person-hours to plan. And before the national conversion was rolled out—successfully, over a period of about sixty days—the changeover was piloted in a test market for nearly eight months.

But we didn't neglect the other laws of leading change. In every discussion of the change, the importance of open date coding to the war with Coke was repeatedly emphasized (the Law of Building a Cathedral), as was our impending loss of market share—the beginning of the end of the Cola Wars—if we failed (the Law of the Burning Platform). The CEO was intimately involved from the first announcement to the final review sessions (the Law of Cascading Sponsorship). And we had learned enough from the Grandma's Cookies fiasco to pay extra attention to the route salespeople and vending machine delivery people, to solicit their input and feedback on our plans, and to act on that feedback (the Law of Ownership).

Leadership is about producing change. But because change is so emotionally fraught, and can involve such a large number of people, change efforts must be meticulously designed in order to ensure predictable results. Hence the focus on planning, controlling, and problem solving in these laws, and hence the irony that change—the cardinal *leadership* task—relies for its success on High-Performance *management*.

Summary: Feiner's Laws of Leading Change

1. The Law of the Burning Platform

If change is not presented as a burning platform decision, it can't hope to succeed.

2. The Law of Cascading Sponsorship

Leaders cannot delegate responsibility for implementing change. While a change process requires the involvement of many, High-Performance Leaders recognize that they must stay continuously and intimately involved from start to finish.

3. The Law of Nuts and Bolts

No matter how obvious the need for change, discipline and planning are essential in cascading change through an organization. This planning needs to anticipate resistance and the need to adjust the process as it evolves.

4. The Law of Ownership

If you want your people to own the outcome of a change process, give them a vote along the way.

10	*Leading Difference*
	THE TREACHERY OF ASSUMPTIONS

The playing field for women and minorities in contemporary organizations is not level. This was true thirty-five years ago, when I
began my career; it was true when I left Pepsi; and the war stories recounted in my class each semester by female or minority students
strongly suggest it's still true today. These students' work experiences
have included unequal performance standards, insensitive or racist
comments, demeaning treatment, and outright sexual harassment.

Feiner's Laws alone can't solve these problems, and I don't pretend for a moment that they can. The Laws of Leadership won't fix
core values, when those values reflect prejudice or bigotry. To fully
eradicate these offensive values, which undermine so many lives
and careers, will require societal change, through, among other
things, our government, our legislation, our corporations, and our
entertainment media. Most importantly, it will require people
being taught in homes and schools that differences are to be em-
braced, not feared.

So this is not a chapter about the need to eliminate racism and prejudice from the workplace, much as we should. This is not a chapter about the torturous struggle women face if they want to be both a mother and a professional. This is not a chapter about the travails of African-Americans in white corporate America. This chapter, rather, focuses on the role of the individual in leading difference—an area where, I've found, the laws can have a positive impact. It examines the problems created by the assumptions we make every day (assumptions that are particularly poisonous where differences of ethnicity or gender are involved); it discusses the critical difference between intentional and unintentional bias; it looks at the value of knowing the whole person—emotions as well as skills and behaviors—in preventing negative assumptions and bias; and it presents one approach to overcoming negative assumptions and bias in others.

Feiner's Laws of Leading Difference are as follows:

1. THE LAW OF THE ONION

We make assumptions about people every day. They're a kind of shorthand for reaching decisions promptly and effectively, and they're generally a helpful and efficient way of navigating our way in the world. Consider, for example, the category of assumptions that tell us that people and objects will tend to behave the same way they have done in the past. We assume that people will behave today much as they did yesterday, that their essential characteristics and motivations will be consistent from day to day. While this isn't always true, it's an assumption that saves us from having to reevaluate our world on a daily basis. Or consider the related group of assumptions that tell us that past experience is a good predictor of future experience. When we see a man stumbling and slurring his words on a busy city street late at night, we quickly assume he's drunk and give him wide berth so as to avoid even the slightest

possibility of an altercation. While there might be alternate explanations for the man's behavior, the assumption allows us to act
more quickly in a potentially unpleasant situation. Few of us
would quarrel with such a decision.

By their very nature, however, assumptions are risky. They depend for their usefulness on making judgments based on an incomplete set of facts—this is what enables us to simplify our world
to the point where we can act with reasonable speed. But the habit
of acting on incomplete information has a dark side to it. There are
bad assumptions and good assumptions, and very often when differences of gender or ethnicity are part of the mix the assumptions
people make are dangerous.

What happens is predictable. It's easy to fall into the trap of assuming, "You're not me, therefore you're different from me." But
all too often the fallacious logic quickly extends from "You're *different* from me" to "You're *inferior* to me." This kind of odious
thinking is at the root of many of the special leadership challenges
for women and minorities.

The antidote here is to take the implicit or assumed facts that
lead to the assumption, and bring them out into the open. There's
a brief story that illustrates this point, and that reminds us how
often issues are present in a relationship that are not acknowledged
because they're perceived to be too sensitive.

Many years ago my girlfriend and I paid a visit to a friend of
hers. As we approached the house, my girlfriend whispered in my
ear, "Don't mention pets. Her dog just died, and she's very upset
about it."

So we went in, and sat down in the living room to talk. The
conversation was awkward, to say the least. I could tell the lady was
grief-stricken, just by the look on her face, but the conversation
danced around the issue—we didn't want to say anything, because
we didn't want to upset her further. But her grief was in the room
with us, acknowledged or not.

So after we'd been there awhile, I decided to try a different tack. I said to the lady, "I guess you miss Sparky, then."

This unleashed a flood of tears and sobbing, all of which lasted for a minute or so. But the atmosphere in the room lifted. Grief was acknowledged and expressed, and it subsided, just through this acknowledgment. The transformation was extraordinary. We had assumed that the dog's death was too painful to talk about, whereas in fact it was too painful *not* to talk about. By bringing the hidden assumption of pain (on our side) and the hidden struggle to conceal emotion (on the owner's side) into the open, both were dissipated. There was no longer an invisible wall separating us.

I first realized the power of getting unspoken issues out in the open in the early eighties, when we persuaded Pepsi there was a need to make the organization more racially pluralistic and diverse. We had a number of innovative programs to do this. At one point, we were hiring one hundred and twenty-five summer interns into an ambitious recruitment program. I interviewed a large number of these candidates. I began to ask them questions such as, "What's it like going to a historically black university after going to a predominantly white high school?" Or, "Have you faced racism at the university you attend and how did you deal with it?" Or, "What's the biggest challenge you anticipate facing as an African-American woman in corporate America?" And I noticed that the minute I began to deal directly and overtly with the unspoken issue of race or gender, the more connecting and comfortable the conversation became. It stopped being a plastic chat between a stuffed suit and a college student twenty light-years removed from each other. Too often, we work hard at avoiding those touchy issues—we expend great amounts of energy to keep the conversation on "safe," emotionally neutral ground—and are uncomfortable raising issues of race or gender. *But I learned to take risks*—or at least, that's how it felt in the beginning—*and to acknowledge and discuss differences, because the very fact that you do so makes those differences recede.*

Now I know there may be some HR managers who think this approach to exposing assumptions is dangerous, that it's too risky to ask an African-American about the issue of race. Needless to say, I disagree. I'm all in favor of making the organization as real and authentic as possible. That doesn't mean that, as a leader, you start off by assuming that racial, cultural, or gender issues are the problem. *It simply means that you check it out if you're not able to get to the root cause of a situation.*

The story of Sparky the dog is a good, if simple, example of what happens when people make faulty assumptions. There the assumption was that it would be unwise to openly acknowledge Sparky's demise. In the following story, however, the assumptions are less benign.

One of the groups reporting to me was an internal consulting team, staffed with a number of Ph.D. industrial psychologists who supported line departments with various HR issues: installing self-directed work teams in some of our factories, designing new training approaches for front-line workers, building new communication processes for keeping employees better informed and more motivated, and establishing better measures for evaluating leadership potential. This may sound a little soft but this Organizational Development (OD) group was very highly regarded at Pepsi, and demand for its services by line managers was high.

We were always on the lookout for top-flight talent for this group. So when my staffing director called one day and told me he had just interviewed a sensational candidate, I was delighted.

"Mike," he said, "you're going to love her. She has all the qualifications we're looking for."

"Don, that's great. Has Jerry [the head of the OD group] seen her?"

"No, Jerry's in L.A. rolling out the sales management performance system."

"Oh yeah, I forgot. Well, try to get her back ASAP so Jerry and I can interview her."

"Well, that's the thing—she's still here, I asked her to wait. It took me six weeks to get her here in the first place and I thought you could see her for a few minutes, just to boost her interest in us."

"I'm really jammed up, Don—today has been a killer."

"Mike, if you could just spend a couple of minutes telling her how much clout the group has around here . . . by the way, she's African-American."

I thought for a few seconds: We were always looking for talented minorities. Hell, I was pushing my entire organization to become more diverse. And the issue of me seeing the candidate first, before Jerry did, was a no-brainer. We were pretty relaxed and unbureaucratic about that kind of stuff. Expediency ruled. I was here. Jerry wasn't. The candidate needed some selling.

"Don, tell you what. Bring her by—just give me five minutes to juggle my schedule."

"Thanks, Mike. I don't think you'll be disappointed."

I spent almost an hour with Joanna, and I wasn't disappointed. She was really a great candidate—bright, poised, and street-savvy, with excellent work experience. I thought she'd be a perfect fit with Pepsi's culture. We talked a lot about the OD group and its stature within the company. She asked very good questions and my responses seemed to jibe with what she was looking for in a new job. I concluded the interview and called Don, who came by to reconnect with Joanna. As I said good-bye, I asked Don to try to get Joanna back to interview with Jerry and other members of the group.

Don called me about thirty minutes later, said that Joanna had enjoyed our talk, was very interested in the job, and would try to return as soon as possible to meet with Jerry.

A month later we extended an offer to Joanna—Jerry was as excited about hiring her as I was—and she joined the OD team, seemingly as charged up about joining us as we were about landing her.

About two months later, at the end of the meeting with Jerry and some of his managers, I asked him to stick around for a minute. When we were alone I asked how Joanna was settling in. This was standard operating procedure for me—my team was accustomed to questions about the progress of our people, how well each was doing, and what, if any, performance issues I ought to know about.

Jerry's response aroused my suspicions immediately. "I guess she's doing all right."

"What do you mean 'you guess'?"

"I mean it's still early and she's still learning her way around."

"What do you have her working on?"

I don't recall the specifics but the projects Jerry recited seemed to be meaty ones that Joanna would find engaging. "Okay, Jerry, but keep me posted on her progress." My instincts told me Jerry was holding back but I didn't want him to feel I was taking over. That might have created a bigger problem.

I purposely chose not to ask about Joanna for a while. But when I did ask again, at the end of a meeting with Jerry a couple of months later, I knew something was definitely awry.

"So how goes it with Joanna?"

He seemed to anticipate my question. "Mike, do you think I'm a good manager?"

I wasn't sure if he was serious. "Come on, Jerry, I've given you lots of feedback that you're one of the best people managers I've ever worked with."

"You think I'm good at motivating people?"

"Jerry, I'll say it again. You're really talented at motivating people—it's one of your towering strengths. So what's this about?"

"She's unmanageable—that's what this is about. She comes in

later than anyone else in the group. She misses her project due dates. And I get the feeling she thinks I'm a lightweight."

I was floored. "Have you talked with her and told her your concerns?"

"Kind of. I don't want to crater her—she's only been here four months. I've tried to hint that she should get with the program in terms of getting to the office earlier. But I'm worried that the group is beginning to think she's getting special treatment 'cause she's black."

"Jerry, this is serious. It's bad enough she's not meeting your expectations. If the race issue is in the mix then we have a real problem on our hands. Don't you think you need to talk with her—and this time not pull any punches about your concerns?"

"Maybe you're right. Maybe I've been too cautious with her. I'll talk with her this week."

"Good. I think that's the way to go. Let's talk after you do."

A few days later Jerry stopped by. He looked troubled.

"Mike, I talked with Joanna. It didn't go very well. She was very guarded and not really communicative. Said something about this culture being hard to figure out. I didn't push but I feel we've got a problem. She and I are definitely not on the same wavelength. Maybe you ought to talk with her. Maybe she'll open up with you."

I met with Joanna the very next day. She seemed upbeat and full of enthusiasm as we chatted for a couple of minutes.

"Anyway, Joanna, you've been here about four months so I wanted to dial in and see how things are going."

She hesitated for a moment. "Fine. I think things are going fine."

Not exactly an expansive response.

"Well, fill in the blanks for me. What projects are you working on? What's been the biggest challenge for you?"

She began to respond in what seemed to me to be an artificial, almost mechanical fashion—a Joe Friday, "facts, just the facts" kind of way.

I interrupted her paint-by-the-numbers routine. "Listen, Joanna, I only look stupid. What's the real story? What's really going on for you here?"

There was a long pause. "To be honest I'm not sure why you haven't been more involved in my projects."

I was confused. "What do you mean?"

"Well, you hired me. I saw you on my first visit and we seemed to hit it off. Obviously it was your decision to hire me. So I thought you'd have direct involvement in supervising me."

"But Jerry's your boss."

"Sure, technically I report to him but you made the hiring decision. That's why I interviewed with you first. He just signed off as a matter of courtesy."

I couldn't believe it. Because I had interviewed Joanna before her immediate boss—a common occurrence at Pepsi given how hectic everyone's travel schedule was—she had assumed that Jerry was a drone and I was the only boss in her solar system. I explained to Joanna that she'd made a faulty assumption based on the sequence of events in her hiring. Then I moved on to even more dangerous terrain. "Joanna, what about your project deadlines. Jerry tells me you've missed some."

"Frankly, Mike, Jerry is so hands-off with me that I've gotten the impression my deadlines really don't matter." She went on to describe how uninvolved Jerry seemed to be in her projects, and how little interest Jerry seemed to have in giving her feedback—camera-lens or any other kind—about her work. Listening to her narrative, it was clear to me why she seemed to have so little regard for Jerry. And that, in turn, probably explained why Jerry felt dismissed as a lightweight by her. I wondered whether Joanna attributed Jerry's indifference to racism but decided Jerry should be the one to delve into that.

I explained to her that I was glad we'd talked and that I hoped I'd clarified that Jerry was her boss. I told her that I wanted to talk with Jerry about his being so hands-off, as he was typically a very supportive and involved coach.

After Joanna left I called Jerry and asked if I could see him right away.

"So how did it go?" he asked.

"Jerry, you asked me last week if you were a good manager. And I said absolutely. In part because you make yourself available when your people need you. You give them plenty of feedback. And you care about your people doing well."

"Thanks. I sure try to do all that."

"You usually do. So why doesn't Joanna feel you've done any of that with her?"

He paused. "To tell you the truth, I guess I haven't done it that much."

"How come?"

Another pause.

"Come on, Jerry," I said. "Be straight with me."

"I guess I wasn't sure how much license I had."

"What in the world does that mean? License?"

"Yes, license. Everyone knows how important hiring women and minorities is to you. It's a crusade with you—well, one of your crusades. So I wasn't sure how much license I had to supervise Joanna closely. Or tell her that coming in at nine in the morning is a nonstarter in my group. I didn't want to come down too hard on someone you really wanted to succeed here."

I couldn't believe it. Another collection of erroneous assumptions. "But what's so hard about telling her she needs to get to work earlier?"

"I figured she'd think I was being racist. As a black she'd probably be very sensitive about the tardiness thing since that's kind of a black stereotype."

By the time I finished talking with Jerry I was totally discouraged. Bad assumptions by Joanna. Still more faulty assumptions by Jerry. Both sets of assumptions exacerbated by differences of race and gender. The result? Two talented professionals misjudging each other's intentions and motives, and failing to deliver the goods as a result.

A few days later I brought Joanna and Jerry together in my office and tried to resuscitate a relationship that was barely on life support. I got the two to discuss the bad start they had made with each other, and tried to help them see that their bad assumptions were the culprit.

They seemed to get it. Their relationship did improve, as did the quality of Joanna's work and Jerry's supervision. Yet the story doesn't have a happy ending. Twelve months later, after only sixteen months with Pepsi, Joanna resigned, accepting a similar position with another company. Assumptions can be treacherous, and sometimes wrong ones can't be righted, even with the best of intentions.

High-Performance Leaders look beneath the surface when assessing another's motives and abilities. These leaders understand that humans are assuming beings, and that they are no exception themselves. So they seek to peel the onion with people, looking for deeper and richer context for another's behavior, and looking to validate or refute their own reflexive or unthinking assumptions. This is another important application of the pull technique. And this is a question of courage, not skills. Chris Argyris has written extensively about the subject of what he calls the *governing values*, the drivers of most human behavior. He suggests that four fundamental motives account for much of what we do: to win and not to lose in a situation, to maintain control, to avoid embarrassment, and to stay (or appear to stay) rational.[1] I'd argue that, in a situation where assumptions play a large part in forming opinions, a natural tendency toward risk aversion also comes into play. We're aware, at some level, that we've made assumptions; we're aware that these assumptions are based on incomplete facts; and *we're worried that, in order to find out the truth of the matter, we will have to reveal our ignorance.* Because avoiding embarrassment is such a profound concern, we prefer the path of safe ignorance. It takes courage (not skill) to reveal one's own ignorance; it takes wisdom (not brains) to see greater strength in this approach, in risking embarrassment in order to more richly understand the world.

My first assumption, when Chris performed his end run on the bonus recommendations, was that he was a duplicitous schemer out to challenge my authority (for me to pause and consider the possibility that he might have a valid reason to change the numbers would have required me to acknowledge the possibility of being wrong—would, in other words, have required me to overcome the *win, don't lose* governing value). As I found out when my bullying him elicited his push-back, I was the insufferable jerk who never listened to others' opinions.

Leaders need to be aware that assumptions are omnipresent. While that's not a problem in itself, it is a problem to rely on assumptions unthinkingly or superficially. *If there's the slightest doubt about motives—with a boss, a peer, or a subordinate, leaders must peel the onion.*

2. THE LAW OF INTENTION

All of us, regardless of our color or gender or cultural heritage, have biases. These biases show themselves in many ways with bosses, peers, and subordinates. When seeing bias, High-Performance Leaders make a careful distinction between biased behavior that is *conscious* and that which is *unconscious*. A great example of this was when, during one of my MBA classes, I suggested, "There are as many stereotypes about Orientals as there are about African-Americans." At the end of class, one of my students asked if she could talk with me privately.

"Of course you can. What's up?"

"Professor, your use of the term Oriental was inappropriate. I know you didn't mean it but it's condescending to us. Today people use the word Asian."

I blushed with embarrassment, apologized, and thanked her for telling me. Departing, she smiled warmly, telling me one more time that she knew I didn't mean to be insulting. (One of the reasons I love teaching is that I learn as much from my students as I hope they learn from me.) Rather than quickly assuming my comment was conscious, the student took the opposite approach, and assumed it was innocent—that is, *unintended*. Touchy issues such as race, gender, or, for that matter, party political allegiance often quickly flare up into full-force conflagrations. The fuel for these fires is our tendency to assume the worst in people, and in particular, to assume conscious prejudice rather than unconscious implication. Read any Internet message board, and you'll see that discussion of these sensitive subjects almost invariably escalates into name calling and other abuse (and when the forum is online—or, in a corporate setting, e-mail—the dangers are increased by the absence of the facial or body language that can signal the difference between a tentative statement, a questioning one, and a definitive one). The Law of Intention teaches us to trust that comments which evidence prejudice are made unconsciously rather than in a deliberate attempt to malign, until we see strong evidence to the contrary. (This law is thus a cousin of the Law of the Mirror, which tells us to look for fault in ourselves before we seek to blame others. The two laws share the notion that leaders who value relationships look first for explanations that are minimally disruptive. Only if these explanations prove insufficient do they proceed to the disruption of suggesting that a colleague is at fault, or has exhibited conscious and intended prejudice.) *In organizational life, leaders recognize that distinguishing between unintended bias and purposeful prejudice is crucial to managing relationships successfully.*

3. THE LAW OF THE WHOLE PERSON

I once asked a boss at dinner how he felt about his stint in Latin America—a taboo subject, since he had reportedly failed in this assignment (though he has gone on to become very successful since then).

He looked at me for a second before replying, warily, "Why do you ask?"

"I don't know—we've worked together for almost a year now. I think you trust me. You know I care about you. So I've always been curious—maybe because you've never mentioned it."

He hesitated. "I've never mentioned it—I've never mentioned it to anybody—because I don't know how to, really. The fact is I failed in the job big-time. I didn't know what the hell I was doing, really. My boss didn't want me in the job and left me out to fend for myself. Juan, my key guy, was sabotaging me behind the scenes so I'd fail and he could replace me . . ."

And for another thirty minutes or so my boss spoke about how difficult the experience of failing was for him. And how difficult it was to openly acknowledge his failure.

The upshot of all this was that we formed an ever more tightly bonded relationship in the years I worked for him. Over time he was able to talk about the experience with others in his inner circle. He had become willing to discreetly let the skeleton out of his closet.

High-Performance Leaders have the courage to connect with their people, not just in the safe and sterile world of projects and deadlines, but in the world of emotions (what we might call the *human* world!). I've found that male leaders in particular have difficulty with this aspect of their jobs—women seem much more comfortable connecting through feelings. This tactic—summoning the courage to broach taboo subjects when they impact a working relationship—applies just as much to unspoken differences of ethnicity and gender as it does to unspoken history. It signals interest and concern, and moves toward a deeper understanding of the situation and a wider fact base, thereby reducing the need for assumptions. I'm not suggesting that you cultivate a reputation of prying into others' affairs, but I am encouraging you, *when there's a body in the living room, to acknowledge it rather than just stepping aside.*

4. The Law of Self-Interest

Despite the spate of scoundrels masquerading as executives we've seen in the past few years, there are a great many leaders who are highly principled. But although you might feel that your holding the moral high ground should be enough in itself to move others to act, that is—I'm sorry to say—seldom the case. A conflict between an individual's values and those of the organization he or she works for is the classic ethical roadblock in career progression. What do leaders do when unsuccessfully pushing others to accept an ethical approach?

Sadly, the outlook here is bleak. In a 2001 survey of MBA students—the future leaders of our corporations—the Aspen Institute found that, in situations where their values conflict with those of the company where they work, most MBA students state they would look for another job.[2] This in itself gives a pretty depressing prognosis for the future of our corporations, if so many young and talented people would leave rather than attempt to influence change. But my suspicion is that, were these students to be removed from the comparatively secure environment of business school and faced with families to support and mortgages to pay, their responses would change, and that inactivity—looking the other way—would become the predominant reaction. But this signals not so much a lack of resolve as a paucity of options. So let me add an option, which, though you might find it less comfortable than simply asserting the moral high ground, is pragmatic and effective—it's similar, in this, to the option of accommodating when dealing with conflict (where Trevor gave me a lesson in being wrong once in a while).

Many ethical or values conflicts arise from issues of difference, be they of gender or ethnicity, and the approach I'm about to discuss can be effective in these cases. But it's worth noting that it also applies, more broadly, to the full spectrum of values-based conflicts.

I'll illustrate this with a story.

Ron was a Columbia Business School graduate whom we'd hired from a prestigious management consulting firm. By his mid-thirties he was a successful sales executive in one of our largest regions. A big job opened up. I went to Barry, my boss—it was my job to come up with slates of candidates for jobs—and said that Ron was perfect for the position.

"You know Ron—he's a great candidate," I said. "I've talked to Jake [our lead sales exec], and he thinks it would be a good idea. Ron's African-American, and he'd be the most senior African-American in our system. He's very talented—let's do it."

Barry agreed with my recommendation and we promoted Ron. We announced it, and a few days later Barry called me into his office and said, "We've got a problem."

"What's the problem?"

"I just heard from Billy."

Billy was one of our franchise bottlers, and he was running one of our largest bottling operations.

Barry said, "I've just heard from Billy, and we've got to renege on Ron's promotion."

"Why do we have to do that?" I asked, slowly.

"Well . . . Billy's a key guy, he's running a vital operation for us . . . and he doesn't want an African-American in his region . . . and, well, we're going to have to renege on the offer."

"Hang on, Ron's got his furniture en route—he's already bought a house. His family is moving. We've already announced it . . ."

"Mike, you're my go-to guy. When I've got a problem, you handle it. You ship. So Mike, ship. But I don't want a problem with Billy. He's a key bottler, a damn good bottler, he's been an ally of ours, I don't want to create World War III with Billy. So see if you can fix it."

So I called Billy.

Billy said, "Mike, I thought I'd be hearing from you."

"Billy, do you have a problem?"

"Mike, I don't have a problem. *You* have a problem."

"Billy, the guy's ex–Boston Consulting Group, Columbia Business School, he's had a great track record out west . . ."

"Mike, let me explain this to you. You're a nice young kid. I like you. I've always liked you, Mike. But I'm telling you right now, that Ron's black behind isn't going to be allowed in my place. Do we understand one another, Mike?"

Now, these are the kinds of issues leaders face every week. It may not be children working in factories in Asia, or the baby formula issue in Africa, but issues will arise where what a leader feels is morally right is threatened, and if a leader deserves the name, then he or she must be prepared to take action.

This was certainly one of those issues. And I was stuck. I was offended—no, outraged—by Billy's position. And I was worried that Barry would ultimately put Billy's interests and our business interests ahead of what was clearly the right thing for us to do.

I decided I should present my case to Billy in person—forcefully but artfully.

So I went to see him. "Billy, I'm coming to see you."

"Mike, you're always welcome in my territory."

He picked me up at the airport and we went to a restaurant—the name of which I'd forgotten about halfway through the dinner. And we were having shooters and silver bullets and two bottles of wine, and I was my most charming self. I was schmoogleing and dancing—he got my best stuff. The moral argument, the political argument, and the Ron's-the-best-person-for-the-job argument. I had the moral high ground, and I knew I did, and I used it as fully as possible.

And I think I remember his slurring at the end of dinner, "Mike, this has been most enjoyable, and I'd like to accommodate you 'cause I know you're in a bit of a bind, but I'm telling you right now, you'd better figure out something else for Ron. Thanks for coming down anyways."

So it was a good plan, but it didn't work. I gave him the most schmoogle-oogle I've ever given anyone—and in my day I was pretty good with the schmoogle-oogle—but it didn't work.

I knew I'd have to call Ron and let him know what was going on. "I just want to post you," I said when I got through to him. "We have a bit of a problem. Billy is underwhelmed with the prospects of your being the sales VP for his division."

"What's the problem?"

"The problem, Ron, is that . . . well, he just doesn't want a black in that job. Obviously the firm's backing you . . . we think you're the best guy for the job . . . but this could get ugly for you. How far do you want us to go on this?"

"Mike, you make the call. I mean, obviously, we've sold our house, the family's en route, but I think if he were to let me inside his tent I'm pretty sure I could convince him in short order I'm talented, I could help him with the business. That doesn't scare me. I've dealt with issues like this my whole life."

So I went back to Barry. And he said, "You fixed it, right?"

"No, I didn't fix it."

"Well what's the deal?"

"I went down to see Billy, he's resolute, and I—well, I just don't have the stroke to jam it through."

He said, "Mike, I thought you were going to fix it. You gave me the sense that you could take care of it. I don't want to take up any more time on this."

I said, "Barry, I tried to fix it." Things were getting testy now between the two of us. "I tried to fix it and couldn't."

"Well, did you try hard enough?"

"Well, Barry"—defiantly, now—"I tried as hard as I can."

"Mike, if I have to fix it, if I have to fix this damn thing, then maybe I ought to do your job and my job at the same time."

"Maybe you ought to. Maybe you ought to—because I can't."

He said, "Look, I know this is difficult. It's as offensive to me as it is to you. We shouldn't care what Billy thinks for two reasons: one, we run the business, and two, he's full of it. But the guy's a profitable bottler, and we have a lot of concentrate revenue riding on this. So it's as much a business issue as a Human Resources issue. And don't forget, he usually takes our side when we're fighting with the Bottlers' Association.

"Let's just promote Ron somewhere else. Give him a double raise. I mean . . . let's not move him to Billy's region, move the guy in Detroit there instead, move Ron to Detroit, I mean . . . there's a large black population in Detroit, he'll even be better there . . . I don't care. We're not going to send him back to L.A. but . . . be creative here."

I thought for a moment and said, "Barry, here's the deal. We've announced to five thousand managers that we've just promoted Ron to this division. And you're going to look like one of the great cowards of all time if we have to go back and tell these people, 'Ron? Oh no, his furniture's on the truck, it's en route, but no, we're moving him to Detroit.' First of all, it'll look like we haven't got the first clue about managing succession in this company. Second, it'll get out in a nanosecond why we're doing it, which will send a terrible signal to every manager in this company, whether they're African-American or not. I don't have the stroke to give Billy the order. You do. So, Barry, this is one where you're either going to have to step up or suffer the consequences. It's your leadership stature that's on the line here. It's your reputation."

And that's what he responded to. The moral high ground, the ethical argument—those alone weren't enough. No, he responded more to a framing of the issue in terms of what it would cost him—his image, his stature. He called Billy, and told him that Ron was the guy. Billy wasn't happy, and wouldn't let Ron in his plant for a couple of weeks. But ultimately, over time, Ron—to his eternal credit—figured it out, figured out how to schmoogle Billy, and two and a half years later, when we wanted to promote Ron again, Billy called Barry in a fury, irate that we were moving the best salesperson he had ever had.

What moved Barry, and what moves many other corporate leaders, is their self-interest. In terms of getting organizations to do what's right, an appeal to self-interest has more stroke, more juice, more power, more influence, and more impact than anything else.

If you have to rely on pitching it as self-interest, then you pitch it. A pragmatic, practical approach like this is not ideal—we'd all like to live in a world where moral arguments consistently carry the day—but it often works. If your choice is between losing the moral argument or winning the pragmatic one, I'd encourage you to consider the latter. *If self-interest is what it's going to take to persuade and influence people to do what you want them to do, then use self-interest.* Competitive and financial pressures prompt many leaders to succumb to a very linear, binary set of forces. I'm disappointed by that, but to my mind the option of leaving a company every time an ethical conflict occurs is not a real one, and this is the best alternate approach I've found.

You might feel that this story is disturbing. In what you might describe as a Machiavellian way (that is, a way that places a higher value on the ends than on the means), I got Barry to do what was right. But right as defined by me, not by him.

Isn't this a dangerous tactic for me to be advocating?

It might well be. In this case, there were mitigating factors. By appealing to his reputation, I was by extension appealing to the societal values that influenced that reputation. While these values are certainly mutable over time (had our conversation occurred fifty years ago, my tactics might have been considerably less effective), in the absence of any other moral true north they're a good proxy for some sort of ethical absolute. Outside the circumstances of this particular series of events, however, I'd agree that there is danger here. Although right and wrong are broadly agreed upon, reasonable people can differ as to the appropriate course of action in a particular circumstance. So if you elect to rely on the Law of Self-Interest, be sure to link self-interest to some sort of external moral reference. In this case, reputation provided that check. In another case, it might be a legal concern, or a fear of adverse publicity. Make a connection between your colleague's self-interest, and how he or she would feel, reading about his or her actions in the newspapers the next day, and you will have successfully understood the role of this law in overcoming damaging assumptions.

Summary: Feiner's Laws of Leading Difference

1. The Law of the Onion

High-Performance Leaders look beneath the surface when assessing another's motives and abilities. They're aware that assumptions are omnipresent, and take care not to make them unthinkingly.

2. The Law of Intention

Leaders make a careful distinction between biased behavior that is conscious and that which is unconscious.

3. The Law of the Whole Person

High-Performance Leaders have the courage to connect with their people, not just in the safe and sterile world of projects and deadlines, but in the world of emotions.

4. The Law of Self-Interest

When your holding the moral high ground isn't enough, frame issues in terms of the other's self-interest to encourage them to do the right thing.

PART IV

Values-Based Leadership

The laws in Parts II and III are necessary but not sufficient for High-Performance Leadership—they enable follower-ship, but they do not ensure it. Part IV looks at two broad reasons why leaders and their organizations fail. The first—the lack of honest push-back to bosses—looks up the organization. The second—the danger of leaders' being seduced by pride, greed, and ambition—takes a top-down view. Together, these two constitute the final ingredient in building followership: a leader's value system.

11	*Why Organizations Don't Work*
	THE EMPEROR'S LOOKING GREAT TODAY

The list of American companies embroiled in controversy seems to grow longer every day. Arthur Andersen was found guilty of obstruction of justice. Enron's executives have been investigated for creating and approving partnerships that kept billions of dollars of debt off the company's books. WorldCom is accused of inflating its earnings by booking expenses improperly. Qwest Communications is being investigated for accounting practices that inflated sales, as is Dynegy. Executives at Tyco face criminal charges connected to their allegedly illegal self-enrichment. Sam Waksal, ImClone's CEO, was sentenced to a federal prison term for his role in an insider trading scandal. And this is only a partial list of businesses now under a cloud. Beyond business organizations one can look at the FBI and its handling of pre-9/11 terrorist threat data, or the Catholic Church and its unwillingness to take action against pedophile priests for over a decade.

Is all this an aberration that casts an unfair cloud over the vast majority of organizations? I don't think so. While most leaders may be basically honest, most organizations simply don't work the way they should. The current list may be longer than usual, but a review over the past quarter century reveals many parallel cases. Consider the Watergate scandal of the seventies. Recall the Savings and Loan crisis of the eighties, and the shenanigans of Charles Keating. Or the junk bond capers of the same decade, brought to us by the likes of Ivan Boesky and Michael Milken, not to mention Drexel Burnham Lambert. The sequence continued in the nineties, with such luminaries as Chainsaw Al Dunlap and his near-killing of Sunbeam Corporation, and the fraudulent accounting at Waste Management. And these are just the firms that reach the point of meltdown. We can only assume that there are plenty of other organizations where unethical behavior either goes unpunished, or skirts just shy of technical illegality. While the examples here are examples of calamities, I suspect that most organizations stop working the way they should long before calamity arrives.

But the assertion that companies don't work the way they should has an impersonal, abstract quality to it. While the newspaper headlines level blame at corporate entities, there are people—*leaders*—behind every scandal. So if organizations are ever going to work, it must be because people exercise positive leadership. This brings us full circle to the notion of leadership with which we began the book—that it is at least as much about the small stuff as about the big stuff, and that it needs to happen at all levels of an organization. Leadership is the aggregation of these daily transactions and decisions that collectively determine an organization's fate. It follows that, if organizations are to work, people both junior and senior, both new and experienced, must exercise positive leadership in hundreds of ways every day. If they don't, the results will be devastating—as we have seen.

Yet exercising leadership can be difficult. More than this, it can be scary. It takes courage to tell the Emperor (or Empress) that he (or she) has no clothes. Bosses have enormous power, over our compensation, our promotions, and our careers, and, more immediately, over our quality of life at the office each day. So taking on the responsibility for telling our superiors when they're heading in the wrong direction can seem daunting. To be a High-Performance Leader, however, requires telling the Emperor when he or she is naked. When his agenda is overloaded, when her objectives are unclear, when his team is splintered, when her leadership is failing. And when the wisdom of his or her decisions is doubtful.

In case you feel that I'm suggesting effective push-back is a silver bullet for all our corporate ailments, I should clarify what I mean here. I'm not claiming this is a one hundred percent solution for the problems that beset most organizations. There are certainly structural problems, related to financial reporting, corporate governance, and industry regulation, that need our urgent attention. But I would argue that more effective push-back would lead to a substantial reduction in the number of organizations that crash and burn, or that make their employees' lives miserable along the way.

And if you feel that the scandal-ridden firms were led by bad leaders, and that bad leaders are just that, and can't be changed, I'd counter with two points. First, most bad leaders begin their lives as good leaders. Second, to pin the blame on a single bad apple, or on a small group of ethically backward executives, requires us to believe that these individuals or senior groups were able to do what they did covertly. I don't believe that's a rational assumption. Do we really suppose no one knew, outside the senior team, what was going on at WorldCom? Do we really suppose no one knew, apart from Sherron Watkins, of the fun and games at Enron? Do we really suppose no one knew what Dennis Kozlowski was up to at Tyco (do we really suppose you can hide a multimillion-dollar apartment, or a lavishly refurbished headquarters office)? And do we really suppose that Sunbeam, Waste Management, Drexel Burnham, and all the others were staffed entirely by blind and deaf employees? Anyone who's worked in an organization for more than a day knows that all too often people don't tell one another what they need to know to make good, honest, and appropriate decisions. Many employees of all these firms knew perfectly well what was going on—they weren't blind. But they were tragically mute. I'd argue that they lacked the tools to push back effectively, particularly in the early stages of aberrant behavior, when the line between ethical and unethical behavior is easy to cross with a very small step.

To do these things is never easy. But there are ways of pushing back with bosses that make it much more probable that leaders up the line receive the information and feedback they deserve—and that their organizations require—to make good decisions.

Feiner's Laws of Push-Back build on the Law of the Emperor's Wardrobe in Chapter 4. That law emphasized the importance of push-back in a productive relationship with your boss. These laws provide more specific tactics as to how to do so.

1. THE LAW OF LOYALTY VS. INSUBORDINATION

Most bosses like the power and authority they've worked hard to acquire. And with the success they've achieved, bosses can come to believe that their way is the right way, the best way—perhaps even the only way. It's what led to their success, and it's why bosses can easily mistake an opposing view from a subordinate not as feedback, but as insubordination. To avoid this trap, *leaders need to establish at the outset that they intend to tell their boss what he or she needs to hear, as opposed to what he or she wants to hear.* Telling a boss *early* in the relationship, before contentious issues arise, that you're sure he or she wants an honest and straight point of view is essential. Because contentious issues *will* arise, and when they do it's too late to prepare a boss for push-back.

Very early in the relationship with your boss it's essential to establish this ground rule, with phrases such as those we saw in Chapter 4: "I assume you want my point of view," or, "I'm sure you feel I owe you the truth." And once you've set your boss's expectations in this way, reiterate your position often, so that your boss understands that you equate intellectual honesty with loyalty, not with insubordination, that your motivation is professional commitment, not mutiny.

Too often people masquerading as leaders agree with the boss and go home hating themselves for their lack of courage. At home they kick the cat, scream at their kids, or argue with their spouse without really understanding why. Their boss, meanwhile, is in the dark about what's wrong, and doesn't have the information he or she needs to make a better decision. It's a lose-lose proposition.

This law was particularly crucial for me to follow when, after a few years in another PepsiCo division, I started working for Linda, a division president. Everyone knew about Linda. She was one of the youngest division presidents—a superstar who had achieved sensational results in her past few assignments. Passionate, intense, and strong-willed, Linda was held in high regard by her peers. But there were caution flags as well. She was known to be impatient, wanted most things done yesterday, and expected her people to do things her way. All in all she was considered an intimidating boss.

I figured I'd better go slow with Linda and not throw my legendary fastball for a few weeks. While she had interviewed me for the position, it was understood that I was the "first-up" candidate for the job, so the interview was more a discussion about what she saw as the key priorities of my job. It was a good but not especially memorable talk. We seemed to get along well, and when Linda asked if I was up for the assignment, I immediately responded in the affirmative.

After a couple of weeks, I saw firsthand Linda's towering strengths—she was very bright, creative, decisive, and obsessive about winning in the marketplace. True to her reputation, however, Linda was all about push—she'd decide, without much consultation with the team, what she wanted to accomplish and how the team should go about delivering it. And she had little patience for debate.

After a particularly bruising meeting, in which Linda expressed her strong dissatisfaction with the implementation of some of her decisions, she brought the session to an abrupt close, and directed that we reconvene the next day after some members of the team took corrective measures to fix the problem. It was obvious that she was pretty angry. I figured it was now or never—this was the moment of truth. As people began leaving the conference room and heading back to their offices, I approached her and asked if she had a minute to talk. She nodded, which I took to mean a reluctant yes.

We entered her office, and her opening made it easier for me to do what I felt was needed. "What'd you think of the meeting?" she asked.

"Do you really want to know?"

"What's that supposed to mean?"

"Linda, I'm the new kid on the block so I don't mean to come across as a professional critic. But I figure you're paying me to give you my best thinking on stuff. I mean—I think you want my honest opinion."

"What are you trying to say, Mike?"

I swallowed but my mouth was dry. I wasn't sure where this was going to end up.

"Linda, I owe you the truth in this job. And I think you want my points of view, even if they don't agree with yours."

"Keep going." I had Linda's attention, although she was clearly uncomfortable.

"You asked me what I thought about the meeting. So let me tell you, even though you may not like what I have to say. But as I said—I think you want me to be honest and give it to you straight. Not only about the meeting issue but on other stuff that comes up. For as long as I work for you. That's the way I plan to operate with you."

"Go ahead, I'm listening."

So I proceeded to tell Linda that I thought chewing out individuals in a team meeting was a mistake. That it wasn't the best way to elicit commitment from subordinates. And that her meetings appeared to be hers, not the team's.

She listened impassively, which I thought was unusual for such a quick-tempered personality. And then she said, "What do you think I should do now?"

"I've got a couple of ideas. First, apologize privately to Kate and Brian. I'd also set aside time at tomorrow's meeting for all of us to build an agenda for next week's meeting—and all our meetings. Probably most important, we should spend most of tomorrow's session trying to figure out how this thing got screwed up. You know, try to sort out as a team what we did wrong so we don't have the same implementation problem again."

Linda listened carefully to this. "Anything else?"

"No . . . just thanks for letting me tell you what was on my mind. Hope it was helpful."

I got up to leave, but Linda had something else to say. "I heard you were independent. That's your reputation, you know."

"Yeah, I guess I am independent—but that has nothing to do with what I hope you see is my commitment to you and this organization. That's exactly why you deserve my honest point of view for however long I work for you." I left her office, breathing a deep sigh of relief that my push-back hadn't set her off. Linda subsequently took my advice—she apologized to Kate and Brian, refrained from chewing out people publicly, and was able to improve the quality of our team meetings.

2. THE LAW OF RE-PLEDGING ALLEGIANCE

Even if leaders let bosses know early in the relationship of their intention to push back, that's not enough. *Leaders must recite the loyalty oath periodically.* Otherwise a boss can forget your initial expression of loyalty and see your push-back as truculence, insubordination, or disrespect. Depending on the boss, it may be necessary to reiterate your commitment each time you push back. Phrases such as "As I promised when we started working together I need to tell you when I disagree . . ." or, "I hope you recognize I'm pushing back here out of concern for our group's success," or, "I'm not trying to be difficult but this issue is important for the team so I'd like to offer a different alternative," are some examples of how to do this. Reciting the loyalty oath and restating it periodically are essential so that bosses don't perceive push-back as a lack of commitment.

When Brett, another boss with whom I had already established the ground rules of giving him the straight scoop, called me to his office, I had an idea of what was up.

"Mike, I've been thinking about it long and hard—I've decided that Helen [the VP-Marketing] is the wrong person for the job."

"Did something happen?"

"No, nothing specific, but my gut tells me we need to make a move."

"I think we're being too quick on the draw. I agree Helen has been slow off the mark, but it's still early, it's only been six months."

"Listen, Mike, I think we need to cut our losses. We can't afford to have anyone but a star in the marketing job. I know you call 'em like you see 'em but on this one I want to move. I'm beyond the point where I need to hear any more discussion. I've already talked with Allen [Brett's boss] and he's on board. So put together a severance package for Helen and I'll talk to her tomorrow."

"Brett, I really think we should go over this again."

"For once, would you quit debating with me? My mind's clear on this. I need your support, not your talk therapy."

So what did I do? I caved. I was afraid Brett would think I wasn't being supportive if I argued with his decision. He'd think I just was being difficult if I pushed back. So, in the face of an unpleasant encounter with my boss, I blinked. I ducked.

It was one of the biggest mistakes of my career. I should have begun by re-pledging my allegiance, by saying that the reason I wanted him to step back and think about this some more was that I cared about his and the group's success. That I wasn't arguing for the sake of arguing, but because I wanted to see him avoid making a mistake—"I know you've thought a lot about this, but isn't it worth a few more minutes of discussion to make sure you've considered all the downsides?" I should have told Brett that Helen's relaxed style was clouding his judgment about her real abilities, and that firing her would hurt the division's success.

But I was so concerned that Brett would feel I was being disrespectful or argumentative that I lost sight of the big picture. *I was so worried about my standing with Brett that I forgot—true allegiance is telling the Emperor when he's naked.*

Shortly after our conversation, Brett suggested to Helen that she "look outside for another job," and Helen left the firm. And we went through two more marketing VPs before Brett realized how hard it was to do this job—and how talented Helen had been. Helen went on to be a hugely successful executive in several companies. And several years later, Brett—no longer my boss—remarked to me one day at lunch that he had made a big mistake in letting her go!

Had I done more to frame my push-back in terms of ongoing loyalty to Brett and the organization, he might have been more willing to listen.

3. THE LAW OF THE STRATEGIC RETREAT

So you've established these ground rules and communicated frequently how committed you are to your boss's success. Yet on this particular day your boss isn't buying your recommendation and is clearly rejecting your push-back. When push-back turns contentious—and it will on occasion—a leader should not continue to advance his or her opposing view. This is the time for a *strategic retreat*. But all is not lost. Often an approach phrased as "let's both think some more about this and talk again when you have some more time" or "let's agree to disagree and revisit the issue when time permits" is a good way of establishing license to revisit the issue at another time. The critical idea here is not that you give up, but that you reserve the right to return to the issue when you're more likely to have a positive impact—you're choosing to lose the battle so as to keep alive the possibility of winning the war.

I first saw the value of this approach when a talented subordinate used it to overcome my own reluctance to heed push-back.

Early on in my job as VP-HR at Pepsi, I realized that we had no system or process for managing our union negotiations. We had over fifty different labor agreements and seemed to approach each as an isolated deal. More troubling to me, we had no real handle on the terms we were prepared to settle for, or what our management objectives were for new labor agreements. Our approach was totally reactive—we seemed to scramble to cut the best deal we could.

So within a few months I asked our Labor Department to implement what we ended up calling the Negotiating Authority Request Process (clearly our marketing folks weren't involved in selecting the name), which required our field managers to come to headquarters and present a review of the upcoming labor negotiations, including a history of collective bargaining in that location, wage rates in the location (including Coke's), and changes we should seek in the upcoming contract talks. These reviews were rigorous, especially for those on the receiving end of my questions. I would ask why we couldn't negotiate a less costly deal, or get more union concessions, and the managers would have to defend the deal they'd proposed.

The process worked. Over a few years we significantly reduced the size of wage increases, reduced absenteeism, and began to regain management control in our sales and manufacturing facilities. So when Luke, my chief labor guy, called and asked if we could spend some time discussing our approach, I told him to stop by right away.

"Mike, I think we need to revise the Authority Request Process," he began as soon as he came into my office.

"Luke, if these reviews get any tougher, we'll need to begin passing out smelling salts to the field people."

"Well, I'm really not talking about making them any more rigorous. Just the opposite."

"It's funny you say that 'cause I was thinking about turning the dial down a little on these reviews. Maybe they're getting too high on the pressure valve."

Luke paused. "Mike, I'm not talking about dialing down the pressure. I'm suggesting we do away with the reviews altogether."

It was my turn to pause. "Come on, you're not serious."

"Yeah, I am. We've achieved what we set out to. The entire field team knows that we need to be smarter and tougher in negotiations."

"Luke, as soon as we take our foot off the gas, the field folks' attention will drift elsewhere. It's not embedded yet in their DNA."

"I'm not suggesting that we eliminate the work or thinking that goes into the process. We can ask the field to submit all the data and their recommendations for a settlement. If we agree, we can sign off. If we have some concerns, we can ask for more info and talk about it by phone. But requiring these people to travel to head-quarters and face the firing squad is unnecessary and unhealthy."

"I'm in violent disagreement. We need to inspect what we ex-pect"—I was right up to date on the latest management apho-rism—"so no way am I prepared to abandon this process." I was really annoyed.

Luke tried a few more arguments: It was expensive to fly peo-ple to headquarters, and it was preventing the field from focusing on their many other priorities. I was buying none of it. "No way, Luke. Absolutely no way." I was adamant.

And Luke did something interesting. "Mike, can we agree to disagree? And table this for another time? You feel strongly about this but I think it's worth picking up at another time."

How could I say no?

And for the next month or so Luke would revisit the subject, never trying to win me over in a single conversation, but rather calmly reprising his arguments, and adding a new one or two each time. Finally, he had moved me to the point where I thought what he had been saying made sense. So I agreed to try his approach for six months.

Instead of forcing a decision which would not have gone his way when he first raised the subject, Luke executed a *strategic re-treat*, thereby avoiding an extended skirmish he could see he would lose. By reengaging me in discussions at other times, he won the war.

4. The Law of the Candy Store

High-Performance Leaders don't shy away from pushing back. Painful and tricky as it sometimes is, push-back is part of a High-Performance Leader's repertoire. Yet no leader, no matter how skillful at push-back, can win every disagreement. So leaders must recognize whose candy store it is—that is, they must show *they know who's the boss*. They recognize that bosses have the right to make the final call, and that, short of that decision being a breach of their personal ethics or a violation of the law, it must stand even if they feel it's wrong. What's crucial, however, is that the leader leave the office that night knowing he or she fought the good fight and told the Emperor or Empress they didn't agree with a course of action.

So, why is it that organizations don't work? They rely, as makes sense, on structures of power and authority (the org chart) in order to get things done. But the same hierarchies that are so essential for efficient operation also inhibit the vital flow of information up the organization to where it's most keenly needed. People experience a tension between the need to push back, to pass critical information and opinions up the organization, and the need to respect the office, to know whose candy store it is and who holds the power. Fundamentally, organizations don't work because the balance is tipped away from the need to push back, and toward the need to follow the boss, and protect our continuing employment. And this imbalance exists because most people lack skills when it comes to telling the Emperor he or she has no clothes. As we've seen, real options exist between the extremes of silence on the one hand or resigning on the other. High-Performance Leaders know these options and use them.

And when they do practice these Laws of Push-Back, the results are dramatic. Bosses with oversized egos begin to listen. "My way or the highway" superiors begin to accept opposing points of view. Executives whose knee-jerk reaction is their own self-preservation begin to realize there are better ways to achieve results. I've worked for very tough bosses who responded to these laws, so I speak from experience, not from naive optimism. Effective push-back can go a long way to properly clothing our corporate leaders.

Summary: Feiner's Laws of Push-Back

1. The Law of Loyalty vs. Insubordination

Leaders must establish early on that they intend to tell bosses what they need to hear, as opposed to what they want to hear. Having set the ground rules, they must reiterate them often.

2. The Law of Re-Pledging Allegiance

Leaders must repeat the loyalty oath periodically so that bosses don't perceive push-back as a lack of commitment.

3. The Law of the Strategic Retreat

If push-back turns contentious, a leader should not continue to advance his or her opposing view, but should reserve the right to return to the issue later.

4. The Law of the Candy Store

Ultimately, leaders recognize whose candy store it is—that is, they know who's the boss.

12	*Values-Based Leadership*
	UP AND DOWN THE SLIPPERY SLOPE

When I left Pepsi, and moved back to the States from Europe, I remember saying to my wife, "I think we're going to need four telephone lines. One is for the home line, one is for a fax line, one is for my own business line, and I'm probably going to need a second line for me, because it's quite likely that I'm going to be getting fifty or a hundred calls a week from Pepsi, given what I was there and who I was there. It's quite likely that we'll need a fourth line."

My wife is a very smart person. So rather than saying, "No, that's ridiculous," which immediately would have prompted me to get a fourth line, she said, "You know, that's probably a good idea, but why don't we just get three. Three lines is already expensive. Let's get three, and see what happens, and we can always get a fourth line."

And because I'm so wonderfully flexible, and so willing to compromise, we argued for two or three days before I decided on three lines. I was concerned about not being able to respond to my constituents at Pepsi, since, as was clear to everyone, I had been a big kahuna there.

Of course, I got hardly any calls. Very few of my former colleagues called for my sage advice. Practically none, in fact. And I had a hard time struggling with the question of how I could be so important, and so powerful, and so acknowledged for my competence and my achievement, yet be left without an identity the moment I departed. My achievement, my success—this was a big part of how I viewed myself, a big part of my persona. Coming to terms with what life is all about after achievement and after success is not such an easy thing—the discovery that you can't take power and prestige with you is a bitter pill to swallow.

But, on reflection, I found that there was plenty that I *could* take away with me. The relationships that I formed during my Pepsi years have lasted to this day, and continue to give me genuine warmth and satisfaction. Those relationships, moreover, are not predicated on what I *did* at Pepsi. They grow from what I *stood for*. Talking to those I worked with over the years, and reflecting on the stories I've shared here, *I realized that there was something behind the laws of leadership, something that motivated much of what I had learned, and something that fueled relationships which endure.*

Think back to the story about Dan, my subordinate who needed to go trick-or-treating in Chapter 3. We saw that, in order to ensure commitment from him, I had to demonstrate personal commitment to him—I put my butt on the griddle for him, and in return secured his ongoing support. But it's also true that, in taking a personal risk to allow him to keep a promise to his kids, I sent a strong signal about what I valued. I demonstrated that I valued his personal well-being—and his own commitments to his family—enough to risk my own neck.

For an opposite example, think back to my interview with sixty-two-year-old, about-to-retire Chuck, where I failed to ask any questions and as a result nearly let my dream job slip through my fingers. The reason this was such a blunder was again the signal it sent about my values—about where people who had grown old in the service of the Queen were placed in my values hierarchy.

Or think of the Law of Expectations, and the signal it sends to subordinates—"I believe in you, I value your capabilities, therefore *you* should believe in you." Or the signal sent by leaders who follow the Law of Competency-Based Coaching—"I value your development, and I'm prepared to commit significant time to ensuring that you improve your performance." Or the signal sent to a boss by the Law of Professional Commitment—"I value your success (however difficult our relationship might be)." Or the Law of the Whole Person—"I value you not just as a professional but as someone with their own story," or the Law of Ownership—"I value your input and participation in our effort to change," or the Law of the Emperor's Wardrobe—"I owe you my honest opinion on how I see the world."

Or think of the stories where feedback of one sort or another was key. My encounter with Scott the doo-wop singer at our division conference, my confrontation of Fred regarding his drinking problem, or my giving feedback to Nicholas about his communication problem, or Ann, about her unit's priorities vis-à-vis my group. We've said many times that feedback is a gift, but why? Obviously, it's a gift to the recipient because it helps them improve performance. And it's a gift to the leader, because that improved performance reflects well on him or her, and makes life easier. But it's also a gift because it sends another signal to the recipient—in many ways the most precious signal of all. The message is that "you matter to me, you count, I respect you." When I failed to ever consider Chris's bonus recommendations—because I thought I knew better—I sent a strong and opposite signal: "Your opinions don't matter to me, and neither do you." No surprise, then, that he was so resentful.

Or consider the lessons from the occasion when Alex tested my integrity by trying to get me to criticize my boss behind his back, or when I took on my boss over the bottler who refused to accept a black sales executive. There, the values signal was obvious—I try to do the right thing, even when that represents the more dicey path.

This is not an exhaustive list—if you look over the laws once more, and consider the values signal that each one sends, you'll discover that there is a link to values in almost every one. If you muster the commitment, the courage, and the integrity to lead through these laws, you will send a strong signal about what you value in life, and what you don't, what you value in relationships, and what you don't, and what you value in people, and what you don't. The values that you signal determine whether the relationships that you build will endure or not, and they determine whether your subordinates, peers, and bosses will follow your lead or not. *Values are the oxygen of followership.*

We all know of executives with great leadership ability who diminish their potential for building followership. They do this in any number of ways: by making unwelcome sexual advances toward fellow employees, by caring about nothing beyond their own success, by abusing their access to corporate perquisites, by failing to honor their personal commitments, by treating employees with rudeness and nastiness, by blaming others for their own mistakes, by behaving arrogantly—well, you get the idea. Other leaders get results by pushing people and using fear as a motivator, or relying on the carrot of financial reward to keep their people working hard. *But over the long run, people will only follow a leader whose values they respect.* Of course, values must encompass meeting business targets and deadlines, keeping commitments, and satisfying customers—clearly, business leaders have to deliver the goods, that is, meet or exceed their objectives. But values must also extend to giving feedback, to knowing your people, and letting them know, through a multitude of activities, that they matter. They must also—critically—extend to treating people decently, to speaking the truth, to saying what you mean, to telling the Emperor when he or she has no clothes, and to doing the right thing. *People follow not just because of what you do, but because of who you are.*

But surely this is all obvious. Why am I preaching here?

I'm preaching because I've seen too many people slide down the slippery slope to unethical behavior. It's usually a small thing that starts the descent—charging expenses to your firm that are strictly personal, say—but once you're on the slope, it frequently leads to far worse things, and the descent can be rapid.

Such as the admission by two Sony Pictures advertising executives that they had concocted gushing quotes from a fictitious movie critic to promote several films in national newspapers. Or the misrepresentation of the true cost of insurance policies by Prudential salespeople in the 1990s. Or the extra interest and late fees charged by Citibank and Chase Manhattan Bank in 2000 to customers whose payments, in fact, arrived on time. Or the failure by Firestone in 2000 to recall tires when it became clear that there was a serious safety problem. Or any of the recent collection of scandals. When we read about these transgressions we often conclude that they've been committed by faceless, monolithic corporate entities. But it's people—leaders at a variety of levels—who make these decisions and sanction these policies!

And if you think that this sort of thing only happens when the stakes are high, consider the case of Craig Spradling, reported a few years back in *The New York Times*. At age twenty, Mr. Spradling graduated Phi Beta Kappa and magna cum laude from Wesleyan University in Connecticut. He obtained a master's in computer science from Yale University. He then attended the University of Texas Law School in Austin, where he graduated with honors and was associate editor of the *Law Review*. He went on to become an associate in a prestigious New York law firm. It's fair to say that Spradling was a person of enormous promise.

But in October 1998 he pleaded guilty to insider trading, and confessed to misusing confidential information about one of the firm's clients. This crime had been committed just *one month* after he was hired. Spradling said he made $48,000 from the information. He sold his soul (not to mention the career he had worked toward for so long) for $48,000.

What led to Spradling's downfall? I'd suggest it was PGA. Not as in the Professional Golfers' Association, but as in Pride, Greed, and Ambition. Because we're all achievement-oriented, because we're all focused on fame and fortune, we all want to make it. But this intense drive to make the numbers, to meet the targets, to ship, to be successful, results in the lethal concoction of pride, greed, and ambition. PGA can lure any one of us into playing it fast and loose.

Stories of unethical behavior are in the pages of the newspapers *nearly every day*. While the headlines report on the CEOs and CFOs at Andersen and WorldCom and Tyco and the like, lots of leaders at different levels in organizations slide down the slippery slope. There is the potential for a Gordon Gecko, an Andrew Fastow, a Michael Milken, in each and every one of us—PGA is too seductive and too powerful for us to be complacent. And while it's easy to say that bad people do bad things, and good people don't, sadly that's an oversimplification. Where values are ignored or compromised, in the majority of cases it is by people who began their careers as good people, and who continue to think of themselves as good people. I'd be surprised, then, if any of the recent parade of disgraced executives thought of themselves as bad. They likely thought that they were good people, who were just doing what it took to deliver results. I suspect they rationalized their behavior by excusing it as something like "real-world pragmatism in the dog-eat-dog world of commerce."

* * *

We said at the beginning of the book that Feiner's Laws seek to bridge the gap between the *whats* of leadership and the *hows*—that while it's often easy to figure out *what* it is that you're trying to do (have motivated, empowered employees who deliver the goods), it's much more difficult to figure out *how* you do this. The final set of laws in this book, Feiner's Laws of Values-Based Leadership, recognize that the same problem applies to ethical and values-based decisions—while it's often easy to figure out what *should* happen, it can be much harder to figure out how to avoid the slippery slope when everything is stacked against you. In particular, these laws seek to combat four forces underlying many ethical lapses. We've already discussed PGA and the pressure to make the targets, but there are two other factors to consider. First, the initial step across the line can seem small when taken in isolation—without a sense of the wider personal consequences, it's very easy to make a slight, but critical, error, after which the slope takes over. Second, the pressure to build a cathedral, to play a great role in fulfilling the mission, can prompt people to cut corners and downplay ethical considerations. The laws that follow attempt to protect you against these forces, and to give you the tactics of ethical decision making.

1. THE LAW OF WYHA vs. WYHB

No one on their death bed gasps that they wish they had spent more time at the office. At least, most won't. Remember Mitch, CEO of Olympia, who resisted my advice about aligning his team, preferring instead to blame them for their mistakes and treat them like imbeciles? In a meeting I had with him about working on improving his relationship with his COO, I asked him what was really important to him—what his long-term objectives were. Obviously there are countless ways to answer this question. I was intrigued how this difficult client would answer it.

He thought for only a few seconds and responded, "One billion."

"I don't understand," I managed to mutter, totally confused by his answer.

"I want to be worth a billion dollars—then I'll hang it up."

I was numbed by his response at first, then I just felt enormous sadness. Mitch was a brilliant guy, yet was struggling with how to align and motivate his disgruntled and fractious team. His direct reports were scared to death of him. His marriage was, by his own admission, on shaky ground. And his youngest daughter had recently been diagnosed with childhood diabetes.

That a billion dollars was his primary objective is, to this day, mystifying to me. I don't claim to know how pervasive this kind of thinking is among today's organizational leaders. What I do know is that High-Performance Leaders come to understand that keeping score of one's worth means much more than *WYHA, What You Have Achieved.* Augmenting this metric, High-Performance Leaders use a second one, *WYHB, What You Have Become.* WYHA stays behind when you leave office, as my silent phone lines demonstrated. WYHB, on the other hand, travels with you wherever you go. Unlike WYHA, WYHB is completely within your control. It's what will enable you to look back on your career with a sense of pride and fulfillment. And it's what others will remember you for.

Without both these measures, there is a danger that leaders will define themselves solely by what they achieve. And it is this powerful drive for achievement, which, unchecked, can lead people down the slippery slope of unethical behavior.

2. THE LAW OF THE SILENT SINNER

Very often, the decisions that take us away from the ethical path are made alone, in isolation. Most of us are smart enough to know an ethical dilemma when we see one, and the natural response, if we're considering bending the rules, is to keep our thoughts to ourselves. You would be unlikely to ask a colleague's advice on whether or not to cheat on your spouse—in the same way, you're hardly likely to ask that colleague whether or not to fudge the numbers or accept an illegal "marketing fee." Many ethical lapses occur because their perpetrators are deprived, by the nature of the situation, of the counsel of others—when it comes to ethical decisions, the Law of Healthy Conflict is generally nowhere to be seen.

So the Law of the Silent Sinner serves as a restraint on rushed, ill-considered decisions. It states that *if you can't tell anyone what you're doing, don't do it!*

3. THE LAW OF CHOOSING A CULTURE

Very often, corporate sins have their root in corporate culture. The most recent and famous example of this is the way that the culture at Andersen—the now-deceased auditing firm—valued client relationships and the revenue they generated over a duty to serve the investing public, as detailed in Barbara Toffler's recent book.[1] The mandate, embedded deep within the culture, to do whatever it took to keep the client happy and protect both audit and consulting revenue was a root cause of Andersen's failure to stand up to the leaders of Waste Management, Sunbeam, and Enron (among others) when their financial statements were inaccurate.

The only lasting solution to these problems is to change the culture. And cultures can certainly be changed. There are examples throughout recent corporate history, from IBM's transformation under Lou Gerstner, to Pepsi's attempt to create a distinctive culture during my tenure. But this is no easy undertaking, and if you're low on the executive ladder, or if you're without allies, it can be virtually impossible. I strongly believe that real leaders try to figure out ways to enlist the support of senior sponsors in changing a culture. For many of us, however, the culture of our firm is a given, at least in the short run. So it's critical that, before you join a firm, you check out not only the requirements of the job, not only the colleagues you'll be working with, not only the compensation and benefits, but also the culture. There are a number of ways to do this—asking to talk to people who joined the firm within the past few years is one; another is inquiring about what criteria and metrics are used in their reward systems. What companies reward—not what they say in their vision statements—is the true guide to their values.

But if you don't realize until you've become an employee that a firm's culture is fundamentally rotten, you might have few realistic options. The Laws of Push-Back in Chapter 11 will certainly help you when you see bad decisions being contemplated, as will the Laws of Leading Bosses—you'll be able to do everything possible to avert disaster while keeping your integrity. But the sad truth is that there are limits to what an individual leader with no allies and no sponsorship can achieve when a culture has gone bad, and in some cases the only pragmatic option is to leave. Remember, though, that Serial Quitters finish last. If you're forced to change jobs in short order more than a few times in your career, you'll be labeled as someone with no staying power. So to avoid becoming a Serial Quitter, take time to check out the culture of your next employer *before* you sign the employment agreement.

4. The Law of the Tombstone

The quest for fame and fortune is so powerful that anyone can fall down the slippery slope, sometimes in one swift, sickening plunge, sometimes in a series of small missteps that we rationalize with increasing ease. And because the pressure to bend the rules or break the law often comes from a need for quick results, there's seldom much time to mull things over. The high road is long—often the low road represents a convenient shortcut to the desired result, and time pressures play a huge part in bad decisions. So the best way to safeguard against ethical lapses is to have thought about your value system in advance, *before* the crisis arrives. One of the goals of military training is to make various actions and reactions automatic, so that when troops have to make life-or-death decisions in the heat of combat they can rely on their instincts. The same principle applies here—this law recognizes that ethical lapses occur because judgment is impaired in the rush of the moment, and so encourages us to refine our ethical instincts, as far as possible, ahead of time.

One way to do this, morbid as it may sound, is to consider your tombstone. Your tombstone won't list the promotions you've earned, the deals you've pulled off, the homes you've owned, or the net worth you've amassed. But it might state what you stood for in your life. What will it say?

Many of us haven't crystallized what our values are and what we stand for. Sure, we're committed to our spouses and kids, and we're loyal to our friends. Yet when I ask people to articulate their values, I usually get a blank stare or banal generalities. But when I ask people to take a few minutes to think about and then *write down* what they'd like the few lines on their tombstone to read, the specifics of what's of core importance to them begin to emerge. They move from statements such as, "Of course I have good values—I'm a good person," to being able to articulate values such as, "What's important to me is that I be remembered for being a parent and spouse who upholds honesty, humility, and respect, for infusing my working life with integrity, courage, and humor, and for making someone smile every day." That kind of detailed written statement will prove much more resilient at the critical moment. This exercise is important for all of us to practice at regular intervals, say every few years. It's especially important for leaders to practice, in light of the enormous pressures they face to produce, excel, and outperform the competition. Without the anchor of a conscious, deeply held, and committed values system to keep us grounded, these pressures make it easy to lose our way. Don't misunderstand me—I'm not telling you what values you should have. Each of us will have a unique set of values that evolve and shift as we grow and mature. But the Tombstone Exercise can help us view our lives with a wide lens, so we're less likely to lose our way in the temptations of the moment.

As I've said, when I talk about values, understand that I include things like making the numbers, meeting targets, and all the things High-Performance Leaders are expected to achieve. High-Performance Leaders want the material things that professional success can buy, and I don't think there's anything wrong with wanting a nice home, clothes, and cars. It's *how* we go about meeting these targets and achieving success that's the issue. Do we intimidate and obfuscate like an Al Dunlap? Do we push and bully? Do we cheat and bribe and cook the books? Or do we treat people with dignity and respect while maintaining high standards of performance? Do we say the right things or do the right things?

High-Performance Leaders understand that while getting results must have quantifiable financial elements, it must also, in the long run, have human elements. They think about results in business terms, but also in terms of the underlying fundamentals of human relationships. And they behave as though every decision they make will be etched on their tombstone as their lasting memorial.

The final piece of the leadership jigsaw, then, the final part of that ninety percent of the iceberg hidden from view, is that leaders must have a strongly held values system, and must understand how to protect and uphold those values. Unless those values grow to encompass not just What You Have Achieved, but also What You Have Become, unless leaders prize not just what they want but also what they stand for, the consequences are sadly predictable: People will not follow, results will not be sustainable, ethical train wrecks will be infinitely more likely, organizations that don't work won't get fixed, and life after work will be empty. *Career achievement, per se, is a hollow journey.*

But when leaders do find this elusive balance, amazing things happen in their organizations. These leaders build followership—people respect and trust and follow them. These are the leaders who make the numbers, grow their businesses, and outperform competitors—not just in the short term but in the long term—by treating people with decency, honesty, and dignity. There's nothing inherently soft or weak about this approach. High-Performance Leaders set very high performance standards and, at the same time, motivate people to meet these standards without the need to cheat shareholders or intimidate employees.

I'm a thirty-year veteran of corporate life, so I recognize that business is a tough institution that requires hard work and commitment. But High-Performance Leadership is what elicits this commitment. Leadership that establishes effective relationships with bosses, peers, and subordinates. Leadership that understands how to drive change, acknowledge human differences, and handle conflict. Above all, leadership predicated on a set of values that rejects the notion that anything goes, so long as the targets are met. *Leadership that believes that how targets and goals are met is crucial to legitimizing their very achievement.*

Business institutions can have a greater impact on the human race over the next two hundred years than any other form of organization. For centuries, the various churches of the world were the most important institutions in terms of defining and leading society, and its values and norms. As the second millennium progressed, it was governmental and political systems that gradually took over this role for many of the world's citizens (think about democracy's struggle with totalitarianism and communism throughout most of the twentieth century). Going forward, it is business institutions that will increasingly shape our view of the world, which will determine how we spend our days, both as employees and as consumers, and which will play a central role in upholding societal values. But the record of our business institutions up to this point has been pretty spotty.

I don't believe that we have any choice about this shift in our society. With the ongoing secularization and globalization of our lives, the trend toward the increasing importance of business institutions is inevitable and irreversible. But we—leaders—can choose how our business organizations behave and perform. We can decide to create businesses that give us not only better results, but also better working relationships; businesses that give us not only new products, but also new ways of preserving and respecting the world we inhabit. We can decide to create business organizations that add value, meaning, and richness to the wonderful mosaic of human existence.

We can do this, I believe, through the laws I've set out in this book, and, most importantly, through values-based leadership. Ultimately, that's the challenge of High-Performance Leadership—and its greatest opportunity.

Summary: Feiner's Laws of Values-Based Leadership

1. The Law of WYHA vs. WYHB

It's important to use two metrics to gauge your success in life—focus not only on What You Have Achieved, but also on What You Have Become.

2. The Law of the Silent Sinner

If you can't tell anyone what you're doing, don't do it!

3. The Law of Choosing a Culture

If a rotten corporate culture is the root cause of ethical lapses in your firm, and you've done everything you can to push back and to tell the Emperor that he or she is naked, you may have little choice but to leave. But remember, Serial Quitters finish last. Check out the culture of your next employer before you sign up.

4. The Law of the Tombstone

Sharpen your ethical reflexes by developing a detailed written statement of what you stand for in life. Do this now, so that you've already thought about your values before you face an ethical dilemma. And remember that your net worth won't be listed on your tombstone.

APPENDIX

The Laws Matrix

I want this book to be usable, not just readable. The Laws Matrix, then, is an attempt to make the lessons in The Feiner Points of Leadership *easier to use. It takes a large number of difficult leadership challenges that each of us encounters on a daily basis, and highlights the three or four laws that are most useful in that situation. It aims to function as a quick reference guide for the Laws of Leadership, and to put Feiner's Laws at your fingertips.*

Leading Subordinates	Primary Laws		Secondary Laws	
My subordinate is not performing up to my expectations.	Expectations (Ch. 3, p. 37)	Competency-Based Coaching (Ch. 3, p. 63)	Feedback (Ch. 3, p. 52)	Intimacy (Ch. 3, p. 39)
My superstar subordinate is not a team player.	Winning Championships (Ch. 5, p.105)		Feedback (Ch. 3, p. 52)	Building a Cathedral (Ch. 3, p.43)
My subordinate is alienating his/her subordinates.	Accountability (Ch. 3, p. 66)		Feedback (Ch. 3, p. 52)	
My subordinate bad-mouths me behind my back.	Pull vs. Push (Ch. 6, p. 121)		Mirror (Ch. 6, p. 126)	
My subordinate is extremely ambitious and career-centric.	Career Covenant (Ch. 4, p. 80)		Intimacy (Ch. 3, p. 39)	Building a Cathedral (Ch. 3, p. 43)
My subordinate is arrogant.	Tough Love (Ch. 3, p. 59)		Feedback (Ch. 3, p. 52)	
My subordinate is disorganized and weak at time management.	Competency-Based Coaching (Ch. 3, p. 63)		Feedback (Ch. 3, p. 52)	Accountability (Ch. 3, p. 66)
My subordinate doesn't seem committed to my objectives.	Personal Commitment (Ch. 3, p. 45)	Career Covenant (Ch. 4, p. 80)	Pull vs. Push (Ch. 6, p. 121)	Building a Cathedral (Ch. 3, p. 43)

Leading Bosses	Primary Laws		Secondary Laws		
My boss is indecisive.	Professional Commitment (Ch. 4, p. 78)	Acting Grown-up (Ch. 4, p. 90)	Emperor's Wardrobe (Ch. 4, p. 82)		Who Is That Masked Man or Woman? (Ch. 4, p. 77)
My boss doesn't know how hard I'm working.	Make Your Own Bed (Ch. 4, p. 76)		Acting Grown-up (Ch. 4, p. 90)		Career Covenant (Ch. 4, p. 80)
My boss ignores me.	Career Covenant (Ch. 4, p. 80)	Emperor's Wardrobe (Ch. 4, p. 82)	Pull vs. Push (Ch. 6, p. 121)		
My boss takes credit for my ideas.	Pull vs. Push (Ch. 6, p. 121)	Career Covenant (Ch. 4, p. 80)	Professional Commitment (Ch. 4, p. 78)		
My boss behaves unethically.	Loyalty vs. Insubordination (Ch. 11, p. 240)	Self-Interest (Ch. 10, p. 225)	Tombstone (Ch. 12, p. 260)		
My boss is not competent.	Professional Commitment (Ch. 4, p. 78)	Class vs. Style (Ch. 4, p. 87)	Who Is That Masked Man or Woman? (Ch. 4, p. 77)		
My boss doesn't give me performance feedback.	Career Covenant (Ch. 4, p. 80)	Acting Grown-up (Ch. 4, p. 90)	Pull vs. Push (Ch. 6, p. 121)		
My boss micromanages me and doesn't give me enough space.	Make Your Own Bed (Ch. 4, p. 76)	Communicating Up (Ch. 5, p. 111)	Pull vs. Push (Ch. 6, p. 121)		

Leading Bosses	Primary Laws		Secondary Laws	
My boss treats me rudely and uncivilly.	Make Your Own Bed (Ch. 4, p. 76)	Professional Commitment (Ch. 4, p. 78)	Acting Grown-up (Ch. 4, p. 90)	Who Is That Masked Man or Woman? (Ch. 4, p. 77)
My boss is insensitive to my need for work-life balance.	Make Your Own Bed (Ch. 4, p. 76)	Acting Grown-up (Ch. 4, p. 90)	Professional Commitment (Ch. 4, p. 78)	Who Is That Masked Man or Woman? (Ch. 4, p. 77)
My boss doesn't like anyone to disagree with his/her opinion.	Loyalty vs. Insubordination (Ch. 11, p. 240)	Re-Pledging Allegiance (Ch. 11, p. 244)	Strategic Retreat (Ch. 11, p. 246)	
My boss doesn't ask for my input.	Pull vs. Push (Ch. 6, p. 121)	Make Your Own Bed (Ch. 4, p. 76)	Loyalty vs. Insubordination (Ch. 11, p. 240)	
My boss is too busy to give me the help or support I need.	Acting Grown-up (Ch. 4, p. 90)	Career Covenant (Ch. 4, p. 80)	Professional Commitment (Ch. 4, p. 78)	
My boss is making a decision I don't agree with.	Loyalty vs. Insubordination (Ch. 11, p. 240)	Re-Pledging Allegiance (Ch. 11, p. 244)	Professional Commitment (Ch. 4, p. 78)	Emperor's Wardrobe (Ch. 4, p. 82)
My boss doesn't seem interested in helping me advance my career.	Career Covenant (Ch. 4, p. 80)	Professional Commitment (Ch. 4, p. 78)	Pull vs. Push (Ch. 6, p. 121)	

Leading Teams	Primary Laws		Secondary Laws
I'm in charge of a task force with a few Lone Rangers.	Winning Championships (Ch. 5, p. 105)	Building a Cathedral (Ch. 5, p. 106)	Nitty-Gritty (Ch. 5, p. 107)
My team seems discouraged and worn-out.	Personal Commitment (Ch. 3, p. 45)	Building a Cathedral (Ch. 5, p. 106)	Winning Championships (Ch. 5, p. 105)
My team meetings are more trouble than they're worth.	Nitty-Gritty (Ch. 5, p. 107)	Healthy Conflict (Ch. 8, p. 185)	Building a Cathedral (Ch. 5, p. 106)
My staff meetings never seem to result in closure on key issues.	Nitty-Gritty (Ch. 5, p. 107)	Mirror (Ch. 6, p. 126)	
We never seem to complete the agenda for my team meetings.	Nitty-Gritty (Ch. 5, p. 107)	First Among Equals (Ch. 5, p. 100)	
I'm never sure if my team is aligned around the decision arrived at.	Nitty-Gritty (Ch. 5, p. 107)	Healthy Conflict (Ch. 8, p. 185)	Team Together, Team Apart (Ch. 5, p. 112)
After team meetings there's lots of grapevine chatter about what went on in the meeting.	Team Together, Team Apart (Ch. 5, p. 112)	Healthy Conflict (Ch. 8, p. 185)	Building a Cathedral (Ch. 5, p. 106)
We agree on lots of stuff during our meetings, but nothing ever gets done.	Healthy Conflict (Ch. 8, p. 185)	Accountability (Ch. 3, p. 66)	Nitty-Gritty (Ch. 5, p. 107)
I'm in charge of a task force with people more seasoned than me.	First Among Equals (Ch. 5, p. 100)	Equality (Ch. 6, p. 121)	Pull vs. Push (Ch. 6, p. 121)
My organization is at odds with another department.	Options (Ch. 8, p. 177)	Healthy Conflict (Ch. 8, p. 185)	Pull vs. Push (Ch. 6, p. 121)
My meetings are filled with soapbox speeches.	Healthy Conflict (Ch. 8, p. 185)	Nitty-Gritty (Ch. 5, p. 107)	Equality (Ch. 6, p. 121)

Leading Peers	Primary Laws		Secondary Laws	
I don't get along with a colleague.	Equality (Ch. 6, p. 121)	Mirror (Ch. 6, p. 126)	Pull vs. Push (Ch. 6, p. 121)	
I don't trust a colleague.	Trust (Ch. 6, p. 130)	Feedback (Ch. 6, p. 127)	Intention (Ch. 10, p. 222)	
A peer is out to undermine me.	Mirror (Ch. 6, p. 126)	Pull vs. Push (Ch. 6, p. 121)	Feedback (Ch. 6, p. 127)	Building a Cathedral (Ch. 5, p. 106)
A peer is not doing his or her job well.	Good Samaritan (Ch. 6, p. 125)	Pull vs. Push (Ch. 6, p. 121)	Interdependence (Ch. 8, p. 172)	
A peer resists my point of view though the facts support my position.	Options (Ch. 8, p. 177)	Pull vs. Push (Ch. 6, p. 121)	Equality (Ch. 6, p. 121)	
A peer bad-mouths our team to his or her people.	Team Together, Team Apart (Ch. 5, p. 112)	Feedback (Ch. 6, p. 127)	Tell Your Cat (Ch. 6, p. 132)	
A peer's team is not cooperative with me or my people.	Feedback (Ch. 6, p. 127)	Options (Ch. 8, p. 177)	Pull vs. Push (Ch. 6, p. 121)	
My colleagues spend lots of time gossiping about our boss.	Tell Your Cat (Ch. 6, p. 132)	Conscientious Objector (Ch. 8, p. 184)	Team Together, Team Apart (Ch. 5, p. 112)	

Leading Conflict	Primary Laws		Secondary Laws
There seems to be friction or rivalry between some members of my team.	Last Chance Saloon (Ch. 8, p. 185)	Building a Cathedral (Ch. 8, p. 177)	Team Together, Team Apart (Ch. 5, p. 112)
Members of my team seem reluctant to openly express their views in meetings.	Healthy Conflict (Ch. 8, p. 185)	Mirror (Ch. 6, p. 126)	Nitty-Gritty (Ch. 5, p. 107)
I always seem to be in a state of disagreement with my colleagues.	Options (Ch. 8, p. 177)	Pull vs. Push (Ch. 6, p. 121)	Equality (Ch. 6, p. 121)
My organization is fighting a civil war.	Options (Ch. 8, p. 177)	Building a Cathedral (Ch. 8, p. 177)	Healthy Conflict (Ch. 8, p. 185)
Two of my subordinates hate each other's guts.	Pull vs. Push (Ch. 6, p. 121)	Last Chance Saloon (Ch. 8, p. 185)	Feedback (Ch. 6, p. 127)
My boss only likes yes-men or yes-women on his team.	Emperor's Wardrobe (Ch. 4, p. 82)	Healthy Conflict (Ch. 8, p. 185)	Loyalty vs. Insubordination (Ch. 11, p. 240)
My boss is fighting his peers for promotion or control.	Conscientious Objector (Ch. 8, p. 184)	Professional Commitment (Ch. 4, p. 78)	Emperor's Wardrobe (Ch. 4, p. 82)
However hard I try to stamp out the conflict, it just keeps getting worse.	Interdependence (Ch. 8, p. 172)	Healthy Conflict (Ch. 8, p. 185)	Options (Ch. 8, p. 177)

Leading Change	Primary Laws		Secondary Laws
I see a need for a major change within the organization (but I'm not the boss).	Cascading Sponsorship (Ch. 9, p. 198)	Burning Platform (Ch. 9, p. 195)	Nuts and Bolts (Ch. 9, p. 200)
I intend to implement a major change in my organization.	Burning Platform (Ch. 9, p. 195)	Cascading Sponsorship (Ch. 9, p. 198)	Nuts and Bolts (Ch. 9, p. 200)
People are anxious about a change that has been announced.	Ownership (Ch. 9, p. 203)	Cascading Sponsorship (Ch. 9, p. 198)	
Some people seem resistant to a change that has been announced.	Nuts and Bolts (Ch. 9, p. 200)	Ownership (Ch. 9, p. 203)	Burning Platform (Ch. 9, p. 195)
My team is on board with the planned change but I'm not sure about the rest of the organization.	Cascading Sponsorship (Ch. 9, p. 198)	Nuts and Bolts (Ch. 9, p. 200)	Burning Platform (Ch. 9, p. 195)

Leading Difference	Primary Laws		Secondary Laws
My boss or peer always seems to have a hidden agenda.	Onion (Ch. 10, p. 212)	Pull vs. Push (Ch. 6, p. 121)	Mirror (Ch. 6, p. 126)
My boss or peer is prone to racially or culturally insensitive comments.	Intention (Ch. 10, p. 222)	Emperor's Wardrobe (Ch. 4, p. 82)	Good Samaritan (Ch. 6, p. 125)
My boss or peer looks after his or her own skin instead of doing what's morally right.	Self-Interest (Ch. 10, p. 225)	Loyalty vs. Insubordination (Ch. 11, p. 240)	Silent Sinner (Ch. 12, p. 258)
My boss or peer is very professional, but very private.	Whole Person (Ch. 10, p. 224)	Onion (Ch. 10, p. 212)	Pull vs. Push (Ch. 6, p. 121)
My peer has come out of the closet at work.	Whole Person (Ch. 10, p. 224)	Equality (Ch. 6, p. 121)	Interdependence (Ch. 8, p. 172)
My boss only likes things done his or her way.	Make Your Own Bed (Ch. 4, p. 76)	Communicating Up (Ch. 5, p. 111)	Pull vs. Push (Ch. 6, p. 121)

Push-Back	Primary Laws		Secondary Laws
I don't agree with my boss's decision.	Loyalty vs. Insubordination (Ch. 11, p. 240)	Re-Pledging Allegiance (Ch. 11, p. 244)	Strategic Retreat (Ch. 11, p. 246)
I still don't agree with my boss's decision.	Re-Pledging Allegiance (Ch. 11, p. 244)	Self-Interest (Ch. 10, p. 225)	Candy Store (Ch. 11, p. 249)
My boss is tired of my push-back.	Re-Pledging Allegiance (Ch. 11, p. 244)	Professional Commitment (Ch. 4, p. 78)	Strategic Retreat (Ch. 11, p. 246)
My boss publicly executed the last person who suggested a different way of doing things.	Loyalty vs. Insubordination (Ch. 11, p. 240)	Self-Interest (Ch. 10, p. 225)	Professional Commitment (Ch. 4, p. 78)
My boss isn't a fan of collaborative decision making.	Professional Commitment (Ch. 4, p. 78)	Emperor's Wardrobe (Ch. 4, p. 82)	Loyalty vs. Insubordination (Ch. 11, p. 240)

Values-Based Leadership	Primary Laws		Secondary Laws	
My boss wants me to make the numbers, "whatever it takes."	Loyalty vs. Insubordination (Ch. 11, p. 240)	Silent Sinner (Ch. 12, p. 258)	Tombstone (Ch. 12, p. 260)	Strategic Retreat (Ch. 11, p. 246)
My boss plays fast and loose with ethical issues.	Emperor's Wardrobe (Ch. 4, p. 82)	Self-Interest (Ch. 10, p. 225)	Loyalty vs. Insubordination (Ch. 11, p. 240)	
A peer plays fast and loose with ethical issues.	Good Samaritan (Ch. 6, p. 125)	WYHA vs. WYHB (Ch. 12, p. 257)	Self-Interest (Ch. 10, p. 225)	
The only thing that matters around here is short-term profit.	Emperor's Wardrobe (Ch. 4, p. 82)	Acting Grown-up (Ch. 4, p. 90)	Choosing a Culture (Ch. 12, p. 259)	
If I turn a blind eye, I can advance my career.	Tombstone (Ch. 12, p. 260)	WYHA vs. WYHB (Ch. 12, p. 257)	Silent Sinner (Ch. 12, p. 258)	

Notes

All the stories in this book are true. I have changed locations and character names so as to preclude identification of those I worked with. The dialogue is accurate to the best of my recollection—which is normally pretty reliable—but if there are mistakes, they're mine and mine alone. The reader should bear in mind that the intent of relating these stories is never to criticize, but to draw lessons from events in my career.

Chapter 1. Beneath the Tip of the Iceberg

1. Warren Bennis, Patricia Ward Biederman, *Organizing Genius* (Perseus Books, 1997), p. 1.

2. The ED-AP-MI model of what leaders do—Establish Direction, Align People, Motivate and Inspire—was devised by John P. Kotter, and is described in his article "What Leaders Really Do," *Harvard Business Review*, May–June 1990, p. 103.

3. "AOL's Need: A New Vision," *The New York Times*, February 2, 2003.

Chapter 2. The Difference Between Leadership and Management

1. These three categories are suggested by Kotter in "What Leaders Really Do."

2. Clayton M. Christensen, *The Innovator's Dilemma* (Harper-Business, 1997).

Chapter 3. Leading Subordinates: Of Expectations, Feedback, and Riding a Bike

1. Students showed average IQ gains of two points in verbal ability, seven points in reasoning, and four points overall. R. Rosenthal and L. F. Jacobson, *Pygmalion in the Classroom* (Holt, Rinehart & Winston, 1968).

2. The concept of the BHAG is discussed in James C. Collins and Jerry I. Porras, *Built to Last* (HarperBusiness, 1994).

3. Bureau of Labor Statistics, JOLTS Historical Data: December 2000–April 2001. The figure quoted is the mean monthly separation rate for this period.

Chapter 4. Leading Bosses: Never . . . Ever . . . Ever . . . EVER Treat Your Boss Like a Bumbling Old Fool (Even if He or She Is One)

1. Recent research suggests that, in a similar way, it's the things you do, or don't do, that determine how lucky you are in life (Richard Wiseman, *The Luck Factor* [Miramax Books, 2003]). If luck is under your control, the quality of your relationship with your boss certainly is!

2. For a fascinating discussion of several other shortcomings of the intelligence obsession, see Malcolm Gladwell, "The Talent Myth," *The New Yorker*, July 22, 2002.

3. "AT&T's Walter Failed to Court the One Man Who Counted: Allen," *The Wall Street Journal*, July 18, 1997.

4. "The Wisdom of Thoughtfulness," *The New York Times*, May 31, 2000. The article reports a Hudson Institute and Lou Harris Associates survey which found that 56 percent of employees said their company does not care for them, and that 40 percent of those who rated their boss's behavior as poor were likely to look for another job, while only 11 percent of those who rated their boss's behavior as excellent were likely to look for another job. The same article cites a Gallup survey which found that most workers rate having a caring boss more important than wages or benefits, and that the length of

tenure and productivity of an employee is directly correlated with the quality of the relationship with that employee's immediate superior.

Chapter 5. Leading Teams: First Among Equals

1. Fred Smith, "How I Delivered the Goods," *Fortune Small Business*, October 2002.

Chapter 7. Leadership Style: The Hadley Paradox

1. "Maytag's Top Officer, Expected to Do Little, Surprises His Board," *The Wall Street Journal*, June 23, 1998.

2. Brian MacArthur (editor), *The Penguin Book of Twentieth-Century Speeches*, p. 335.

3. David McCullough, *Truman* (Simon and Schuster, 1992), p. 359.

4. White House press conference, Washington, D.C., July 8, 2002.

5. Stockton, California, August 23, 2002.

6. Franklin D. Roosevelt, speech to Congress, December 8, 1941.

7. John F. Kennedy, Inaugural Address, January 20, 1961.

Chapter 8. Leading Conflict: The Art of the Productive Disagreement

1. Robert F. Kennedy, *Thirteen Days* (W. W. Norton, 1971).

2. *Thirteen Days*, p. 25.

3. *Thirteen Days*, p. 35.

4. *Thirteen Days*, p. 36.

5. *Notes Taken from Transcripts of Meetings of the Joint Chiefs of Staff*, October–November 1962, p. 13, National Security Archive, Washington, D.C.

Chapter 9. Leading Change: The Burning Platform

1. This phrase is attributed to Virginia Satir, a pioneer in the field of family therapy, who lived from 1916 to 1978.

2. Boeing Company Web site: http://www.boeing.com/news/feature/747evolution/747facts.html.

Chapter 10. Leading Difference: The Treachery of Assumptions

1. Chris Argyris, Robert Putnam, and Diana McLain Smith, *Action Science: Concepts, Methods, and Skills for Research and Intervention* (Jossey-Bass, 1985).

2. *Where Will They Lead?*, Aspen Institute Initiative for Social Innovation Through Business, 2001.

Chapter 12. Values-Based Leadership: Up and Down the Slippery Slope

1. Barbara Toffler with Jennifer Reingold, *Final Accounting* (Broadway Books, 2003).

Acknowledgments

Writing a book is a lonely and solitary process—all the more so when you're doing it for the first time. Yet it turned out to be a very satisfying experience, one in which I was required to crystallize and clarify and codify many of the leadership principles and practices I have learned over the course of my career.

For this experience I have many to thank. My wife, Lisa, strongly encouraged me to undertake a venture I wasn't sure, at first, I was up to.

I'm indebted to the many hundreds of my former MBA students at Columbia Business School, who over the past few years have urged me to translate the course I teach, "High Performance Leadership," into book form. As well, there were many managers in Columbia's executive programs who felt the material I presented on leadership was deserving of wider dissemination.

Dean Meyer Feldberg and Vice Dean Safwan Masri of Columbia Business School were very supportive and understanding of my need to take a year's sabbatical from my teaching responsibilities to write this book.

Of course, writing a book is an iterative process and the manuscript evolved along the way, based on incredibly helpful feedback from a variety of sources. Suggestions from Holly Bennet, John Berisford, Kevin Cox, Ken DiPietro, Tom Hardy, David Harper, Wayne Mailloux, Foster Mobley, Bruce Nathanson, and David Pace were especially valuable. As were comments from the two oldest of my four children, Matt and Allison, both of whom are making their mark in their corporate careers.

Finally, three people deserve special acknowledgment:

Denise Marcil, my agent, who took me on as a client and first-time author, believing in my excitement for this book and my passion for the ideas in it.

Rick Wolff, my editor at Warner Books, whose support and sponsorship from start to finish were uncompromising and unflagging.

Ashley Goodall, a former MBA student (who can't miss as a High-Performance Leader), now with Deloitte Consulting, whose assistance was incalculable. His organizational skills in helping me structure the book and his editorial skills in helping me write it were truly heroic. For all his support I am forever grateful.

Last, I'm indebted to the late Doug Boles, who worked in my organization at Pepsi for almost fifteen years. It was through watching Doug grow and develop as a leader that I began to realize that kindness, authenticity, and decency were in no way incompatible with intellectual rigor, drive for results, and High-Performance Leadership. Doug's untimely death robbed me of a great friend and the planet of an extraordinary human being.

Readers who wish to contact the author
can do so by accessing his Web site:
www.feinerpoints.com